Global Sex Workers

Global Sex Workers

Rights, Resistance, and Redefinition

edited by
Kamala Kempadoo
and
Jo Doezema

Routledge
New York and London

Published in 1998 by
Routledge
29 West 35th Street
New York, NY 10001

Published in Great Britain by
Routledge
11 New Fetter Lane
London EC4P 4EE

Library of Congress Cataloging-in-Publication Data
Global sex workers : rights, resistance, and redefinition /
edited by Kamala Kempadoo and Jo Doezema.
p. cm.
Includes bibliographical references.
ISBN 0-415-91828-6 (cloth). —— ISBN 0-415-91829-4 (pbk.)
1. Prostitution—Cross-cultural studies. 2. Prostitutes—Civil
rights—Cross-cultural studies. I. Kempadoo, Kamala.
II. Doezema, Jo.
HQ111.G56 1998   97-45759
306.74—dc21   CIP

Contents

Acknowledgments

Many people made this collaborative effort possible. First, thanks must go to Chandra Talpade Mohanty and Rickie Solinger. Without their encouragement and practical advice at early stages this collection would never have materialized. Thanks also to Licia Brussa, whose contribution was far more than just the chapter included here. As one of the founders of this project, we are grateful to her for the time and energy she gave at the beginning of this endeavor.

Jo would like to acknowledge the activists of the Network of Sex Work Projects, whose commitment to a truly global and diverse sex worker rights movement provided the inspiration for this book, especially Cheryl Overs, Paulo Longo, Brett Macmillan, Alison Murray, and Monocca Momocco. Jo Bindman and everyone at Anti-Slavery International gave loads of humor and support, (not to mention computer access!) keeping panic at bay throughout a very busy last year. Tons of love and thanks to her partner Ruth Mackenzie for the great companionship, encouragement and commitment.

Kamala would like to thank the Women's Studies Program at the University of Colorado for providing the space to conclude this book. Nan Alamilla Boyd and Michiko Hase were two colleagues in particular who read parts of the manuscript and gave helpful comments, as well as warmth and friendship. At different stages, Yamila Azize Vargas and Cyndi Mellon were important long-distance life-lines. The start of the book was made possible due to support by the Department of Ethnic Studies at the University of Colorado. Many, many thanks to David Barsamian, her partner and best critic, for his love and constant reminder that most of the world cannot read postmodernese.

At Routledge, editors Cecilia Cancellaro and Melissa Rosati were both enthusiastic about the idea of this book, but it was Eric Nelson who coached us along in the later stages, giving advice and feedback as well as gentle prods at times when we were flagging. Thanks also to production editor Brian Phillips for his competence and care. Kris Gilmore, at the University of Colorado, came on board towards the end of the process and provided welcome assistance for the completion of the manuscript.

Finally, thanks to the contributors and to each other for all the enthusiasm, cooperation and patience it took to compile this book. Working so successfully across continents and oceans has truly affirmed our belief in a global sex workers' movement and transnational solidarity.

Introduction Globalizing Sex Workers' Rights

Kamala Kempadoo

When I first heard about prostitutes organizing for their rights in Suriname in 1993, I was both excited and puzzled by the news. Was it a singular incident spurred by an outsider, or did it reflect a local movement? I wanted to know. Also, in this part of the world, were women serious about staying in the sex industry or anxious to have prostitution abolished? What were the aims of such an organization, and who were the activists? Was this an isolated group, and what was the response to this initiative from the rest of the women's movement in this corner of South America? Questions outweighed any answer I could find in libraries or books—I decided to travel to Suriname to find out more.

Curiosity opened my world to a movement not just in Suriname, but in other parts of the "Third World." I realized that sex workers' movements were no longer exclusive to the United States or Western Europe. Prostitutes and other sex workers were fighting to keep brothels open, challenging the various stigmas about prostitution, and exposing corruption within sex industries in many different countries—yet very few people had heard about these courageous steps. The voices and activities of sex workers outside the industrialized North went unheard, nearly invisible to all but those in the immediate surroundings. As someone trained to think that a documentation of social history is absolutely vital for the construction of knowledge, I believed the one thing I could do was to facilitate the recording of this new international movement.

During a 1994 meeting in Amsterdam, Licia Brussa and I exchanged the initial ideas on compiling a book about these international initiatives. Jo Doezema soon joined the project. Within a year we had mapped out the terrain we needed to cover. Since then, Jo and I worked long distance to create a forum for those rarely heard outside of their own environment, yet who are at the forefront of sex workers' rights activism internationally. The result is a collection presenting a variety of voices and analyses by women and men who are organizing globally to change the exploitations and oppressions associated with prostitution and other forms of commercial sex work, a collection foregrounding Third World women at home and in migratory contexts.[1] Through interviews, reflective essays, research papers, reports, and critical writings from Asia, Australia, the Caribbean, North and South America, West and South Africa, and Western Europe, this collection challenges complacent knowledges and enduring misconceptions about prostitution. It explores various understandings of sexual labor and traces activities that are culturally specific as well as transnational in scope.

This collection testifies to the courage and determination of sex workers to tell their own stories. Since prostitution is a criminal and highly stigmatized activity in many countries, speaking out can be a dangerous act—exposing the individual sex worker, sex worker organization, or rights advocate to easy identification by the authorities, parents and the community, possibly giving rise to harassment. Furthermore, a book like this may provide leads for tabloid journalists, leaving contributors vulnerable to sensationalist press coverage. Still, all authors were eager to participate, and it was this commitment that made the volume not only possible, but an important contribution to the understanding of sex work and prostitution. And despite the differences in access to technology to communicate easily across the globe, we are grateful that so many sex workers and rights advocates trusted us and gave their full cooperation in this effort. In putting together this collection, we did not attempt to streamline the writings to conform to any particular writing style or format, thus it represents the heterogeneity and diversity that makes up the contemporary movement. Each piece appears with the full consent of the organization and sex workers involved, written with their own words and sentiments, and offering some of the flavor of the various languages and cultural contexts.

Ultimately, this book is not about the details of sexual acts themselves but instead about what some women and men who perform these acts and sell sex for a living consider to be important in their everyday lives. It does not offer much for the reader who is seeking titillation and cheap thrills, or for those who wish to confirm their ideas about the exotic sexuality of brown or black women. However, it does give us a glimpse into the priorities, hardships and resistances of people who are marginalized and outcast in many societies today—of those women and men who service vast sections of the worlds' male populations and render what many consider vital to the well-being of manhood yet who are often despised, criminalized and rejected for doing so.

Global Sex Workers is about the politics of a worldwide sex workers movement, about how ordinary women and men in prostitution define and shape their struggles for social change and justice. We hope it will cast some light on knowledges, actions, and transformations that pertain to sex work on a global scale, at the end of the twentieth century.

Sex Worker, Prostitute or Whore?

Identity, rights, working conditions, decriminalization, and legitimacy have been central issues collectively addressed by prostitutes for many years. Through these struggles the notion of the sex worker has emerged as a counterpoint to traditionally derogatory names, under the broad banner of a prostitutes' rights movement, with some parts recovering and valorizing the name and identity of "whore." In this book we have chosen the term "sex worker" to reflect the current use throughout the world, although in many of the essays "sex worker" and "prostitute" are used interchangeably. It is a term that suggests we view prostitution not as an identity—a social or a psychological characteristic of women, often indicated by "whore"—but as an income-generating activity or form of labor for women and men. The definition stresses the social location of those engaged in sex industries as working people.

The idea of the sex worker is inextricably related to struggles for the recognition of women's work, for basic human rights and for decent working conditions. The definition emphasizes flexibility and variability of sexual labor as well as its similarities with other dimensions of working people's lives. In particular, the writings here illustrate the ways in which sex work is experienced as an integral part of many women's and men's lives around the world, and not necessarily as the sole defining activity around which their sense of self or identity is shaped. Moreover, commercial sex work in these accounts is not always a steady activity, but may occur simultaneously with other forms of income-generating work such as domestic service, informal commercial trading, market-vending, shoeshining or office work. Sex work can also be quite short-lived or be a part of an annual cycle of work—in few cases are women and men engaged full-time or as professionals. Consequently, in one person's lifetime, sex work is commonly just one of the multiple activities employed for generating income, and very few stay in prostitution for their entire adulthood. In most cases, sex work is not for individual wealth but for family well-being or survival; for working class women to clothe, feed and educate their children; and for young women and men to sustain themselves when the family income is inadequate. For many, sex work means migration away from their hometown or country. For others, it is associated with drug use, indentureship or debt-bondage. For the majority, participation in sex work entails a life in the margins.

The concept of sex work emerged in the 1970s through the prostitutes' rights movement in the United States and Western Europe and has been discussed in various publications.[2] Than-Dam Troung's study of prostitution and tourism in Southeast Asia produced one of the first extensive theoretical elaborations on the subject (1989). Defining human activity or work as the way in which basic needs are met and human life produced and reproduced, she argues that activities involving purely sexual elements of the body and sexual energy should also be considered vital to the fulfillment of basic human needs: for both procreation and bodily pleasure. Troung thus introduces the concept of sexual labor to capture the notion of the utilization of sexual elements of the body and as a way of understanding a productive life force that is employed by women and men. In this respect she proposes that sexual labor be considered similar to other forms of labor that humankind performs to sustain itself—such as mental and manual labor, all of which involve specific parts of the body and particular types of energy and skills. Furthermore, she points out, the social organization of sexual labor has taken a variety of forms in different historical contexts and political economies, whereby there is no universal form or appearance of either prostitution or sex work. Instead, she proposes, analyses of prostitution need to address and take into account the specific ways in which sexual subjectivity, sexual needs and desires are constructed in specific contexts. Wet-nursing, temple prostitution, "breeding" under slavery, surrogate child-bearing, donor sex, commercial sex and biological reproduction can thus be seen as illustrations of historical and contemporary ways in which sexual labor has been organized for the re-creation and replenishment of human and social life.

Perhaps one of the most confounding dimensions in the conceptualization of prostitution as labor concerns the relation that exists in many people's minds between sexual acts and "love," and with prevailing ideas that without love, sexual acts are harmful and abusive. After all, isn't sex supposed to be about consensual sharing of our "most personal, private, erotic, sensitive parts of our physical and psychic being," as some would argue?[3] And aren't women in particular harmed or violated by sexual acts that are not intimate? In such perspectives, the sale of one's sexual energies is confused with a particular morality about sexual relations and essentialist cultural interpretations are imposed upon the subject. This conflation of sex with the highest form of intimacy presupposes a universal meaning of sex, and ignores changing perceptions and values as well as the variety of meanings that women and men hold about their sexual lives. In *Live Sex Acts*, Wendy Chapkis proposes that if we are able to understand how women experience and define their sexual acts in commercial transactions, then it is possible to move beyond a universalistic moralizing position and to develop some knowledge of the complex realities of women's experiences of sexual labor. Through extensive interviews with sex workers in the Netherlands and the United States, Chapkis concludes that prostitution can be likened to the sociological category of "emotional labor," activities and jobs for which care and feeling are required, commodified and commercialized, such as airline service work, acting, psychotherapy, massage work, or child-care (1997). The objectification of emotion that occurs in the process of this kind of work, including sex work, is not inherently destructive or harmful, she points out, rather the worker is able to "summon and contain emotion within the commercial transaction," to erect and maintain boundaries that protect the worker from abuse, and to develop a professionalism toward the job (76). Sex workers are thus able to distinguish intimacy and love from the sexual act itself, much in the same way that an actor or therapist is able to separate their work from private life, preserving a sense of integrity and distance from emotionally demanding work. Similarly, contributor Heather Montgomery describes perceptions and experiences for children in the Thai sex industry. She explains that the children are able to form a distinct ethical system that allows them to sell sex while preserving a sense of humanity and virtue.

While our approach suggests that social relations involving sexual labor are not inherently tied to specific gendered roles or bodies, there is a persistent pattern through much of history that positions the social gendered category "women" as the sellers or providers of sexual labor and "men" as the group deriving profits and power from the interactions. The subordination of the female and the feminine is the overriding factor for this arrangement in a variety of cultural, national and economic contexts, producing stigmas and social condemnation of persons who defy the socially defined boundaries of womanhood. Categories of "good" and "bad" women (virgin/whore, madonna/prostitute, chaste/licentious women) exist in most patriarchal societies, where the "bad" girl becomes the trope for female sexuality that threatens male control and domination. Female sexual acts that serve women's sexual or economic interests are, within the context of masculinist hegemony, dangerous, immoral, perverted, irresponsible and indecent. Construed in this fashion, the image of the whore disciplines and divides women, forcing some to conform to virginity, domesticity and monogamy and demonizing those who transgress these boundaries. Sex work positions women in dominant discourse as social deviants and outcasts. Today the majority of the world's sex workers are women, working within male-dominated businesses and industries, yet while the social definition of the provider of sexual labor is often closely associated with specific cultural constructions of femininity, and "the prostitute" rendered virtually synonymous with "woman," these gendered relations are clearly also being contested and redefined in different ways throughout the world. Various trends acutely challenge the tendency to essentialize the sex worker with biological notions of gender. In the Caribbean for example, so-called romance tourism is based on the sale by men of "love" to North American and European women, and "rent-a-dreads" and beach boys dominate the sex trade in the tourism industry in some islands (Press 1978, Pruit and Lafont, 1995). In essays in this volume, Thai sex workers in Japan report to sometimes buy sex for their own pleasure from male strippers, Brazilian "miches"—young male hustlers—get by through selling sex to other men, and in Europe and Malaysia male-to-female transgender sex workers also service men. Across the globe, "genetic" men and boys engage in sex work, selling sex to both men and women in homosexual and heterosexual relations, as feminine and masculine subjects.

Nevertheless, even with the increasing visibility of genetic men and boys in sex work, gender inequality and discrimination remain evident. Julian Marlowe argues that if we compare beliefs about male and female sex workers, two prominent yet very different sets of assumptions emerge with men commanding a more liberated and independent position in the discourse than their female counterparts (1997). In this volume Dawn Passar and Johanna Breyer discuss a setting in the U.S. where even though men are entering stripping and exotic dancing in greater numbers than before, they are paid different—and better—kinds of wages than women in clubs under the same management. In an attempt to address such gender inequalities, the women filed a case of sexual harassment and discrimination with the California Equal Employment Opportunity Commission. For Brazil, contributor Paulo Longo describes a situation where young men and boys resist inferiorization that is associated with being defined and viewed as "feminine" by asserting a "macho" identity, and for Malaysia, Khartini Slamah contends that transgendered persons are female, either through self-definition, medical operations or definition by others. As Gail Pheterson notes, "male homosexuals and transvestites also provide sexual service in a minority of cases, but this does not change the gender pattern because like women, they service men and their role is often feminine" (1996:

27). Within the sex industry, a gendered hierarchy and systematic privileging of the male and the masculine continues to be prevalent.

Children, both boys and girls, are also increasingly evident in prostitution, particularly in Third World settings, making the picture of gendered relations even more complex. However, child participation in sex industries invariably raises other questions and problems than those to do with gender, and it is within the international debates on "child prostitution" that a discourse of sexual labor and sex work is also apparent. While some attribute the rise of adolescents and pre-pubescent children in prostitution to the insatiable sexual appetites of depraved western men, or to cultural preferences in Third World countries for sex with virgins, a highly compelling explanation involves an analysis of the global political economy and processes of development and underdevelopment. Studies by the International Labor Organization (ILO) show that the proliferation of earning activity by children is associated with the development process "with its intrinsic features of population and social mobility, urbanization, and progressive monetization of all forms of human activity," and the growth of the modern tourist industry based on the accumulation of wealth and disposable incomes in the industrialized world (Black 1995). The disruption that such development brings to the organization of production in developing countries, draws children into marginal and servile occupations sometimes requiring parents to deploy the income-generating capacity of their children in order to ensure that the household survives. The research suggests we include child prostitution in the context of the global exploitation of child labor in order to effectively address the problem. Such understandings of child labor undergirds various child worker movements around the world, some of which were represented at the 1997 Amsterdam Conference on Child Labor.[4] The organization of young male hustlers in Brazil described in this volume is also premised on the articulation of child prostitution as work.

Sex work, as we understand it here, is not a universal or ahistorical category, but is subject to change and redefinition. It is clearly not limited to prostitution or to women. but certainly encompasses what is generally understood to fall into these two categories. However, even though human sexual and emotional resources have been organized and managed in different ways and acquired different meanings, capital accumulation, liberal free market politics and the commodification of waged labor has transformed various social arrangements in a consistent fashion. Louise White notes in her study of prostitution in colonial Nairobi, Kenya, "prostitution is a capitalist social relationship not because capitalism causes prostitution by commoditizing sexual relations but because wage labor is a unique feature of capitalism: capitalism commoditized labor" (1990:11). White's study proposes that capitalism shapes sex work into commoditized forms of labor rather than causing sex work as a category of social activity. She understands prostitution as another form of domestic labor. Both White and Troung point out that the exploitation of sexual labor is intensified under systemic capitalism, leaving it open to similar kinds of pressures and manipulations that any other waged labor faces. Sexual labor today forms a primary source for profit and wealth, and it is a constituent part of national economies and transnational industries within the global capitalist economy.

If sexual labor is seen to be subject to exploitation, as with any other labor, it can also be considered as a basis for mobilization in struggles for working conditions, rights and benefits and for broader resistances against the oppression of working peoples, paralleling situations in other informal and unregulated sectors. And by recognizing sexual labor in this fashion, it is possible to identify broader strategies for change. Jo Bindman, from Anti-Slavery International, explains that "we first need to identify prostitution as work, as an occupation susceptible like the others to exploitation. Then sex workers can be included and protected under the existing instruments which aim to protect all workers from exploitation, and women from discrimination."[5] Anne McClintock observes that "historically the international labor movement has argued for the radical *transformation* of labor, not its abolition" (1993:8). She thus marks the difference between a movement that advocates the eradication of prostitution and that which is premised on understandings of prostitution as a form of sexual labor, highlighting the need to address issues of social transformations that are linked to the political economy. Situating prostitution as *work* allows then, for a recognition of what Chandra Talpade Mohanty sees as concrete "common interests" based on a shared understanding of location and needs, creating "potential bases of cross-national solidarity" between women (1997:7). The conceptualization of prostitutes, whores, strippers, lap dancers, escorts, exotic dancers etc., as "sex workers" insists that working women's common interests can be articulated within the context of broader (feminist) struggles against the devaluation of "women's" work and gender exploitation within capitalism. Indeed, sex worker Carol Leigh, inventor of the term "sex worker," recalls that she coined it out of a feminist priority to end divisions between women (1997).

Despite the marginality and vulnerability of sex workers internationally, the notion of sex workers as exclusively "victims" is rejected by the authors of this volume. Even in cases where women, men, boys and girls are clearly harmed within the sex industry or are caught in debt-bondage and indentureship situations, it is the respectful recognition of subjectivity and personal agency that creates continuity in this collection. Explorations of agency encountered in *Global Sex Workers* identify sites of transformative practices within the context of both structural constraints and dominant relations of power in the global sex industry. By underlining agency, resistances to, and contestations of, oppressive and exploitative structures are uncovered, and the visions and ideologies inscribed in women's practices made visible. Such analyses position sex workers as actors in the global arena, as persons capable of making choices and decisions that lead to transformations of consciousness and changes in everyday life.

The approach taken here, regarding agency, is embedded in social theory that is informed by a notion of *praxis* (human activity) as central to the construction and reconstruction of society and social knowledge.[6] According to Judith Kegan Gardiner the recognition of agency is integral to feminist theories of social transformation, in ". . . that any theory that denies women 'agency' retards the changes in patriarchal social structure for which feminism strives, because it denies the existence of an entity to attack those structures" (1995: 9). Feminism, from this understanding, is grounded in a notion of the social category "women"—the dominated, oppressed social collectivity within patriarchal relations—as the primary and necessary agents in processes of change. Chapkis (1997) confirms this approach in relationship to sex workers. "Practices of prostitution," she writes, "like other forms of commodification and consumption can be read in more complex ways than simply as a confirmation of male domination. They may also be seen as sites of ingenious resistance and cultural subversion . . . the prostitute cannot be reduced to one of a passive object used in male sexual practice, but instead it can be understood as a place of agency where the sex worker makes active use of the existing sexual order" (29–30). However, even with such general acknowledgement that agency is an integral part of feminism, the idea of women's agency in prostitution is often vehemently rejected by feminists. Indeed, few are able to extend the theoretical position summarized by Gardiner and Chapkis to women's praxis in the sex trade. Sex workers who fight for changes within sex industries, and not for its abolition, are often charged by feminists, as Cheryl Overs remarks in her interview here, with acting with a "false consciousness," or as handmaidens to patriarchal capitalism. Clearly the "good girls" are privileged in much feminist theorizing, while sex workers remain relegated to the status of objects, seen to be violently manipulated and wrought into passivity and acquiescence. Prostitution appears to be one of the last sites of gender relations to be interrogated through a critical feminist lens that assumes that women are both active subjects and subjects of domination.

Sex Work and Racism

Besides the location of women in the sex trade as workers, migrants and agents we address the specificity of racism in positioning Third World sex workers in international relations. Two distinct dimensions are discussed in this collection: racisms embedded in structures and desires within specific local industries, and cultural imperialism refracted through international discourses on prostitution.

The first is analyzed in the studies of prostitution in Australia, Curaçao and Cuba where various ideologies and stereotypes of particular racial-ethnic categories of sex workers are evident. In each place, images of "the exotic" are entwined with ideologies of racial and ethnic difference: the "prostitute" is defined as "other" in comparison to the racial or ethnic origin of the client. Such boundaries, between which women are defined as "good" and "bad," or woman and whore, reinforce sexual relations intended for marriage and family and sets limits on national and ethnic membership. The brown or black woman is regarded as a desirable, tantalizing, erotic subject, suitable for temporary or non-marital sexual intercourse—the ideal "outside" woman—and rarely seen as a candidate for a long-term commitment, an equal partner, or as a future mother. She thus represents the unknown or forbidden yet is positioned in dominant discourse as the subordinated "other." Trends presented in this collection echo those identified in other studies, where it is argued that the exoticization of the Third World "other" is as equally important as economic factors in positioning women in sex work.[7] In other words, it is not simply grinding poverty that underpins a woman's involvement in prostitution. Race and ethnicity are equally important factors for any understanding of contemporary sex industries. To some scholars, racial/ethnic structuring visible in the global sex industry highly resembles the exoticist movement of the eighteenth and nineteenth centuries in which "labelling the anthropological Other as exotic legitimated treating the peoples of the 'third world' as fit to be despised—destroyed even . . . while concurrently also constituting them as projections of western fantasies" (Rousseau and Porter 1990:7). The movement valorized peoples and cultures that were different and remote while simultaneously imposing a status of inferiority upon them. The eroticization of women of Third World cultures was an integral part of the approach whereby female sexuality was defined as highly attractive and fascinating, yet related to the natural primitiveness and lower order of the other cultural group. According to Porter, it was the exotic lands and peoples which provided Europeans in past centuries with "paradigms of the erotic." Away from the repressive mores of Western Europe, these strange cultures and particularly the women in them became sites where sex "was neither penalized, not pathologized nor exclusively procreative" (Porter 1990:118). Enslaved, indentured and colonized womanhood thus came to represent uninhibited and unrestricted sexual intercourse, a situation that in many ways is today reflected in the global sex industry. As the *New York Times* reports "Exotic

Imports Have Captured Italy's Sex Market," referring to the increased importance of African women in sex work in Rome, and simultaneously illuminating
the connection that is still made between Third World women and the exotic
(July 9, 1997). However, as several essays point out here, prostitution is a realm of
contradictions. Thus, even with the heightened exoticization of the sexuality of
Third World women and men, they are positioned within the global sex industry second to white women. White sex workers invariably work in safer, higher
paid and more comfortable environments; brown women—Mulatas, Asians,
Latinas—form a middle class; and Black women are still conspicuously overrep-
resented in the poorest and most dangerous sectors of the trade, particularly
street work. Whiteness continues to represent the hegemonic ideal of physical
and sexual attractiveness and desirability, and white sexual labor is most valued
within the global sex industry.

The second dimension of racism is somewhat less obvious, yet concerns the
neo-colonialism that is evinced in much recent feminist and pro-sex worker
writings that have come out of the United States and Western Europe. Kathleen
Barry's work on the trafficking of women best illustrates this tendency (1984).
Her definition has captured many a feminist imagination regarding Third World
women and has produced an emphasis and fascination with the subject of sex
slaves in developing countries. While Barry argues that "trafficking" could
involve any woman in the world, and that any woman could become a sex slave,
on closer reading of her work another meaning emerges. She constructs a hierarchy of stages of patriarchal and economic development, situating the trafficking of women in the first stage that "prevails in pre-industrial and feudal societies that are primarily agricultural and where women are excluded from the
public sphere" and where women, she states, are the exclusive property of men
(1995: 51). At the other end of the scale she places the "post-industrial, developed
societies" where "women achieve the potential for economic independence"
and where prostitution is normalized (1995:53). Quite simply and without
shame, she evokes an image of non-western women, that various Third World
feminists have identified as common to much western feminist theorizing. The
Third World/non-western woman is positioned in this discourse as "ignorant,
poor, uneducated, tradition bound, domestic, family-oriented, victimized etc"
and is conceptualized as leading a "truncated" sexual life (Mohanty 1991: 56). She
is not yet a "whole or developed" person, but instead resembles a minor needing
guidance, assistance and help. The construct stands in opposition to that of the
western woman who is believed to have (or at least has the potential to have)
control over her income, body and sexuality: the emancipated, independent,
post-modern woman.

In true colonial fashion, Barry's mission is to rescue those whom she considers to be incapable of self-determination. And along with this mission, goes a particular cultural definition of sex itself. Subaltern understandings and lived realities of sexuality and sexual-economic relations, such as found in various African or Caribbean countries for example, where one can speak of a continuum of sexual relations from monogamy to multiple sexual partners and where sex may be considered as a valuable asset for a woman to trade with, are ignored in favor of specific western ideologies and moralities regarding sexual relations.[8] Likewise the meanings young women and men have about their own sexuality, such as described in two essays here on Brazil and Thailand, are denied legitimacy and validity. Barry's work has informed a plethora of activities and inquiries by women's organizations into the subject of prostitution and has helped form an international consciousness and discourse about the sex trade that is solely informed by western, non-sex working women's definitions of sexual relations and prostitution.

The neo-colonialism that surfaces in such representations of the lives and situations of Third World women across the globe does not, however, end with radical feminists or the anti-trafficking lobby. Some prostitute's rights advocates assume that western development, capitalist modernization and industrialization will enable women in developing countries to exercise choice and attain "freedom."[9] Seen to be trapped in underdeveloped states, Third World prostitutes continue to be positioned in this discourse as incapable of making decisions about their own lives, forced by overwhelming external powers completely beyond their control into submission and slavery. Western women's experience is thus made synonymous with assumptions about the inherent superiority of industrialized capitalist development and Third World women placed in categories of pre-technological "backwardness," inferiority, dependency and ignorance. Jo Doezema demonstrates in her chapter that this distortion has crept into even some of the more progressive prostitutes' rights debates concerning "forced" and "voluntary" prostitution, resulting in a negation of Third World sex workers' rights to self-determination.

The surge of writing about the position and identity of prostitutes, the redefinitions that have occurred, the various subject positions that are evident in the present discourse, and the struggles for recognition and rights have also contributed, albeit indirectly, to the creation of an hegemonic western script about prostitution. Shannon Bell's *Rewriting the Prostitute Body* presents an example. In her reading, the categorization and othering of the prostitute is located unequivocally in dichotomies that lie "at the heart of Western thought"—in short, a western concern (1994:40). Bell recovers and celebrates prostitute knowledge through a re-reading of western philosophy and U.S. prostitute performance art, validating distinctly culture-bound practices and knowledges. In so doing, she produces notions of a "new prostitute identity" that trace back to the sacred prostitute in Ancient Greece. Thus, while she argues for a feminist postmodern reading of the subject position that allows for a recognition of differences within the category women represented by class, race, language, national boundaries, sexual orientation and age, and for a theorizing that creates space for new marginal political subjects, her work results in an essentialist definition of the prostitute. Through an homogenization of the origins of prostitution and an erasure of contextual differences, she not only fails to validate histories and subjectivities that lie beyond her purview but subtly infers that the West defines the rest.[10]

The "canon" in prostitution studies reinforces this script.[11] For the most part, contemporary writers on sex work construct the prostitute/sex worker from testimonies and analyses that are derived from struggles of "First World" women in the United States and Western Europe. While all these writings are important in uncovering prostitute politics and identities in some parts of the world, and certainly contribute to a fuller apprehension of sex work, without historicization and geo-political contextualization, they run the risk of universalizing the subject from bounded locations and experiences. Lacking an analysis of international relations and notions of differing cultural constructions and meaning of sexuality and gender, this body of literature appropriates the "non-western" woman's experience without any investigation into the matter. Little research or theorizing to date is, for example, grounded in the lives, experiences, definitions and perspectives of Third World people in sex work, allowing western categories and subjects to be privileged in the international discourse on sex work. The distortion of relations between the First and Third Worlds, and privileging of the western prostitute subject thus places some prostitutes' rights activists and allies in danger of a political alignment with movements that consolidate western hegemony.

Third World and anti-racist feminisms have over the past two decades intensely critiqued the universalism and totalizing effect of unnuanced western (feminist) theorizing—modernist and postmodernist—arguing that many of the concepts and theories produced about women's oppression are, and have been for many years, grounded in struggles of middle-class white women and may be quite antithetical to other women's experiences, if not representative of imperialist feminist thought.[12] Nevertheless the need for feminist theory to engage with racialized sexual subjectivities in tandem with the historical weight of imperialism, colonialism and racist constructions of power has only been raised recently in the context of this feminist theorizing on prostitution.[13] In view of histories of the oversexualization of non-western women in western cultures and the colonial legacies of the rape and sexual abuse of indigenous, and other Third World women, a hesitancy to explore topics of Third World women's sexual agency and subjectivity in prostitution is quite understandable. Yet in an era when women can no longer be defined exclusively as victims, where Third World women speak for themselves in various forums, where increasingly analyses have shifted focus from simple hierarchies and dichotomies to the problematization of multiple spaces, seemingly contradictory social locations and plural sites of power, it would seem that experiences, identities and struggles of women in the global sex industry cannot be neglected. This book has taken shape in direct counterpoint to a North American-Western European hegemony within contemporary feminist and prostitute writings about the sex trade.

Transnational Sex Work and the Global Economy

Sex work across national boundaries is not new to the world. Donna Guy observes that "foreign prostitutes and pimps were already ensconced in Buenos Aires (Argentina) by 1860" and that between 1889 and 1901, seventy-five percent of the registered working women hailed from Europe and Russia (1990:14–16). Between 1865 and 1885, around one quarter of the registered prostitutes in Bologna, Italy, were migrants, and during the 1880s young British women worked in Belgium and other parts of Europe (Gibson 1986, Walkowitz 1980). In India, a number of European women worked as prostitutes in the latter part of the nineteenth century, the majority of whom originated from Central and Eastern Europe, but also among them were English women (Levine 1994). In Russia, in the late 1880s, "non-Russian and foreign prostitutes" comprised around one-sixth of the registered prostitute population (Bernstein 1995: 97). During World War II, "haole" (white) women were the majority in brothels in Hawaii. Korean and Thai women were forced to "comfort" the Japanese military, and Cuban and Venezuelan women serviced the Dutch and American navies in Curacao (Bailey and Farber 1992, Hicks 1994, Kempadoo 1994). Specific political, economic and social events shaped the women's involvement in the sex trade at different times, in different places, within the context of a globalizing capitalist system, colonialism and masculinst hegemony.

In the late 1980s, Licia Brussa estimated that between thirty and sixty percent of the prostitutes in the Netherlands were from Third World countries, particularly Latin America and Asia (1989). Today, the migrant sex working population has been joined by women from Eastern Europe and West Africa. In 1991, around seventy percent of the sex workers in Japan were reported to be Filipino, and young Afghan and Bangladeshi women worked in prostitution in Pakistan (Korvinus 1992). In the same period, the red-light district in Bombay, India, relied predominantly upon migrant female labor, much of which originated in Nepal. By the mid-1990s, Eastern European, Russian and Vietnamese prostitutes were reported to be working in China while Russian women appeared in the Egyptian sex industry, and Mexican women moved into sex work in Japan (*BBC World Service*, April 28, 1994, *New York Times*, June 9, 1995, Azize et al, 1996). Besides these trends, chapters in this volume point to Thai sex workers in Australia and Japan, Brazilians and Guyanese in Suriname, Dominicans and Colombians in Curaçao, Ghanaians in the Cote d'Ivoire and Austria, Nigerians in Senegal and Italy, Polish, Bulgarian, Czech and Ukrainian women in Germany and Austria and so forth.

Indeed, transnational sex work has continued over the past hundred years, but the question arises about whether it has intensified, as many will argue, during the twentieth century and particularly over the last two decades. Given the lack of figures and documentation of what in most countries is an outlawed and underground activity, and the multiplicity of activities worldwide that constitute "sex work," it is virtually impossible to state with certainty that numbers have increased. Also, as with any activity in the informal sector, information on populations involved, income, types of activities, and international migration or trafficking routes is imprecise. A glaringly obvious example of the inaccuracies that exist is related to the number of prostitutes in Asia. Figures for the city of Bombay in India range from 100,000 (*Asia Watch* 1993) to 600,000 (Barry 1995)—a difference of half a million. In the case of Thailand, figures for "child prostitutes" range between 2, 500 and 800,000, with the age range being equally as imprecise (Black 1995). To any conscientious social scientist, such discrepancies should be cause for extreme suspicion of the reliability of the research, yet when it comes to sex work and prostitution, few eyebrows are raised and the figures are easily bandied about without question.[14]

Nonetheless, since the 1970s a global restructuring of capitalist production and investment has taken place and this can be seen to have wide-scale gendered implications and, by association, an impact on sex industries and sex work internationally. New corporate strategies to increase profit have developed, involving the movement of capital from industrial centers to countries with cheap labor, the circumvention of unionized labor, and so-called flexible employment policies. Unemployment and temporary work plagues the industrialized centers as well as "developing" countries. The ILO estimated that in January 1994, around thirty percent of the world's labor force was unemployed and unable to sustain a minimum standard of living (Chomsky 1994:188). The power and influence of transnational institutions such as the World Trade Organization, the World Bank and various corporations has superseded that of national governments and national businesses.[15] Measures imposed by the International Monetary Fund (IMF) for national debt-repayment, such as Structural Adjustment programs, and international trade agreements, such as the North American Free Trade Agreement (NAFTA) and the General Agreement on Tariffs and Trade (GATT) squeeze national economies, creating displacement from rural agricultural communities, rising unemployment in urban centers, drops in real wages, and increasing poverty. Free Trade and Special Economic Zones for export-oriented production, cuts by governments in national expenditures in the social sector and the removal of trade restrictions, local food subsidies and price controls accompany these measures and agreements and impose even further hardships on working people.[16] The corporate drive to increase consumption, and hence profit margins, has also led to a proliferation of new products, goods and services and the cultivation of new desires and needs. Alongside apparel, automobile, electronic, computer and luxury good industries, sex industries have grown since the mid-1970s to fully encompass live sex shows, sex shops, massage parlors, escort services, phone sex, sex tours, image clubs, and exotic dancing, and to creating, as Edward Herman states, "one of the booming markets in the New World Order—a multi-billion dollar industry with finders, brokers, syndicate operations and pimp 'managers' at the scene of action" (1995:5). Sex tourism has become a new industry. Recruitment agencies and impresarios link the local sites and sex industries in various parts of the world, indicating a parallel with transnational corporations in the formal global economy. "The 'success' of the sex industry," write James Petras and Tienchai Wongchaisuwan about Thailand, "is based on a 'special relation' of shared interests among a complex network of military leaders, police officials, business tourist promoters, godfathers and pimps. At the international level, airline and hotel chains have worked closely with the local business-military elite to promote the sex tourist industry. The World Bank's support for the open economy and export oriented development strategy results in financial support of tourism" (1993: 36). In Thailand, the authors estimate, direct and indirect earnings from sex enterprises is about $5 billion a year. Elsewhere, as in Cuba and the Dominican Republic, the specter of sex tourism has become embedded in the economy. The sexual labor of young brown women in these playgrounds of the West has become increasingly important to the national economies, while prostitution remains condemned as degrading and destructive. In Cuba's case, it is viewed as a counterrevolutionary engagement. Nevertheless, State support or tolerance of this form of tourism is evident. Sex work fills the coffers of countries whose economic survival is increasingly dependent on global corporate capitalist interests.

The emerging global economic order has already wreaked havoc on women's lives. Recent studies document an increasing need of women to contribute to the household economy through waged labor, yet having to deal with declining real wages, lower wage structures than men and longer working hours.[17] Seasonal or flexible employment is the norm for women all over the world. Skilled and unskilled female workers constitute the main labor force in the new export-oriented industries—for shoe, toy, textile and garment production, in agribusinesses and electronic factories—where they are faced with poor working conditions, are continually threatened with unemployment due to automation and experience mass dismissals due to relocations of whole sectors of the industry. In many instances, minimum wage, health and safety laws are overridden by the transnational corporations in these new production zones, leaving women workers in particularly hazardous situations. Furthermore, with disruptions to traditional household and family structures, women are increasingly becoming heads of households, providing and nurturing the family. With dwindling family resources and the western emphasis on the independent nuclear family, women must also increasingly rely on the state for provisions such as maternity leave and child-care, yet fewer funds are allocated by governments for social welfare and programs.[18] Informal sector work and "moonlighting" is growing and engagement in the booming sex industries fills a gap created by globalization.

Migration is a road many take to seek other opportunities and to break away from oppressive local conditions caused by globalization. A 1996 ILO report describes the "feminization" of international labor migration as "one of the most striking economic and social phenomena of recent times" (1). This "phenomenon" according to the authors of the report, is most pronounced in Asian countries where women are migrating as "autonomous, economic agents" in their own right, "trying to seize economic opportunities overseas" (1). The Philippines has put more women onto the overseas labor market than any other country in the world (Rosca 1995). Within all this dislocation and movement, some migrant women become involved in sex work. However, laws prohibiting or regulating prostitution and migration, particularly from the South, combine to create highly complex and oppressive situations for women if they become involved in sex work once abroad. The illegal movement of persons for work elsewhere, commonly known as "trafficking" also becomes a very real issue for those who are being squeezed on all sides and have few options other than work in underground and informal sectors. Traffickers take advantage of the illegality of commercial sex work and migration, and are able to exert an undue amount of power and control over those seeking political or economic refuge or security. In such cases, it is the laws that prevent legal commercial sex work and immigration that form the major obstacles.

A related dimension to globalization with the expansion of sex industries, a heightened necessity for transnational migration for work, and increasing immiseration of women worldwide, is the spread of AIDS. Paul Farmer links the pandemic in sub-Saharan Africa to the social realities of the migrant labor system, rapid urbanization, high levels of war with military mobilization, landlessness and poverty that have been exacerbated by an economic crises caused by "poor terms of trade, the contradictions of post-colonial economies which generate class disparities and burdensome debt service" since the mid 1970s (1996:71). These factors, he contends, are intricately intertwined with pervasive gender inequality and specific socially constructed meanings of gender and sex, creating a very complex situation regarding the epidemiology and, consequently, the prevention of AIDS. Around eighty-two percent of AIDS cases worldwide in 1996, he points out, were found in Africa, with women and children bearing the brunt of the epidemic. A similarly complex interrelationship between changing agriculture systems to meet New World Order demands, fueled by gendered traditions and inequalities, inadequate subsistence, a felt lack of desired consumption, goods, tourism and the drug trade enables the spread of AIDS in Asia (Farmer 1996:82–88). For the Americas, Bond et al. note that labor migration between the Caribbean and the United States has been an important factor in the spread of HIV and AIDS, and that "the development of tourist industries, frequently based on U.S. capital as a replacement for the decline in profits from older colonially established sources such as sugar cane, has also traced the routes for HIV to follow" (1997:7). With only an estimated four percent of the world's AIDS cases being registered in North America and Western Europe, it is particularly evident that it is the rest of the world that is at greatest risk (Farmer 1997).

This relatively new sexually transmitted disease and identification by world health authorities of a concentration of the epidemic in developing countries has led to government interventions. The attention has produced contradictions for sex workers around the world. As in the past, with state concern for public health matters, prostitutes are placed under scrutiny, subject to intense campaigning and roped into projects that define them as the vectors and transmitters of disease (Zalduondo 1991, Murray and Robinson 1996). Sex workers are continually blamed for the spread of the disease, with Eurocentric racist notions of cultural difference compounding the effect for Third World populations. Consequently, inappropriate methods of intervention have been introduced and sex workers burdened with having to take responsibility for the prevention and control of the disease. Farmer points out that ". . . while public health campaigns target sex workers, many African women take a different view of AIDS epidemiology and prevention. In their view, the epidemiology of HIV and Africa's economic crises suggest that HIV spreads not because of the "exotic sexual practices" of Africans but because of the daily life within which women struggle to survive" (1996:74). Bond et al, in their studies of AIDS in Africa and the Caribbean apply a similar analysis. Arguing that there is "more to AIDS than 'truck drivers' and 'prostitutes'" the authors consider it of vital importance to examine relations of political and economic power in relationship to the spread of AIDS, with specific attention to the disempowered such as women and children (1997:xi). Placing the focus and blame on sex workers does not necessarily address the root of the problem, but serves to push them further into marginality and social isolation. On the other hand, some AIDS-prevention work has contributed to the formation of new sex worker organizations, inadvertently empowering sex workers in other areas than just in health matters. Some of these initiatives are described in this collection.

The Global Movement

Since the 1970s sex work has been an organizing basis for women, men, and transgenders in different parts of the world. But while the emergence of prostitutes' rights groups and organizations in Western Europe and North America up to the early 1990s has been well documented, there is little written on the global movement. Over the past ten years, the main recorders of the prostitutes' rights movement, Frederique Delacoste and Priscilla Alexander (1987), Laurie Bell (1987) Gail Pheterson (1989), Nicky Roberts (1992), Valerie Jenness (1993), Shannon Bell (1994), Wendy Chapkis (1997) and Jill Nagle (1997), describe the beginning of a self-identified prostitutes movement with the establishment of the prostitute organization, (COYOTE) Call Off Your Old Tired Ethics, in San Francisco in 1973 and sister or similar kinds of groups in various part of the United States around the same time. They locate the emergence of a highly politicized prostitute rights advocacy movement in Europe, starting with the strike by French prostitutes in 1975 which led to the creation of the French Collective of Prostitutes and which in turn inspired the formation of such groups as the English Collective of Prostitutes in England (1975), the New York Prostitutes Collective (1979), that later became USPROS, the Australian Prostitutes Collective (1981), which is now known as the Prostitutes Collective of Victoria (PCV) and the Italian Committee for the Civil Rights of Prostitutes (1982). CORP—the Canadian Organization for the Rights of Prostitutes—the Dutch Red Thread and HYDRA in Germany also assume a significant place in the history of the sex workers rights movement as chronicled by these authors. The writings also signal the formation of the International Committee for Prostitutes Rights (ICPR) in 1985, the two World Whores Congresses held respectively in Amsterdam, the Netherlands in 1985 and Brussels, Belgium in 1986, and the creation of the World

Charter of Prostitutes Rights through these two congresses, as epitomizing a worldwide prostitutes' rights movement and politics. Nonetheless, the international character of the movement has been more wishful thinking than political reality. As Pheterson, rapporteur on the two congresses and co-director of ICPR, notes about the first congress, Third World sex workers did not formally participate and prostitute advocates represented sex workers for three countries, Singapore, Thailand and Vietnam(1989). At the second congress, a similar dominance of the West was evident. Pheterson further points out in her reflection on the ICPR's work at the end of the 1980s, "the numerous nationalities not represented point to work yet to be done in building a truly world movement of whores." Thus, much of what was laid out in the Charter and discussed at the congresses was defined by (white) western sex workers and advocates. Third World prostitutes' rights organizations, such as the Ecuadorian Association of Autonomous Women Workers, established in 1982, or the Uruguayan, Association of Public Prostitutes (AMEPU), founded in 1985, were at this point not an integral part of the "international" movement, although Pheterson attempted to correct this omission by including "new voices" in her report on the prostitutes' rights movement (1989). And despite Pheterson's awareness of the problem and her insistence that the movement needed to truly "internationalize," many writings in the 1990s have continued to reproduce a skewed representation of the prostitutes rights movement and to ignore sex workers' rights groups in developing countries.

Despite this lack of recognition, sex workers in Third World and other non-western countries have been busy, taking action, demonstrating against injustices they face, and demanding human, civil, political and social rights. Thus not only was an Ecuadorian association formed in 1982, but they held a sex workers' strike in 1988. In Brazil, a national prostitutes conference took place in 1987, giving rise to the establishment of the National Network of Prostitutes, Da Vida. In Montevideo, Uruguay, AMEPU inaugurated its childcare center and new headquarters after making its first public appearance in the annual May Day march in 1988. The Network of Sex Work Projects, founded in 1991, began to make links with sex workers' rights and health care projects in the Asian and Pacific region, slowly creating a truly international network that today includes at least forty different projects and groups in as many different countries around the world. 1992 witnessed the founding of the Venezuelan Association of Women for Welfare and Mutual Support (AMBAR), with the Chilean group Association for the Rights of Women, "Angela Lina" (APRODEM) and the Mexican Unión Única following suit in 1993. Two national congresses were held by the Ecuadorian sex workers' rights association in 1993 and 1994. The Maxi Linder Association in Suriname, the Indian Mahila Samanwaya Committee, and the Colombian Association of Women (Cormujer), were also all established by 1994. In the same year, around 400 prostitutes staged a protest against the closing of a brothel in Lima, Peru, with the slogan "We Want to Work, We Want to Work" and in Paramaribo, Suriname, sex workers made a first mass public appearance on AIDS Day, marching through the city with the banner "No Condom, No Pussy," drawing attention to their demands for safe sex. Also, 1994 witnessed the founding of The Sex Worker Education and Advocacy Taskforce (SWEAT) in South Africa. In 1996, groups in Japan and the Dominican Republic—Sex Workers! Encourage, Empower, Trust and Love Yourselves! (SWEETLY) and Movement of United Women (MODEMU)—were formed, and in the same year the Indian organization held its first congress in Calcutta, as well as organizing several protests and demonstrations against harassment and brutality. In 1997, with the help of AMBAR in Venezuela, the Association for Women in Solidarity (AMAS) became the first Nicaraguan group, comprised mainly of street workers. Other sex worker organizations have been reported to exist in Indonesia, Tasmania, Taiwan, and Turkey. Several of these hitherto unrecognized or new groups and activities are described in this volume, through the eyes and words of the leading activists.

While this list of organizations is not exhaustive, and keeps growing, we must keep in mind that each group has a history that pre-dates its formal founding date. Sex workers as individuals and in informal groups have battled against stigmas and discriminatory laws, denounced social and political injustices, and fought for their basic human rights in non-western settings for many years and there are often several years of organized activity before a formal organization appears on the map. Furthermore, in some instances the seeds of a contemporary organization are much older. The present Uruguayan organization, for example, claims a history lodged in the struggle of Polish sex workers during the nineteenth century in that country. Everyday resistances have also been documented for the mid-nineteenth century in Lucknow, India (Oldenburg 1990) and Guatemala (McCreery 1986), and in colonial Kenya in the 1920s–30s (White 1990). Sex workers' struggles are thus neither a creation of a western prostitutes' rights movement or the privilege of the past three decades.

The lack of Third World sex worker representation in the international arena began to be redressed in the 1990s, as the international AIDS conferences provided a new opportunity for sex workers to get together. Jo Doezema writes, "AIDS was an issue that gave new impetus to the flagging international movement by providing an issue around which to organize much needed funds and new alliances with gay organizations. Under-funded sex worker organizations in both the First and Third Worlds who would have been hard pressed to persuade their funders of the necessity of sending a representative to a 'whores conference' found it easier to get money when public health was, supposedly, at stake."[19] Thus, the AIDS conferences provided a platform for a revitalization of the international movement, and, for the first time, signaled the presence of Third World sex workers as equal participants on the international scene. A notable instance, as Doezema further notes, was the AIDS Conference in Yokohama, Japan, in 1994, when the Network of Sex work Projects organized its first Asia-Pacific regional conference, parallel to the AIDS Conference. Sex worker delegates from around the world put together an action plan for activism during the AIDS Conference itself and beyond. During the Conference, delegates were addressed by a panel of sex workers from countries including Brazil, Mexico and Malaysia, who presented their own analysis and strategies of AIDS prevention in the context of sex workers rights. The United Nations Fourth World Conference on Women in Beijing, China, in 1995 also drew various international sex workers' rights activists—many of whom formed a united delegation, spearheaded by the NWSP.[20]

In 1997, an international prostitution conference took place in California, U.S., divided into a sex worker-only pre-conference organized by NWSP and COYOTE and a conference for sex workers, academics, activists and others working with or for sex workers, organized by COYOTE and the University of California at Northridge. Sex workers representing organizations from countries including Mexico, Guatemala, Venezuela, Brazil, Nicaragua, India, Thailand, Japan, and Malaysia helped insure that the pre-conference worked to an agenda that reflected a truly international perspective.

New Directions

Building upon the definition of sex work, prostitutes in the state of New South Wales in Australia became the first to gain acceptance as an official sex workers' union in 1996, under the umbrella of the Australian Liquor, Hospitality and Miscellaneous Workers' Union. Exotic dancers working at the "Lust Lady" in San Francisco in the United States followed suit. In April 1997, they entered into an agreement with the management of the theater and labor union, Local 790, the Service Employees International Union of the AFL-CIO which includes provisions on discrimination, sexual harassment, family and personal leave, pay, job evaluation, breaks and lunches, and dismissals. The notion of "sex worker" has then enabled prostitutes and others in the sex trade to not only articulate their needs as working peoples, but has brought a legitimacy hitherto unknown, and these examples may provide models for other groups in the future.

And while participation by Third World sex workers in the international movement is on the rise generally, not all regions participate equally. Central and South American, and increasingly, Asian sex workers' organizations are becoming a major voice in the international movement. In the former Soviet Union, Eastern Europe, Africa, and in the majority of Asian countries, however, independent organizing by sex workers is not yet visible. Here, as elsewhere, the AIDS pandemic has meant an upsurge in interest in sex workers as vectors of disease. While this has led, in some cases, to repressive measures against sex workers, it has also provided an opportunity for possible sex worker organizing. The projects such as Bliss without Risk in the Czech Republic, SYNVEV in Senegal, EMPOWER in Thailand, ZiTeng in Hong Kong, and others included in this volume, while not run by sex workers, are committed to the empowerment of sex workers. It is from groups such as these that autonomous sex worker organizations have begun. Continued AIDS prevention work of the type described here could thus lead to a strengthening of the movement, and to many more sex workers' rights groups worldwide.

Finally, in the global movement, struggles against western imperialism and racism within prostitutes' rights activism continues. The 1997 international conference provides a example of this struggle. Early Internet discussions between sex workers about the conference planning was dominated by those with access in the U.S., and focused almost exclusively on western, especially United States issues. This focus was later challenged by other sex workers, and resulted in fierce debate on the nature of an international conference.[21] Sex workers from Chile also frustratedly pointed out prior to the conference, that the organizers claim to internationalism was empty, given that there was an absence of travel funds and facilities for translation to enable Third World sex workers to participate in the conference. From Australia, Alison Murray withdrew from the conference, noting, among other things, that the conference was overly "North America centered."[22] The main conference reflected deep-seated ignorance of the importance, and even the existence, of sex worker organizations outside the United States and Europe. Third World and non-western sex workers felt marginalized, hurt and angry as promised interpretation facilities never materialized and as sessions highlighting the activities and issues of importance to Third World sex workers were relegated to difficult time-slots or even canceled when, due to scheduling problems, they threatened to conflict with "more important" sessions. This led to a storming of the podium during the final plenary session by Central and South American sex worker delegates, who, with full support from other sex workers and activists, denounced the academic organizers for the ill treatment they received. The conference thus ended in a strong anti-imperialist, anti-racist demonstration with the uproar forcing western sex workers to recognize and deal with these dimensions of power and inequality. Such consciousness within the movement can only continue to grow.

This collection, then, remains a sketch of activities and definitions that shape a global sex workers movement, and posits some clear directions that such a movement could take in the coming years. While clearly there is a need for autonomous organizing and consolidation of each groups position, within its own political, economic and cultural context, it is evident that sex workers do not view the struggle as isolated from that of other members of society. As prostitutes, migrant workers, transgenders, family breadwinners, single parents, HIV-positives, or teenagers, many recognize the multiple arenas in which their lives play, and consequently the multiple facets of social life that must be addressed. Gay, lesbian, bisexual, and transgender organizations, legal and human rights activists, health care workers, labor unions, and other sex industry workers are potential allies in the struggle to transform sexual labor into work that is associated with dignity, respect and decent working conditions. The coalitions that are taking shape through everyday resistances of sex workers also brings new meanings to the women's movement and feminism. It is hopefully from this matrix of resistance and coalitions that sex workers' rights will be embraced in the decades to come.

Notes

1. "Third World Women" is used here in keeping with the definition proposed by various "Third-World feminists," which captures the notion of a collectivity whose lives are conditioned and shaped by the struggles against neo-colonialism and imperialism, capitalism and gender subordination. See for example, the writings by Chandra Telpade, "Under Western Eyes: Feminist Scholarship and Colonial Discourses," in C. T. Mohanty, Ann Russo and Lourdes Torres, eds., *Third World Women and the Politics of Feminism* (Bloomington: Indiana University Press, 1991) and "Women Workers and Capitalist Scripts: Ideologies of Domination, Common Interest and the Politics of Solidarity," in M. Jaqui Alexander and C. T. Mohanty, eds., *Feminist Geneologies, Colonial Legacies, Democratic Futures* (New York: Routledge, 1997) 3–29; Chela Sandoval, "U.S. Third World Feminism: The Theory and Method of Oppositional Consciousness in the Postmodern World," *Genders*, vol. 10 (Spring 1994) 1–24; Uma Narayan, "Contesting Cultures: 'Westernization,' Respect for Cultures and Third-World Feminists," in Linda Nicholoson, ed., *The Second Wave: A Reader in Feminist Theory* (New York and London: Routledge, 1996) 396–414; Geraldine Heng, "'A Great Way to Fly': Nationalism, the State and Varieties of Third-World Feminism," in M. Jaqui Alexander and C. T. Mohanty, eds., *Feminist Geneologies, Colonial Legacies, Democratic Futures* (New York: Routledge, 1997) 30–45.
2. See Frederique Delacoste and Priscilla Alexander, *Sex Work: Writings by Women in the Sex Industry* (Pittsburgh: Cleis Press, 1987); Laurie Bell, ed., *Good Girls: Feminist and Sex Trade Workers Face to Face* (Toronto: The Women's Press, 1987); Gail Pheterson, ed., *A Vindication of the Rights of Whores* (Washington: Seal Press, 1989); Nickie Roberts, *Whores in History: Prostitution in Western Society* (London: Harper Collins, 1992); Valerie Jenness, *Making It Work: The Prostitutes' Rights Movement in Perspective* (Hawthorne, NY: Aldine de Gruyter, 1993); Anne McClintock, "Sex Workers and

Sex Work: Introduction," *Social Text*, vol. 37 (Winter 1993) 1–10; Shannon Bell, *Reading, Writing and Rewriting the Prostitute Body*, (Bloomington: Indiana University Press, 1994); Wendy Chapkis, *Live Sex Acts: Women Performing Erotic Labor* (New York: Routledge, 1997); Jill Nagle, ed., *Whores and Other Feminists* (New York: Routledge, 1997).

3. A position argued by Kathleen Barry, *The Prostitution of Sexuality: The Global Exploitation of Women* (New York: New York University Press, 1995).

4. Antony Swift reporting on the conference for the *New Internationalist*, describes perspectives and demands of child worker organizations from South and Central America, West Africa, and Asia. The entire issue of the magazine documents the emergence of vocal and articulate organized struggles for the rights of working children.

5. This perspective also underpins the Anti-Slavery International examination of existing international human rights and labor standards and instruments in relation to prostitution. See Jo Bindman and Jo Doezema, *Redefining Prostitution as Sex Work on the International Agenda* (London: Anti-Slavery International, 1997) and NSWP: The Network of Sex Work Projects.

6. Antony Gidden's *The Constitution of Society: Outline of the Theory of Structuration* (Cambridge: Polity Press, 1984) and Pierre Bourdieu's *Outline of a Theory of Practice* (Cambridge University Press, 1977) are of particular interest here. Both stress the interwovenness of human agency and social structure whenever, according to the Marxian idea, humans "make their own history, but not in circumstances of their own choosing" stressing the ways in which humans produce and reproduce social, economic and political life. Sherry Ortner notes in her elaboration of practice theory, in *Making Gender: The Politics and Erotics of Culture*: "The challenge is to picture indissoluble formations of structurally embedded agency and intention-filled structures, to recognize the way in which the subject is part of larger social and cultural webs, and in which social and cultural 'systems' are predicated upon human desires and projects" (Boston: Beacon Press, 1996:12).

7. See Luise White, *The Comforts of Home: Prostitution in Colonial Nigeria* (Chicago: University of Chicago Press 1990); Than-Dam Troung, *Sex, Money and Morality: The Political Economy of Prostitution and Tourism in South East Asia* (London: Zed Books, 1990), James A. Tyner, "Constructions of Filipina Migrant Entertainers," *Gender, Place and Culture*, vol. 3:1 (1996), 77–93; Anne McClintock, "Screwing the System: Sexwork, Race and the Law," *Boundary* 2 vol. 19, (Summer 1992), 70–95.

8. See Paola Tabet, "'I'm the Meat, I'm the Knife': Sexual Service, Migration and Repression in Some African Societies," in Gail Pheterson, ed., *Vindication of the Rights of Whores* (Washington: Seal Press, 1989) 204–226; Gloria Wekker, "'I am Gold Money' (I Pass Through All Hands, But I Do Not Lose My Value): The Construction of Selves, Gender and Sexualities in a Female Working-Class, Afro-Surinamese Setting." Dissertation, University of California, 1992; Luise White, *The Comforts of Home: Prostitution in Colonial Nigeria* (Chicago: University of Chicago Press, 1990); Barbara de Zalduonda and Jean Maxius Bernard, "Meanings and Consequences of Sexual-Economic Exchange: Gender, Poverty and Sexual Risk Behavior in Urban Haiti," in *Conceiving Sexuality: Approaches to Sex Research in a Postmodern World*, ed. Richard G. Parker and John M. Gagnon (New York: Routledge, 1995): 157–80. These are studies of culturally specific "sexual-economic" relationships, in which women's bodies are not regarded as sacred sites, but rather sexuality is experienced as a resource that is strategically employed. See Lyn Sharon Chancer, "Prostitution, Feminist Theory and Ambivalence: Notes from the Sociological

Underground," *Social Text*, vol. 37 (Winter 1993) 143–181. Chancer suggests that we can speak of "bodily" or "sexual capital" to distinguish the type of human resources that women and men draw upon for sex work.

9. See Hazel Carby, "White Woman Listen! Black Feminism and the Boundaries of Sisterhood," in Centre for Contemporary Cultural Studies' *The Empire Strikes Back: Race and Racism in 70s Britain* (London: Hutchinson, 1982). Carby writing about this general trend in 1982, notes that " too often concepts of historical progress are invoked by the left and feminists alike, to create a sliding scale of "civilized liberties". When barbarous sexual practices are to be described, the "Third World" is on display and compared to the "First World" which is seen to be more "enlightened" and progressive" (216). In a similar vein, Marchand argues that "the implicit assumption is, of course, that when non-Western women have reached our level of modernization, they will subscribe to western feminist ideals. As a result the western feminist agenda can be presented (and defended) as embodying universal feminist values. . . ." See Marianne H. Marchand, "Latin American Women Speak on Development: Are We Listening Yet?", in M. H. Marchand and Jane L. Parpart, eds., *Feminism, Postmodernism, Development* (London: Routledge, 1995) 59.

10. Similarly, McClintock, while stating that "sex workers do not speak with a univocal voice: there is not a single, authoritative narrative of prostitution . . ." nevertheless manages successfully to make generalizations about "the prostitute" that are drawn exclusively from Western European and North American contexts (1993). See also Floya Anthias and Nira Yuval-Davis, *Racialized Boundaries: Race, Nation, Gender, Colour, Class and the Anti-Racist Struggle* (London: Routledge, 1992). Anthias and Yuval-Davis urge caution about such theorizing under the name of postmodernism, concluding that "there is a danger that 'the specificity of a particular experience' may itself become an expression of essentialism. To posit diversity therefore does not necessarily imply the abandonment of static and a-historical categories but may merely proliferate them" (99).

11. Apart from McClintock see also Jenness (1993), Gail Pheterson (1989), and Delacoste and Alexander (1987) as examples where the assumed reference point for developing generalized claims about "the" prostitutes' rights movement derive primarily from Western European and Euro-American contexts and experiences. In contrast, analyses of the sex industries and sex work in non-western and Third World countries are highly contextualized in terms of history, culture, gender relations, and location in the global economy. See for example, Troung *Sex, Money and Morality* (London: Zed Books, 1990); Saundra Pollock Sturdevant and Brenda Stoltzfus, *Let the Good Times Roll: Prostitution and the U.S. Military in Asia* (New York: The New Press, 1992); Anne Allison, *Nightwork: Sexuality, Pleasure, and Corporate Masculinity in a Tokyo Hostess Club* (Chicago: University of Chicago Press, 1994); Cleo Odzer, *Patpong Sisters: An American Woman's View of the Bangkok Sex World* (New York: Arcade Publishing, 1994); and Carolyn Sleightholme and Indrani Sinha, *Guilty Without Trial: Women in the Sex Trade in Calcutta* (New Brunswick: Rutgers University Press, 1996).

12. Within this argument is also the notion that what may be defined for one race/ethnic, class or gendered group as oppressive could under conditions of racial domination or colonialism, be a site of resistance and potential liberation or at least a site of multiple meanings and contradictions. The construct of the family as singularly oppressive for women has thus been

challenged. Likewise concepts of "the erotic," "patriarchy" and "womanhood" have been rescued from white feminist theory and redefined from Third-World/Black/anti-imperialist feminist perspectives to reflect the history and experiences of "the other."

13. See Patricia Hill Collins, *Black Feminist Thought: Knowledge, Consciousness and the Politics of Empowerment* (New York: Routledge, 1990); and Laurie Shrage, *Moral Dilemmas of Feminism: Prostitution, Adultery, and Abortion* (New York: Routledge, 1994). In the U.S., Collins notes "Perhaps the most curious omission has been the virtual silence of the Black feminist community concerning the participation of far too many Black women in prostitution. Ironically, while the image of African-American women as prostitutes has been aggressively challenged, the reality of African-American women who work as prostitutes remain unexplored" (164). Taking her cue from Collins, Shrage insists that "few researchers have explored how race and gender together condition one's participation in prostitution" (142). Sadly, even with these sharp observations neither author is able to get any further. In Collin's brief coverage of the subject, Black women in prostitution are situated as "victim and pet," with the force of her analysis attacking the relations of dominance that historically constructed this position. She gives no consideration to notions of Black female sexual agency but rather positions Black women as objects that have been formed by purely external forces and conditions. Shrage on the other hand, remains safely within an examination of representations and images. Both, in the end, manage to leave the void they signalled, unfilled.

14. As an example of this careless use, see Robert I. Friedman, "India's Shame," *The Nation* (April 8, 1996) 11–20.

15. See Sarah Anderson and John Cavanagh, *The Top 200: The Rise of Global Corporate Power* (Washington, DC: Institute for Policy Studies, 1996). In this survey of the world's largest corporations, Anderson and Cavanagh, found that "of the top 100 largest economies in the world, 51 are now global corporations, only 49 are countries" with Wal-Mart, bigger than 161 countries, Mitsubishi "larger than the fourth most populous nation on earth: Indonesia" and Ford's economy larger than that of South Africa.

16. See Noam Chomsky, *World Orders Old and New* (New York: Columbia University Press, 1994); Jeremy Brecher and Tim Costello, *Global Village or Global Pillagea; Economic Reconstruction, From the Bottom Up* (Boston: South End Press, 1994); see also, Kevin Danaher, ed., *Fifty Years is Enough: The Case Against the World Bank and the International Monetary Fund* (Boston: South End Press, 1994).

17. For details on gender inequalities worldwide see the United Nation publications: *Human Development Report 1995* and *The World's Women 1995: Trends and Statistics.*

18. Among the many who have written specifically on women in the New World Order, see Carmen Diana Deer, et. al., *In the Shadows of the Sun: Caribbean Development Alternatives and U.S. Policy* (Boulder: Westview, 1990); Sheila Rowbotham and Swasti Mitter, eds., *Dignity and Daily Bread: New Forms of Economic Organizing Among Poor Women in the Third World and The First* (London: Routledge, 1994); M. Jaqui Alexander and Chandra Talpade Mohanty, eds., *Feminist Geneologies, Colonial Legacies, Democratic Futures* (New York: Routledge, 1997); Edna Bonachich, et. al., eds., *Global Production: The Apparel Industry in the Pacific Rim* (Philadelphia: Temple University Press, 1994); and Annie Phizacklea and Carol Wolkowitz, *Homeworking Women: Gender, Racism and Class at Work* (London: Sage Publications, 1995).

19. Doezema, E-mail correspondence, July 25, 1997.

20. Ibid.
21. Ibid.
22. In an E-mail correspondence sent in January 1997 to James Elias, co-organizer of the conference.

Part One

Rethinking Sex Work

Introduction

Trafficking, slavery and pathology have defined prostitution since the mid-nineteenth century. In the past two decades, however, ideas about forced and voluntary prostitution, female migration and sex workers' rights have entered the discourse, shifting and changing the terms of debate and conceptualizations of prostitution. In this section, various sex workers' rights activists and feminists review and discuss the old and new definitions in policies, laws and theory, examining the implications for sex workers in the global sex industry. Each essay signals an urgency for a liberated and informed discourse by and about women and men in the contemporary sex industry.

In the first chapter "Forced to Choose: Beyond the Voluntary v. Forced Prostitution Dichotomy," Jo Doezema argues that the distinction between forced and voluntary prostitution needs to be rethought, as it produces a framework that implicitly supports an abolitionist agenda and serves to deny sex workers their human rights. She analyzes assumptions embedded in UN conventions and international campaigns on prostitution, showing that from the late nineteenth century to the mid-1980s an abolitionist perspective dominated the discourse, defining prostitution as a violation to human rights, and aiming to ultimately abolish prostitution itself. The prevention of trafficking of women for prostitution was the lynch-pin around which arguments revolved and instruments designed. Since the 1980s, however, a shift in definition is discernible, and two ideological positions are today evident in the anti-trafficking debate. One is characterized by the Coalition Against Trafficking in Women (CATW) founded by Kathleen Barry, which furthers the older abolitionist position, the second is internationally represented by the Global Alliance Against Trafficking in Women (GAATW) which distinguishes between forced and voluntary prostitution and respects the rights to women's self-determination. The two positions are also reflected in various UN declarations and conventions, although much ambiguity and confusion reigns when the two positions meet in one document. Doezema observes that while the "forced v. voluntary" distinction is now dominant in the international discourse and is supported by various sex workers' organizations, it remains problematic. Even though this position recognizes workers' human rights and self-determination, the international instruments, organizations and campaigns against trafficking do not actually deal with voluntary prostitution or offer any support for sex workers who are not trafficked. Policies, conventions and activities still remain exclusively focussed on eradicating trafficking and forced prostitution. Furthermore the distinction has created a false dichotomy between sex workers. Ideas have been constructed of, on the one hand, liberated Western "whores" who are free to choose their professions, and on the other, forced, trafficked Third World victims. Combined with the idea of a difference between "guilty" and "innocent" prostitutes, the dichotomy reinforces the notions that (Western) women who freely transgress sexual norms deserve to be punished, while (non-Western) young, innocent women forced into prostitution by poverty, traffickers or age, need to be rescued. As yet, no international conventions or anti-trafficking organizations exist that explicitly support sex workers' human rights.

Alison Murray's essay "Debt-Bondage and Trafficking: Don't Believe the Hype" extends the analysis in the first chapter. Writing from an Australian and Southeast Asian sex worker's perspective, she critiques the Asia Watch Report on the trafficking of Burmese women into Thailand, and anti-trafficking campaigns at the Beijing conference, stressing the importance of the sex worker's voice. Murray contends that the report, despite the publicity and widespread acceptance it gained, is flawed in many ways. Not only did the researchers fail to contact sex workers organizations that work with Burmese women and know the field, but based their report on a highly selective sample of prostitutes. The voices and experiences of all but a few trafficked sex workers were thus completely ignored by the researchers. Furthermore she shows that the definition of trafficking in the report remains extremely vague, yet is used in a sensationalist and hyperbolic fashion. Statistics, figures and claims are not substantiated or referenced, yet the document has been widely embraced as irrefutable truth. Both the report and anti-trafficking campaigns informed by the report have detrimental effects on sex workers, and in particular reproduce the stereotype of the passive, diseased Asian woman. Sex workers' perspectives have had some impact on changing this discourse. Nevertheless, Murray concludes, it is still imperative that existing law and conventions that are aimed to protect women, young men and girls from slavery, non-consensual sex and exploitation, need to be ratified by all states, and that governments need to start decriminalizing prostitution, eradicating racism and providing support for sex workers' organizations.

The following two chapters are illustrations of the recent anti-trafficking approach both providing insights and details into the reconceptualization of prostitution from this perspective. Jo Bindman's contribution, "An International Perspective on Slavery in the Sex Industry" is from a talk she gave to one of the oldest feminist prostitution-abolitionist organizations, the Josephine Butler Society, in London. She describes the position held towards prostitution by Anti-Slavery International, the London-based organization that led the nineteenth-century British campaign against Black slavery and which today continues to fight against all forms of slavery. Bindman defines slavery as a condition that exists whenever and wherever workers are denied basic human rights and freedoms. Explaining that although slavery is not inherent to the sex industry, she points out that it is still possible because laws on prostitution and social distinctions made between prostitutes and other women in society exclude those working in the sex industry from the human rights that are offered to other women and workers in society. A labor analysis of prostitution that makes visible commonalities and shared forms of exploitation between prostitutes and other workers is the approach that Bindman advocates. It is an analysis through which it becomes evident that existing human rights and anti-slavery conventions are sufficient to eradicate slavery in the sex industry.

The chapter by Marjan Wijers "Women, Labor and Migration: The Position of Trafficked Women and Strategies for Support" is a reflection on ten years of work with the Dutch Foundation Against Trafficking in Women (STV), a sister organization of the GAATW. She defines trafficking as a form of exploitation within informal and formal labor market sectors, and more specifically as the process through which migrant women are brought into prostitution through the use of violence, coercion, deceit, abuse or violence, and are denied human rights and freedoms. The essay identifies basic principles of support that the STV has developed over the years to assist trafficked women, principles that are based on the needs and aspirations of the women themselves. Wijers argues that it is important to recognize that trafficked women are first and foremost migrants—persons seeking economic, social and political opportunities away from home—yet, due to restrictive laws and policies and limited opportunities for women, are relegated to informal sector work. State polices and laws furthermore serve to position migrant women as "undesirable aliens" and criminals, yet yield benefits for traffickers. The author outlines the four main types of legal state systems towards prostitution: the prohibitionist, regulationist, abolitionist, and decriminalist, pointing out that it is only in the latter system that women can make claim to legal protection. In the other systems, women are severely disadvantaged and their lack of confidence in the police system, fear of deportation and fear of reprisals from the traffickers forces them into silence and extreme forms of dependency. Wijers underlines the fact that migrant women find themselves in trafficked situations precisely because they are enterprising and courageous agents, willing to take initiatives to improve their living conditions—quite the opposite to the "passive victim" stereotype that is widely circulated about them. She concludes with describing two types of strategies—repressive and empowering—that are commonly employed to combat trafficking.

The final two chapters in this section critique dominant discourses on prostitution in specific areas of the world. "Discourses on Prostitution: The Case of Cuba," by Amalia Cabezas, leads us into the Americas with an essay that examines U.S. media coverage of, and studies about, sex workers in Cuba. She argues that this discourse positions Cuban *jineteras* as pathological deviants, failing to produce an analysis that takes into account women's resistances and the current economic situation in Cuba. This dominant discourse, she explains, draws from paradigms informed by nineteenth-century scholarship on prostitutes as well as Christian religious mores about sexuality. Whereas in the United States, such discourse has been challenged and changed through the efforts of new social movements and new scholarship—this shift is barely evident regarding the situation in Cuba. Cuba's realities indicate that the country's economic crisis in the 1990s and the globalization of capitalism has disproportionately affected women, yet when they turn to sex work to make a living they are usually blamed for doing so—or are charged with exhibiting a lack of revolutionary consciousness. This treatment of *jineteras* stands in contrast to the way in which Cuban men are represented, the latter being either completely ignored as sex workers or portrayed in neutral or heroic terms when described with coping with the economic crisis. It is the young women who are singled out for condemnation and stigmatization. Cabezas seeks to shift the level of analysis for the Cuban situation, proposing that what is needed is an analysis that encompasses the complexity of forces that inform sex work.

"Prostitution, Stigma and the Law in Japan" is a roundtable discussion between a group of six Japanese feminist intellectuals who examine the assumptions that underlie definitions of prostitution in Japan. The chapter is a translated, abbreviated version of an article that appeared in the Annual Report of the Women's Study Society in Japan in 1995, and represents an attempt to shift the debate in Japan from an abolitionist perspective to one that empowers women. The group "Sisterhood" addresses the construct "women who have sex with unspecific men" as used in the context of Japanese laws on prostitution to define prostitutes, noting the way in which this construct supports a division between women and morally condemns the prostitute. Evoking the "voluntary v. forced prostitution" distinction the group grapples with the conceptualization of free will and choice in the sex industry, their discussion reflecting some of the pitfalls Doezema and Murray point out about the dichotomous framework. Nevertheless, the members of Sisterhood agree that the criminalization of prostitution in Japan forces women in the sex industry into underground sectors and organized crime, and propose that legalization of prostitution would solve part of that problem. Furthermore, they suggest, if prostitution is defined as work in Japan, within a framework of legality, women in the sex industry would be able to claim labor rights and could press for secure working conditions. Ultimately Group Sisterhood argues for the abolition of the existing Prostitution Prevention Law in Japan and, in its place, laws that punish sexual violence, such as rape, sexual harassment and forced prostitution, based on women's rights to sexual freedom and self-determination.

Kamala Kempadoo

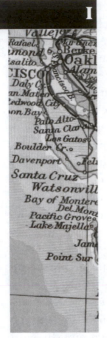

I Forced to Choose Beyond the Voluntary v. Forced Prostitution Dichotomy

Jo Doezema

Introduction

At the 1995 United Nations Fourth World Conference on Women in Beijing, I and other delegates from the Network of Sex Work Projects (NSWP) and the Global Alliance Against Trafficking in Women (GAATW) lobbied to ensure that every mention of prostitution as a form of violence against women in the final conference document would be prefaced by the word "forced."[1] Because sex workers' human rights were not mentioned in the draft document, it was impossible to introduce this concept at the Conference. The best we could do was "damage limitation;" keeping abolitionist language out of the final document. Ironically, I found myself lobbying for a recognition of the distinction between voluntary prostitution and forced prostitution, a distinction I and other sex worker activists had come to realize had been subverted in such a way that it had become a new justification for denying sex workers their human rights.

Does this mean that I deny that some women in the sex industry work in slavery-like conditions or that I deny that it is possible to choose prostitution as a profession? It does not. It means that I argue that the voluntary/forced dichotomy is the wrong theoretical framework with which to analyze the experience of sex workers. The necessity to critically examine the form this theory is taking is all the more pressing now that it is replacing abolitionism as the dominant model of prostitution at the international level.

In this chapter I examine the rise to prominence of the "voluntary" versus "forced" model of sex worker experience, and the implications and consequences of this rise for sex workers' rights. In the first section, I give a short history of feminist attempts to get prostitution on the international political agenda. Second, an examination of relevant international instruments demonstrates that the voluntary/forced dichotomy is replacing the abolitionist model of prostitution. Finally, I seek to show that this dichotomy has become another way of denying sex workers their human rights.

Prostitution and International Politics

A Brief History

Early attempts to deal with prostitution internationally were heavily influenced by nineteenth-century feminist activism. It was women like Josephine Butler who first brought the issue of the "white slave trade" to international attention, via a campaign to protect morals of both men and women. The feminist campaign, founded by Butler, began with attempts to repeal the Contagious Diseases Acts in Britain.[2] Under the acts, any woman identified as a "common prostitute" was forced to undergo a fortnightly internal examination. Infected women were interned in specially designated hospital wards, "pseudo-medical prisons for whores."[3]

Feminists in the repeal movement were ambivalent in their attitudes to prostitutes. They recognized a commonality of interests with prostitutes, realizing that the Acts were a threat to the civil liberties of all women. Because any woman could be identified on the word of a police officer as a "common prostitute," any woman, especially a working-class woman, on her own in a certain area at a certain time could be detained and forced to submit to an internal examination. On the other hand, prostitution was seen as "the great social evil," and prostitutes as victims of male vice, who needed to be rescued. Thus, controlling male vice was seen as the key to ending prostitution. Regulation of prostitution was condemned as an official licensing of male vice.

After the repeal of the Acts in 1883, the focus of the campaign shifted from the rejection of government attempts to monitor sexuality to the promotion of repressive measures designed to end vice. The agenda of the social purity movement was dominated by the mirages of white slave trade and child prostitution. This campaign was helped enormously by sensationalist journalists who seized on the titillating tales of deflowered innocence. According to Nicky Roberts, "The typical story involves white adolescent girls who were drugged and abducted by sinister immigrant procurers, waking up to find themselves captive in some infernal foreign brothel, where they were subject to the pornographic whims of sadistic, non-white pimps and brothel-masters."[4] Research indicates that most of the "trafficking victims" were actually prostitutes migrating, like thousands of others, in hope of finding a better life. Roberts notes that, by this stage in the repeal movement, the image of the prostitute had to be "pitched to appeal to the charitable reflexes of middle class Christians" who by then provided the main body of support for the campaign.[5] She calls the results of the social purity campaign "catastrophic" for prostitutes. Although the Contagious Disease Acts were finally repealed in 1886, in many places their regime was continued under a different name, with purity activists now patrolling the streets instead of the police.[6]

The movement for social purity had success in the US and the continent as well as in Britain. By the turn of the century, most of the existing regulatory systems in Europe and the United States had ended, and international efforts had begun to target the "white slave trade." In the five years before the end of the nineteenth century, three international conferences on the prevention of trafficking in women were held.[7] In the early years of the century, two international instruments concerning the trade were created.[8] The League of Nations adopted two conventions dealing with the traffic in women and children.[9] In 1949, the UN adopted the Convention for the Suppression of the Traffic in Persons and the Exploitation of the Prostitution of Others, which combined and superseded the earlier agreements.

Current Approaches

After the 1949 Convention was adopted, both feminist and international concern for prostitution and the traffic in women abated for a time. But since the middle of the 1980s, there has been a new wave of feminist-backed campaigning against trafficking in women, child prostitution and sex tourism. Campaign efforts have succeeded in putting prostitution back at the top of the international agenda.

Prostitution has been a deeply contentious issue for feminists. Women's bodies have been the site of women's oppression: "Female subordination runs so deep that is still viewed as inevitable . . . rather than as a politically contracted reality. . . . The physical territory of this struggle is women's bodies. The importance of control over women can be seen in the intensity of resistance to laws and social changes that put control of women's bodies in women's hands."[10] Not that feminists agree as to what "control of women's bodies in women's hands" means. Shannon Bell observes that the prostitute body has been a site of struggle for feminists because "The prostitute body is a terrain on which feminists contest sexuality, desire, and the writing of the female body."[11]

The modern anti-trafficking campaign is split along ideological lines on views of prostitution. The fundamental difference of opinion concerns the question of whether or not a person can choose prostitution as a profession. Some feminists argue that all prostitution constitutes a human rights violation. The strongest advocate of this "neo-abolitionist" view internationally is the Coalition Against Trafficking in Women (CATW), founded by Kathleen Barry. Their "Convention on the Elimination of All Forms of Sexual Exploitation of Women," defines prostitution as a form of sexual exploitation just like rape, genital mutilation, incest and battering.[12] Sexual exploitation is defined as "a practice by which women are sexually subjugated through abuse of women's sexuality and/or violation of physical integrity as a means of achieving power and domination including gratification, financial gain, advancement."[13] Prostitution is explicitly named as a violation of women's human rights, and is also held responsible for "subordinating women as a group."[14]

The distinction between free and forced prostitution was developed by the prostitutes' rights movement in response to feminists (and others) who saw all prostitution as abusive.[15] The World Charter for Prostitutes Rights (1985) states "Decriminalize all aspects of adult prostitution resulting from individual decision."[16] This distinction was included in the analysis of some anti-trafficking organizations, such as the Global Alliance Against Trafficking in Women (GAATW) based in Thailand. The GAATW objects to international instruments for "disregarding the will of adult persons engaged in prostitution" and demand that instruments to combat trafficking be "based on respect for human rights, specifically the right of all persons to self determination." [17] Traffic in persons and forced prostitution are "manifestations of violence against women and the rejection of these practices, which are a violation of the right to self determination, must hold within itself the respect for the self determination of adult persons who are voluntarily engaged in prostitution."[18]

Changing the Dominant Discourse

The abolitionist viewpoint has defined the terms of the international discourse on prostitution for almost 100 years. This discourse is being challenged by those who see sex work as a legitimate occupation. An examination of relevant UN instruments shows that there has been a shift away from mechanisms based on abolitionist ideology and towards an approach that respects the right to self-determination. This trend is most evident in those UN instruments dealing specifically with women's human rights and violence against women.

The watershed for the shift can be located in the mid-1980s.[19] Before then, UN instruments were abolitionist in character. Since that time, the majority make a distinction between voluntary and forced prostitution. Prostitution is dealt with in many different UN bodies; it is beyond the scope of this chapter to examine them all. Rather, I will focus on key documents and the work of the main bodies to illustrate the shift towards a new discourse .

Abolitionist Instruments

The Preamble to the 1949 Convention for the Suppression of Traffic in Persons and of the Exploitation of the Prostitution of Others states that "prostitution and . . . traffic in persons for the purposes of prostitution are incompatible with the dignity and worth of the human person. . . ." The convention has come under attack from both "sides" in the anti-trafficking debate. There is fundamental disagreement about the ideological approach of the convention. An examination of this disagreement is useful for the light it sheds on the issue of "voluntary" and "forced" prostitution.

Modern abolitionists, ironically, criticize the Trafficking Convention for making a distinction between "voluntary" and "forced" prostitution.[20] Laura Reanda calls this distinction traditional: "A distinction has traditionally been made between prostitution as *a manner of personal choice and a form of work*, perhaps reprehensible but unavoidable, and enforced prostitution, or traffic in persons, considered a slavery-like practice to be combated by the international community. . . . This distinction was formalized in international law from the beginning of this century. . . . These instruments regard prostitution as a human rights violation only if it involves overt coercion or exploitation. They are silent, however, concerning the human rights implications of prostitution per se."[21]

This statement is misleading. The distinction between "voluntary" and "forced" prostitution, as it is currently understood, had no relevance at the time the international instruments to combat trafficking in women were drafted. For the regulationists, the prostitute was a fallen woman, whose personal pathology or inclination to vice, weakness, stupidity, and/or vanity led inevitably to life as a prostitute. Abolitionist ideology firmly fixed the prostitute as a victim. The image of the prostitute as agent, who willingly chooses her occupation, was unimaginable in either of these models. *Prostitution as a matter of personal choice and a form of work* is a concept developed by sex workers that radically contradicts both the regulationist and abolitionist versions of prostitute reality. To equate or collapse the very different analysis of the regulationists and prostitutes' rights supporters denies the radical implications of sex workers' politics.

Apart from abolitionists themselves, there is general agreement that the Trafficking Convention reflects an abolitionist viewpoint. According to the Advisory Committee on Human Rights and Foreign Policy to the Dutch Government:

> Generally speaking, the UN adopts an abolitionist approach and does not make a distinction between forced and voluntary prostitution. It regards both types as morally unacceptable. This attitude emerges forcefully from the 1949 Convention for the Suppression of Traffic in Persons and of the Exploitation of the Prostitution of Others of 1949 (sic) which states that prostitution violates human rights and human dignity and represents a threat to the welfare of the individual, the family and the community.[22]

Jean Fitzpatrick concurs: "The 1949 Convention does not draw an explicit distinction between coerced and voluntary prostitution and represents the then-current consensus on an 'abolitionist' model."[23] The Working Group on Contemporary Forms of Slavery (WGS) is responsible for reviewing developments in the field covered by the 1949 Convention and for recommending action to be taken.[24] This body has from the beginning taken an abolitionist view, in line with the Trafficking Convention, and their attitude reflects the regular attendance of the International Abolitionist Federation at the WGS meetings.

The Convention on The Elimination of All Forms of Discrimination Against Women (CEDAW) was adopted in 1979. Article 6 deals with prostitution and trafficking in women. It uses the same wording as the 1949 convention, calling upon state parties to "take all appropriate measures . . . to suppress all forms traffic in women and the exploitation of prostitution of women." This would seem to imply that the drafters' intent was abolitionist. However, when the text was being drafted, Morocco introduced an amendment to Article 6 which called for the suppression of prostitution in addition to the suppression of the exploitation of prostitution. This amendment was found unacceptable by the Netherlands and Italy, because they considered that the new element of suppression of prostitution unacceptable.[25] The amendment was rejected, thus it can be argued that Article 6 does not consider all prostitution inherently coercive.[26] The Mexico Declaration on the Equality of Women, adopted at the Second UN Conference on Women in 1975, makes no distinction between forced and voluntary prostitution: "Women all over the world should unite to eliminate violations of human rights committed against women and girls such as rape, prostitution, . . ."[27]

Toward a New Perspective

General Recommendation 19 of CEDAW (1992) on violence against women includes specific paragraphs relating to Article 6 (see above) of the Convention. It reaffirms the requirements of Article 6 for states to "suppress all forms of traffic in women and exploitation of the prostitution of others," but also states that "Poverty and unemployment force many women . . . into prostitution. Prostitutes are especially vulnerable to violence because their status, which may be unlawful, tends to marginalize them. They need the equal protection of laws against rape and other forms of violence." Though this text does not specifically distinguish between forced and voluntary prostitution, an important shift in emphasis is apparent. Rather than focusing on repressive measures to eliminate the practice of prostitution, the Committee instead focuses on the prostitute as a subject whose rights can be violated.

The first document to make a clear departure from an abolitionist view of prostitution is the Declaration on the Elimination of Violence Against Women (1993). "Violence against women shall be understood to encompass, but not be limited to, the following: Physical, sexual and psychological violence occurring within the general community, including rape, sexual abuse, sexual harassment and intimidation at work, in educational institutions and elsewhere, trafficking in women and forced prostitution."[28] Jean Fitzpatrick notes that "The Draft Declaration on Violence Against Women includes only "trafficking in women and forced prostitution" despite notice that the 1949 convention considers all prostitution to have been compelled.[29]

The Declaration on Violence Against Women is the standard against which the activities of the international community must be measured.[30] The implicit distinction between forced and non-forced prostitution recognized by the Declaration signalled that the international community's view of prostitution had changed. Since the adoption of the Declaration, the majority of international agreements denote forced prostitution and trafficking, rather than prostitution itself, as violence against women. The Vienna Declaration and Program of Action of the 1993 World Conference on Human Rights, recognized women's rights as human rights, and urged state parties to adopt the Declaration on Violence Against Women.[31] At the Fourth World Conference on Women, Beijing 1995, the draft of the Platform for Action included abolitionist language in a number of paragraphs, but this language was not retained in the final document. The final document condemns only forced prostitution, not prostitution as such.[32]

Radhika Coomaraswamy, the UN Special Rapporteur on Violence Against Women, also distinguishes between voluntary and forced prostitution: "Some women become prostitutes through 'rational choice,' others become prostitutes as a result of coercion, deception or economic enslavement."[33] Arguably, the most convincing evidence for a displacement of the abolitionist discourse is the fact that she commissioned the GAATW to write a report on trafficking, rather than the CATW.[34]

This shift towards a new perspective on prostitution, while clearly evident, is not occurring at the same speed in all areas of the United Nations dealing with prostitution and trafficking. There is no commitment in the United Nations to an integrated and coordinated prostitution policy.[35] As a result, UN approaches are highly fragmented, with different UN instruments and bodies taking different ideological stances, and even with contradictory positions within the same body or agreement.[36] Some UN organizations, such as UNESCO and the Working Group on Contemporary Forms of Slavery, continue to argue that prostitution itself is a human rights violation.

Beyond Voluntary / Forced

So should sex worker organizations be jumping for joy that the right to self determination is being recognized, at least implicitly, at international level? Does this mean that the United Nations and other international organizations are now going to start taking sex workers' human rights seriously, instead of cloaking moral condemnation of sex work under paternalistic "save us for our own good" rhetoric? Before we break out the party hats, we should look at how the concept of self-determination and the distinction between free and forced prostitution are interpreted and being translated into policy by NGOs, governments and intergovernmental agencies. Are the same old stereotypes and moral judgements now being expressed as loathing of forced prostitution?

Criticisms of the Campaigns

The distinction between free and forced prostitution has implicitly been recognized by the international community. But international actors and agreements are rarely as vocal about promoting prostitutes rights as they are in condemning forced prostitution. No international agreement condemns the abuse of human rights of sex workers who were not "forced."

I believe that this is the result of two factors. Firstly, though the international community may be agreeing on condemning only forced prostitution as a human rights violation, this does not imply agreement on how to deal with voluntary prostitution; how it is to be defined, if it should be regulated by the state or left to the workers to organize, or even if it exists at all. In fact, it is because there is no agreement about "voluntary" prostitution in the first place that the consensus on "forced" prostitution has come into being. It can be seen as a compromise: those who, for whatever reason, wish to eliminate all prostitution can at least be satisfied that the "worst" abuses are being dealt with and those who support self-determination are relieved that this right is not threatened.

Secondly, most organizations that acknowledge and support the right to self-determination place much more emphasis on stopping forced prostitution than on sex workers' rights. Partly this is because it is felt that this is more properly the domain of sex worker organizations. Given the fact that sex workers have long demanded the right to speak for themselves, this hesitance is somewhat justified. However, this reluctance to address sex workers' rights can also be attributed to the fact that it is easier to gain support for victims of evil traffickers than for challenging structures that violate sex workers' human rights.

The campaigning efforts of anti-trafficking groups have been instrumental in creating a climate wherein the great majority of sex work, and practically all sex work involving young men and women and women in developing countries is seen as abuse. Forced prostitution, child prostitution and sex tourism are linked together and made indistinguishable. In the race to produce yet more horrifying stories, and higher numbers, concern for rights loses out to hysteria over victims.

Though most of the criticism of the prostitutes rights' movement has focused on the abolitionist view of sex work, sex workers are now increasingly critical of anti-trafficking campaigners and human rights activists who distinguish between voluntary and forced prostitution, yet who place all their campaigning energy into stopping forced prostitution. They have been criticized for initiating their campaigns without consultation with sex workers and for using the same emotive language as abolitionists thus perpetuating "the stereotype of Asian sex workers as passive and exploited victims."[37] Such victimization, "has grave consequences for all sex workers as it perpetuates the old stereotype that prostitution is bad and should be abolished."[38] Others, such as Alison Murray in her contribution to this book, point out how the dichotomy between voluntary and forced prostitution creates false divisions between sex workers. The "voluntary" prostitute is a Western sex worker, seen as capable of making independent decisions about whether or not to sell sexual services, while the sex worker from a developing country is deemed unable to make this same choice: she is passive, naive, and ready prey for traffickers.[39] Potentially the most frightening division, however, created by the voluntary/forced dichotomy is that of sex workers into guilty/"voluntary" and innocent/"forced" prostitutes, which reinforces the belief that women who transgress sexual norms deserve to be punished. This division is thus a threat to the entire concept of women's human rights.

Innocent Victims

"In any given year, many thousands of young women and girls . . . are lured . . . into forced prostitution."[40] For the general public and bodies concerned with this issue, forced prostitution is very much a matter of coerced innocence. The picture of the "duped innocent" is a pervasive and tenacious cultural myth.[41] High profile campaigns by NGOs and in the media, with their continued focus on the victim adds yet more potency to the myths. The public is convinced that huge numbers of innocent (read, sexually pure) women and children are being subjected to the perverse whims of degenerate Western men.

In the new discourse of voluntary/forced prostitution, the innocence of the victim determines which side of the dichotomy she will fall under. One of the consequences of thinking about prostitution in terms of choice and force is that it becomes necessary to show that instances of abuse are in fact "forced prostitution." In reports on trafficking, it is often stressed that the women did not "choose" to be prostitutes. Emotive words like "duped", "tricked" or "lured" are used time and time again to show that the women involved did not know what they were letting themselves in for. A good example of the standard scenario runs as follows: "Many women from Russia, Hungary, Poland and other countries in the region are tricked into prostitution in the West, where they had been promised jobs in offices, in restaurants, or as domestic servants. Instead, they find themselves locked up in a brothel, their papers are taken away and their earnings are kept back to repay their 'debts'."[42]

Human Rights Watch, who did a study of Burmese women and girls trafficked into Thailand, conclude that the "combination of debt-bondage and illegal confinement renders the employment of the Burmese women and girls tantamount to forced labor, which is prohibited under international law."[43] However, the researchers found it necessary to state that only four of the twenty-nine women they interviewed knew they were going to be prostitutes.[44] It is hard to see what relevance this has: surely debt bondage and illegal confinement amount to slavery, whether or not there was initial agreement to be work as a prostitute. Still, the innocence of the victim is seen to be of primary importance.

Other reports of "forced prostitution" focus on the aspect of poverty. "Susie is the face of contemporary poverty. That her job as a debt-bonded sex worker is the best economic option available to her is a metaphor for most of the world's women, whose grinding impoverishment in the Third World is accelerating."[45] This "poverty as force" approach has been criticized for its underlying racist and classist implications; even those who would accept "voluntary" prostitution, on the part of well-off Western women, refuse to respect the choice of a woman from a developing country.[46] On the one hand, this shows an underlying rejection of prostitution as a profession—no "normal" woman would chose the work unless "forced" by poverty. On the other, equating poverty with "force" is, like the focus on deceit, a way of establishing the innocence of "trafficked victims" and thus their eligibility for human rights protection.

A third way "innocence" is established is by focusing on the youth of the "victim" as children are assumed to be sexless and thus beyond "guilt."[47] Campaign pamphlet titles like "The Rape of the Innocents" and sickening stories of child abuse galvanize public opinion and get donations.[48] Tellingly, the distinctions between child and adult are blurred so as to include as many as possible in the category of unquestionable innocents. According to a United Nations report on trafficking in Burma "With the growth of sex tourism and the commercial sex trade in neighboring countries of the region, child abuse and exploitation has assumed a new form: sexual trafficking of children across international borders . . . the number of Myanmar [Burma] girls working in Thai brothels has been conservatively estimated at between 20,000 to 30,000, with approximately 10,000 new recruits brought in yearly. *The majority are between 12 and 25 years old.*"[49]

Reality: So What's Going On?

When subjected to scrutiny, the image of the "trafficking" victim turns out to be a figment of neo-Victorian imaginations. Just as the turn of the century obsession with the "white slave trade" turned out to be based on actual prostitute migration, the Dutch Foundation Against Trafficking in Women (STV) and the GAATW, in their report on trafficking to the UN Special Rapporteur on Violence against Women, conclude that slavery-like conditions in sex work are primarily problems for those already working in the sex trade: thus for prostitutes who migrate.[50] But the campaign juggernaut remains unaffected by fact. From the Arab sheikh's harem slave to the village girl chained to her bed in the brothels of Bangkok, the image of the defiled innocent has a particular fascination.[51] It is reminiscent of sentiment expressed during a meeting of anti-white slave trade activists at the turn of the century. The women present were exhorted by the speaker to "Remember, ladies . . . 'it is more important to be aroused than to be accurate. Apathy is more of a crime than exaggeration in dealing with this subject.'"[52]

Parallels between the two movements are easily drawn. As a symbol, the "white slave" personified conservative moral fears of women's sexuality and economic independence, and of the growing power of the working class, and reflected racist stereotypes. The nineteenth-century sex slave was a white woman, victim of the animal lusts of the dark races. In the modern myth, the racism has changed focus: "passive," unemancipated women from the developing world are the new sex slaves.

A number of today's campaigns have become a platform for reactionary and paternalistic voices, advocating a rigid sexual morality under the guise of protecting women, and incorporating racist and classist perceptions in their analysis of the sex industry in developing countries. This is particularly the case when campaigners actually succeed in getting governments to do something about "trafficking," for then the focus shifts from women's rights to a hysterical and paranoid reaction to women's increasing sexual autonomy, the "breakdown of the family" and migration. Often, "trafficking" is used by states to initiate and justify restrictive policies.[53] There are still many governments with moral objections to prostitution. At the international level, however, most are politically savvy enough to cloak moral indignation in terms of "victimization of women."

If it is recognized that the majority of those in the sex-industry who end up in debt-bondage or slavery-like conditions were *already* working as sex workers, it is impossible to avoid the conclusion that it is prostitutes whose human rights are being violated on a massive scale. Of course this is unpalatable to the international community: it is one thing to save innocent victims of forced prostitution, quite another to argue that prostitutes deserve rights. It is not only governments who prefer saving innocent women to giving rights to guilty ones. Most feminist discourse on trafficking limits itself to the fight against "forced prostitution," the "voluntary" prostitute is not condemned—she is ignored.

Many governments place the distinction between "guilty" and "innocent" women at the heart of their legislation on prostitution and trafficking. In Germany, the penalty for trafficking is reduced in cases where the victim knew she was going to be a prostitute or when deceit was used on a person who is "not far from being a prostitute."[54] In Columbia, the use of violence to force a person into prostitution is only prohibited in cases where the woman concerned is "of undisputed virtue."[55] Other countries, including Uganda, Canada, Japan, Brazil and El Salvador, have similar provisions.[56] But even in those countries where "the virtue of the woman is not mentioned as an explicit criterion in law," it still "implicitly or explicitly plays a crucial role in the interpretation and enforcement of the law."[57] In the Netherlands, for example, police will refuse to investigate complaints of trafficking by women who continue working as prostitutes. "Supposedly there is no victim: she wanted it all the time, at least, that is what they can conclude from the fact that the woman is willing to work again in prostitution after having filed charges."[58]

Because feminists are undecided about whether or not "voluntary" prostitution exists or how it should be dealt with, their analysis of forced prostitution reinforces rather than challenges stereotypical views of female sexuality. For example, Human Rights Watch Women's Rights Project, in their report on global human rights abuses of women, states that it "takes no position on prostitution per se. However, we strongly condemn laws and official policies and practices that fail to distinguish between prostitutes and victims of forced trafficking."[59]

Focusing on forced prostitution provides a way out for those who are unwilling to admit that the issues raised by the prostitutes' rights movement have to be faced. Governments do not have to be challenged about their treatment of voluntary prostitutes, i.e., "While we recognize the right of governments to make and enforce laws that regulate national borders, they must distinguish between those who purposefully violate immigration laws and others who are victims of forced prostitution."[60] The report is not clear about how a prostitute is to be distinguished from a victim of trafficking. In order for a "victim" to be eligible for the protection recommended by Human Rights Watch, she would have to prove her innocence, i.e. that she didn't know she was going to be a prostitute. This bears a frightening resemblance to rape trials, in which a victims chastity status will determine the severity of the crime.

The peculiarities of viewing sex work through the distorting lens of the voluntary/forced dichotomy cause what are clearly abuses of sex workers' rights to be condemned as examples of forced prostitution. Human Rights Watch reports that women in India who are arrested for prostitution are sent to "protective homes" where "inmates complained of grave mistreatment, including branding with hot irons, rapes, and sexual assaults. Almost all inmates were suffering from malnutrition. Many also had skin diseases and tuberculosis."[61] Yet, in the face of this horrific abuse of sex workers' human rights, the best Human Rights Watch can do is reiterate that "victims of trafficking" should be treated differently from prostitutes. Sex workers who are imprisoned and detained, subjected to cruel and degrading mistreatment, who suffer violence at the hands of the state or by private individuals with the state's support, are disqualified from human rights considerations if their status is "voluntary." This is the voluntary/forced dichotomy taken to its extreme and logical conclusion. Human rights organizations and bodies in the United Nations seem content to let governments trample on the rights of sex workers, as long as the morals of "innocent" women are protected.

Conclusion

The distinction between "voluntary" and "forced" prostitution has largely replaced the abolitionist model of prostitution in international discourse. This would seem to imply a recognition of the right to self-determination. However, this dichotomy creates divisions between sex workers. The most frightening division created by the voluntary/forced dichotomy is that it reproduces the whore/madonna division within the category "prostitute." Thus, the madonna is the "forced prostitute"—the child, the victim of trafficking; she who, by virtue of her victim status, is exonerated from sexual wrong-doing. The "whore" is the voluntary prostitute: because of her transgression, she deserves whatever she gets. The distinction between voluntary and forced prostitution, a radical and resistive attack on previous discourses that constructed all prostitutes as victims and/or deviants, has been co-opted and inverted, and incorporated to reinforce systems that abuse sex workers rights.

The campaign for sex workers' rights began with challenging the myths surrounding prostitution and women's sexuality. Claiming that prostitution could be a choice was a major step. Yet now, as old myths are being given new impetus under the guise of accepting choice, it is time to reconsider the usefulness of "choice" versus "force" as the model of sex workers' experience.

Notes

1. The Beijing Declaration and Platform for Action, 1995.
2. These acts, passed in 1864, 1866, and 1869, targeted prostitutes in an attempt to control the spread of venereal disease. See Judith Walkowitz, *Prostitution and Victorian Society. Women. Class and the State* (Cambridge: Cambridge University Press, 1982).
3. Nicky Roberts, *Whores in History: Prostitution in Western Society* (London: HarperCollins, 1992) 248.
4. Ibid., p. 252. It is startling how little this "standard story" has changed in the intervening 100 years: accounts very similar to this are reported in today's media.
5. Ibid., p. 252.
6. Ibid., p. 258.
7. See Lenke Fereh, "Forced Prostitution and Traffic in Persons," in Marieke Klap, Yvonne Klerk and Jaqueline Smith, eds., *Combating Traffic in Persons: Proceedings of the Conference on Traffic In Persons* (Utrecht: IMS, Netherlands Institute of Human Rights, 1995) 68.
8. The International Agreement for the Suppression of the White Slave Traffic, Paris (1904), and the International Convention for the Suppression of the White Slave Traffic (1910).
9. The International Convention to Combat the Traffic in Women and Children (1921) and the International Convention for the Suppression of the Traffic in Women of Full Age (1933). Nicky Roberts links the League's concern with the traffick in women with the re-opening, after World War 1, of actual international migration networks and routes used by prostitutes (279).
10. Charlotte Bunch, "Transforming Human Rights from a Feminist Perspective," in Julie Peters and Andrea Wolper, eds., *Women's Rights as Human Rights—International Feminist Perspectives* (London: Routledge, 1996) 15.
11. Shannon Bell, *Reading, Writing and Rewriting the Prostitute Body* (Bloomington: Indiana University Press, 1994) 73.
12. Developed as a replacement for the United Nations 1949 Convention For the Suppression of the Traffic in Persons and of the Exploitation of the Prostitution of Others by The Coalition

Against Trafficking in Women (CATW). (Draft) Convention on the Elimination of All Forms of Sexual Exploitation of Women, 1993 Art. 2(b).

13. CATW: (Draft) Convention on the Elimination of All Forms of Sexual Exploitation of Women, 1993 Art. 1.

14. Ibid.

15. For a history of the development of sex worker politics to 1986, see Gail Pheterson, ed., *A Vindication of the Rights of Whores* (Washington: The Seal Press, 1989) 3–30.

16. International Committee for Prostitutes Rights, printed in Pheterson, 1989, 40–42.

17. GAATW/STV, "A Proposal to Replace the Convention for the Suppression of the Traffic in Persons and of the Exploitation of the Prostitution of Others," Utrecht, 1994, par II.2 and. par III.1, emphasis added.

18. Ibid., par.III.1.

19. This was also the time when the international movement for sex workers' rights reached its peak of organization, with two international conferences held in 1985 and 1986. For documentation of these conferences, see Gail Pheterson, ed., *A Vindication of the Rights of Whores* (Washington: Seal Press, 1989).

20. See Laura Reanda, "Prostitution as a Human Rights Question, Problems and Prospects of United Nations Action," *Human Rights Quarterly* 13 (1991) 209–211, and UNESCO/ CATW, "The Penn State Report," 1–2. Pennsylvania, 1992.

21. Reanda, 1991, p. 202, emphasis added.

22. "The Traffic in Persons Report" of the Advisory Committee on Human Rights and Foreign Policy, (The Hague 1992) 16.

23. Jean Fitzpatrick, "Using International Human Rights Norms to Combat Violence Against Women," in Rebecca J. Cook ed., *Human Rights of Women: National and International Perspectives* (Philadelphia: University of Pennsylvania Press, 1994), p. 552. See also Yvonne Klerk, "Definition of Traffic in Persons," in Klap et al., and Alice M. Miller, "United Nations and Related International Action in the Area of Migration and Traffic in Women," in the *Report of the International Workshop on International Migration and Traffic in Women* (Chiangmai: The Foundation for Women, 1994) 13.

24. The WGS was established in 1974 by the Sub-Commission on Prevention of Discrimination and Protection of Minorities of the UN Human Rights Commission.

25. See Lars Adam Rehof, *Guide to the Travaux Preparatoire of the United Nations Convention on the Elimination of all Forms of Discrimination Against Women* (Dordrecht: Martinus Nijhoff/ Kluwer, 1993) 91.

26. This conclusion is supported by R. Haverman and J. C. Hes in "Vrouwenhandel en Exploitatie van Prostitutie," A.W. Heringa et. al., eds., *Het Vrouwenverdrag: Een beeld van een Verdrag* (Antwerpen and Amersfoort: MAKLU, 1994).

27. Declaration of Mexico on the Equality of Women, UN 1975, par. 28 34.

28. Declaration of Mexico on the Equality of Women, UN 1975, Art. 2.

29. Fitzpatrick, 1994, p. 552.

30. Maria Hartle, "Traffic in Women as a Form of Violence Against Women," in Klap et al., eds., *Combating Traffic in Persons: Proceedings of the Conference on Traffic in Persons* (Utrecht: IMS, Netherlands Institute of Human Rights, 1995).

31. The Vienna Declaration and Program of Action, par.38.
32. Draft Platform For Action (A/CONF.177 .1, 24 May 1995) notably paragraphs 122, 131d, 225; and the Beijing Declaration and Platform for Action, Paragraphs 123, 131 d, 224.
33. UN EICN 411995142.
34. Marjan Wijers and Lin Lap-Chew, *Trafficking in Women. Forced Labor and Slavery-like Practices in Marriage. Domestic Labor and Prostitution* (Utrecht: The Foundation against Trafficking in Women and the Global Alliance Against Trafficking in Women, 1996), 198.
35. Miller, 1991, p. 1.
36. The above instruments are not all inherently consistent in that several call upon states to ratify the abolitionist Trafficking Convention. However, in calling for the elimination of only "forced prostitution and trafficking" rather than prostitution itself, an implicit recognition of the right to self-determination is evident.
37. See "A Joint Statement of Policy," by the Prostitutes' Rights Organization for Sex Workers; the Sex Workers Outreach Project; Workers in Sex Employment in the ACT; Self-help for Queensland Workers in the Sex Industry; The Support, Information, Education, Referral Association of Western Australia; The South Australian Sex Industry Network; The Prostitutes Association of South Australia; The Prostitute Association Northern Territory for Health, Education, Referrals; Cybelle, Sex Worker Organization Tasmania; Sydney Sexual Health Center, Sydney Hospital; The Queer and Esoteric Workers Union and representatives of Asian sex working communities in New South Wales (1996) 3.
38. Ibid., 3.
39. See also Jo Doezema, "Choice in Prostitution," in *Changing Faces of Prostitution* (Helsinki: Unioni-The League of Finnish Feminists, 1995).
40. *The Human Rights Watch Global Report on Women's Human Rights* (New York: Human Rights Watch, 1995) 196.
41. Roberts, p. 253.
42. Tasha David, *Worlds Apart, Women and the Global Economy* (Brussels: International Confederation of Free Trade Unions, 1996) 43.
43. *Human Rights Watch*, 1995, p. 213.
44. Ibid., p. 210.
45. Angela Matheson, "Trafficking in Asian Sex Workers," *Green Left Weekly* (26 October 1994) 1.
46. See J. Doezema, "Sex Worker Delegation to the Beijing Conference," in Network of Sex Works Projects internal communication, Amsterdam, March 1995, and Alison Murray's contribution to this book. Abject poverty is not usually the primary reason for women to chose sex work or to migrate as a sex worker. Apart from the obvious fact that not all poor women chose to become prostitutes, research shows that there are other important considerations motivating someone's choice to do sex work. See, in this book, Kamala Kempadoo's chapter on the Dutch Caribbean and the research from COIN in the Dominican Republic.
47. In her contribution to this book, Heather Montgomery challenges some of the myths surrounding "child prostitution." See also Maggie Black, "Home Truths," *New Internationalist* (February 1994), 11–13, and Alison Murray, forthcoming, "On Bondage, Peers and Queers: Sexual Subcultures, Sex Workers and AIDS Discourses in the Asia-Pacific."

48. For example, see Ron O'Grady, *The Rape of the Innocent, End Child Prostitution in Asian Tourism* (Bangkok: ECPAT, 1994).

49. *Children and Women in Myanmar: A Situation Analysis* (UNICEF 1995) 38, emphasis added.

50. Marjan Wijers and Lin Lap-Chew, *Trafficking in Women. Forced Labor and Slavery-like Practices in Marriage. Domestic Labor and Prostitution,* (Utrecht: The Foundation against Trafficking in Women and the Global Alliance Against Trafficking in Women, 1996), 198.

51. This fascination has an erotic element: at an 1885 demonstration in London in the wake of a sensational articles about the white slave trade "street vendors shifted record numbers of the pornographic magazine *The Devil.*" See Roberts, 1992.

52. Roberts, 1992, p. 264.

53. Wijers and Lap-Chew, p. 111–152.

54. Ibid., p. 126.

55. Ibid., p. 128.

56. Ibid., p. 126–130.

57. Ibid., p. 153.

58. Marga de Boer, *Traffic in Women: Policy in Focus* (Utrecht: Willem Pompe Institute for Criminal Law, 1994) 29.

59. *Human Rights Watch,* 1995, p. 198.

60. Ibid., p. 200.

61. Ibid., p. 253.

2 Debt-Bondage and Trafficking
Don't Believe the Hype

Alison Murray

The anti-trafficking lobby built up through the early 1990s to a peak at the UN Conference on Women/NGO Forum held in Beijing during September 1995, yet trafficking is an aspect of the mythology surrounding Asian sex workers which remains poorly defined even in conventions and laws against the trafficking of women (David 1995). One of the goals of the anti-trafficking lobby at the UN conference was a new UN Convention to replace the 1949 Convention on the Suppression of Trafficking in Persons and the Exploitation of the Prostitution of Others, in which Article 1 condemns anyone who "procures" or "exploits" a prostitute, "even with the consent of that person." There was relatively little attention paid to "trafficking" after the 1949 convention, until the late 1980s surge of concern about "sex tourism." In April 1993 a conference was organized by the Coalition Against Trafficking of Women (CATW) "to heighten awareness of the sex trade and to stem the sale of humans into bondage" (*Asia Watch* 1993,149). The latest intense phase of publicity began with two conferences on trafficking held at the end of 1994: The First International Conference on the Trafficking of Women in Chiang

Mai, Thailand on October 17–21 (which established the feminist-based Global Alliance Against Traffic in Women, the GAATW), and the International Conference on Traffic in Persons in Utrecht, the Netherlands on November 15–19, 1994.

Many people have been misled into thinking that trafficking (and child prostitution and sex tourism) are enormous problems for Australia and Southeast Asia. Meanwhile Australian and other sex workers, at the UN conference and through its aftermath, set out an alternative view so that before people dig in their pockets for a donation, sign a petition, or join an anti-trafficking group, they would try to consider the sex workers' perspective and the implications of this lobby for the workers in sex trades. A version of this chapter and a position statement supported by most of the Australian sex workers' rights organizations formed part of the vigorous discussions at Beijing, where the anti-trafficking movement lost much of its credibility.

Sex work is diverse and context-specific, related to the combination of local conditions and the forces of economic globalization, the AIDS discourse and legislation which creates the space for exploitation and violence by criminalizing prostitutes and restricting travel. The most extreme lobby, represented by the Coalition Against Trafficking in Women, formed in the United States in 1991, has an underlying agenda of abolishing prostitution. They try to fulfil this agenda by linking all forms of the sex trade together beneath an emphasis on emotive words like "trafficking," "slavery" and "child prostitution." Meanwhile, in discussion at Beijing, the Global Alliance has distinguished itself from the Coalition by clarifying that it does not take an abolitionist stand on prostitution and is also open to the sex workers' perspective. Support of sex workers' rights is part of a larger postmodern challenge to conventional feminism, which allows for a cacophony of voices and refuses the binary dichotomy in which all women are constituted as "other." Feminism which fails to overcome binary oppositions ends up supporting the status quo, impoverishing women and aligning with right-wing fundamentalism and a discourse which has its genesis in homophobia.

Defining Trafficking

There are at least three different "camps" with different ideas about trafficking: the Coalition Against Trafficking in Women lead by Kathleen Barry, the Global Alliance which also claims to be feminist but only opposes "forced" prostitution, and various sex workers' rights activists who dismiss the free/forced distinction and claim that the "harms" of prostitution are actually caused by moral attitudes and their legal consequences. The word trafficking can be applied to any kind of commodities being traded or bartered, however it also has sinister and illicit implications, in this case being used with the implicit assumption that it is women and girls who are being transacted as non-consenting prostitutes to fulfil male sexual desires. The position of Barry and the Coalition is that trafficking is part of the general exploitation of women according to the feminist principle that male sexuality under patriarchy is about power, not sex and thus all prostitution is coercive (see also Sullivan 1996).

If all prostitution is violence against women, it seems that any migration of sex workers can become "trafficking," as in Coalition member Sheila Jeffreys' statement: "As men use women in sex tourism in different countries they then demand these women to be trafficked into their country" (*West Australian*, 13 December 1995). Jeffreys has also said that, "prostitution is a form of sexual violence affecting women's bodies, their health and self-image, and undermines other gains women have made. . . . Once we remove women's subordination in society there will not be prostitution" (*West Australian*, 13 December 1995). In the *LA Times* another Coalition member Janice Raymond has published an editorial, "Prostitution is rape that's paid for" (December 11, 1995).

The Utrecht conference produced a definition emphasizing force rather than the nature of work to be performed in its final statement (1994):

> The traffic in persons is not only for purposes of prostitution, but for a range of other activities as well. . . . It is important to emphasize that the element that defines traffic is force and not the nature of the labor to be performed. . . . The trafficker cannot use as a defense the fact that the person is or was at any time, for example, a prostitute or a domestic worker. . . .

Similarly, after the Chiang Mai conference, the Global Alliance defined trafficking as forced labor where people are lured or deceived into forms of contemporary slavery: more specifically, as a feminist alliance they refer to the movement of "women" in order to "subject them to power" (*STV News Bulletin #3*, July 1995). A draft document, "Standard Minimum Rules for the Treatment of Trafficked Persons" published in the *STV News Bulletin*, says, "the trafficked persons shall be treated as migrant laborers and therefore be protected by the International Labor Organization," the emphasis being on opportunities for retraining and the chance to "start a new life," the meaning of which is unclear, but implies a moral preference for anything else over prostitution. The Global Alliance worked with sex worker groups at Beijing but their conceptual position is confused, since the "free/forced" distinction is untenable.

The movement of sex trade workers into and out of Thailand has been a major focus for lobbyists and the subject of the Asia Watch report, *A Modern Form of Slavery: Trafficking of Burmese Women and Girls into Brothels in Thailand* . The report was publicized with a tour of Australia by the researchers from May 1–13, 1995, supported by the International Women's Development Agency (IWDA). *A Modern Form of Slavery* was also the main source for the trafficking section of the Joint Standing Committee on Foreign Affairs, Defense and Trade report on Burma (JSC 1995: 48–53). This report refers to appalling conditions, social ills, victims etc, without any other evidence, and extends the supposed trafficking to Sydney: "the main center appears to be Sydney where there were at least twenty brothels" (1995: 52). Scarlet Alliance's response notes that the committee failed to contact Australian sex worker organizations which are in touch with Burmese and Thai workers (correspondence, January 4, 1996). While the report says "there might be 200 Asian prostitutes working in Australia," there are actually around two thousand of whom ninety percent are Australian residents (Brockett and Murray 1994).

In other usages, the IWDA leaflet says that Burmese women and girls are "trafficked—sold lured or tricked—into slavery in Thai brothels," while in the media, "the traffic in flesh is a horror of exploitation that shames the world's conscience" (Hornblower 1993: 14). It is not only the media which sensationalizes the issues. A UNESCO report on Contemporary Forms of Slavery (1995) uses the terms trafficking, prostitution and sexual exploitation interchangeably and refers to them as sordid, dangerous and inhuman. As David comments, "exploitation of prostitution" is a vague term which in itself is not an adequate reason to prohibit prostitution (1995: 1–5). The UNESCO document also makes a reactionary, unsupported and culturally vague demand for "strengthening the family nucleus and respect for moral values," as a solution to the "problem." Conversely, sex workers state that it is precisely the moral hypocrisy of global capitalism and sexual repression, including the criminalization of prostitutes, which creates the space for exploitation, discrimination and negative attitudes towards female sexuality (PROS et al. 1995).

The UN Special Rapporteur on Violence Against Women, Radhika Coomarasway, has made a contextualized report on prostitution and trafficking which states, "A discussion of prostitution must accept the premise that prostitution as a phenomenon is the aggregate of social and sexual relations which are historically, culturally and personally specific. The only common denominator shared by the international community of prostitutes is an economic one: prostitution is an income generating activity" (Coomarasway 1995, Article 205, see also Rubin 1975: 175). She goes on to make the point that sex workers are generally well-paid compared to other workers. Coomarasway's section on trafficking appears to be largely based on the Asia Watch report, describing conditions in Thailand as "appalling" and referring to an incident where five workers were burned to death when they were chained to the beds in a brothel and could not escape. A contrast can be made with the case of more than two hundred Thai women who burned to death in a Thai toy factory because the exit doors were locked, and similar cases in U.S. sweatshops (Priscilla Alexander, personal correspondence August 18, 1995, also reports in the *New York Times*, August 4, 1995, August 12, 1995, February 25, 1996), the point being that exploitative and dangerous conditions can be found across a range of industries internationally.

The shadowy nature of "trafficking" may be due to the cunning of the "traffickers," or it may be because they don't exist, at any rate it is difficult to estimate the scale of these issues. The link with child prostitution makes the debate even more emotive and can be manipulated to sideline the position of Western sex workers (Murray, forthcoming). The Norwegian government has very boldly informed the Council of Europe that "Every year, one million children are either kidnapped, bought or in other ways forced to enter the sex market" (Black 1994:12). Estimates of "child" sex workers in Thailand range up to 800,000 under-18-year-olds, according to U.S. Secretary of State for Human Rights John Shattuck, which would mean about a quarter of all teenage girls (*Bangkok Post*, 25 December 1994).

The End Child Prostitution in Asian Tourism (ECPAT) brochure says, "On a global scale millions of children have been forced into prostitution" and "tourists create a demand for more than one million 'fresh' child prostitutes every year." None of these figures are referenced, nor do they explain what research has been done, if any. Thai NGOs apparently estimate that there are two million sex workers in Thailand (Asia Watch 1993: 16), while the IWDA campaign says that over ten thousand women and girls are trafficked into Thailand each year, as in the Asia Watch report, which also says that fifty to seventy percent of them become infected with HIV.

A Modern Form of Slavery

While it is not clear where the figures for "trafficking" come from originally, it is books like *A Modern Form of Slavery* which help them to become accepted fact through the repetition of the rhetoric. This report from Asia Watch is written in a quasi-academic style, where tabloid journalism is footnoted, referenced, and hence legitimated. The book is referred to in academic papers, and it is the major source behind sections of Australian government and UN documents. The book and speaking tour put the issue back in the news, although the expert researchers conveniently chose to remain anonymous.

The authors did not actually visit brothels, but interviewed thirty workers ("victims") who had been arrested and taken to shelters or detention centers. While ostensibly giving these workers a voice, their statements are selectively reinterpreted by the "experts," and may be read differently by other sex workers.

On the one hand, it is emphasized that the women say that they did not know the type of work they were going to do. Since prostitution is illegal in Thailand and the workers were interviewed in detention, it seems logical that they would say this to avoid prosecution, as do migrant sex workers everywhere in an effort to avoid deportation. On the other hand, it seems to be the norm for the women to find their own way out of Burma with prior knowledge of where to find brothel agents. The report claims that they are tricked, but if this is the case they seem to be so stupid they can be duped twice, as they are "taken for deportation to the Thai-Burmese border where they are often lured back into prostitution by brothel agents." Where they have made it home and boasted about the money they made, this is described as lying to "save face," even when they have gone on to recruit others for the brothels or returned to work themselves. "Their return to prostitution was voluntary only in the sense that they saw their first experience as having rendered them unfit for anything else" (*Asia Watch* 1993: 74).

The women are described as fleeing the repressive regime and poverty in Burma, which contradicts the stated aim of "rescuing" the women and returning them home. There is a fairly well-substantiated rumor that HIV-positive Burmese women returned to Burma have been executed by the ruling SLORC authorities: even if this is untrue it seems inhumane to advocate returning these women to a country where there is no care, support or treatment available for HIV-positive people. The women are described as having limited understanding of HIV or AIDS, in fact the demand for them in Thailand is said to be linked to the myth that Burmese women are free of AIDS. The rapid rise in HIV infections may be related to the growth of the heroin trade and injecting drugs in the border area, or to the sharing of needles for antibiotics and contraceptives at health centers and among the workers themselves, however there is little information available about this.

There is evidence to support the claims of serious abuses by Thai police and immigration authorities. This abuse has been made possible by criminalizing the industry while there continues to be a high demand for female sex workers. The large amounts of money at stake encourage the bribery and corruption of the Thai authorities, and unregulated, substandard working conditions (*Asia Watch* 1993: 67–8). At a conference launching the Asia Watch report in a Thai translation, a Thai police officer named Surasek disputed its findings: "At present, most of these Burmese girls come here to work in brothels of their own free will. Very few of the women we meet in our day-to-day work say they were lured into the business" (*The Nation*, 5 April 1995). He also pointed out that "police had great difficulty securing convictions against agents who recruit women for the flesh trade since very few prostitutes are willing to identify or testify against these agents in a court of law."

It is tempting to wonder why the Asia Watch women want to expose the "horrors" in Thailand as opposed to some cases in the United States such as HIV prevalence among sex workers in the black housing projects in Oakland, or the treatment of immigrants (even legal ones) in sweatshops and in the United States in general. Meanwhile UNICEF reports that the United States has 300,000 prostitutes under 18, more than its own estimates for all Asian countries put together (*Far Eastern Economic Review*, 14 December 1995). Perhaps the "researchers" know that as guests in Thailand, which is so dependent on tourism income, they enjoy a level of protection which they would not find in US housing projects.

Trafficking and Female Labor Migration

The IWDA campaign over Burmese women tried to link the situation with Thai women arriving in Sydney in its media release. By equating Australian conditions with those in Thailand, they conjured up dens of iniquity full of juveniles held against their will, such as the media periodically sensationalizes. Matheson introduces a typical article:

> One of thousands of women from Thailand, the Philippines, Malaysia and China trafficked to Australia and other First World countries by crime syndicates each year, Susie is the face of contemporary poverty. That her job as a debt bonded sex worker is the best economic option available to her is a metaphor for most of the world's women, whose grinding impoverishment in the Third World is accelerating (Matheson 1994).

The exaggerations of the anti-trafficking groups only make things worse for the workers, such that representatives of three sex worker organizations in Sydney PROS, SWOP, QEWU, the Sydney Sexual Health Center multicultural health promotion project, and Asian sex workers, met to develop a policy statement on the alleged trafficking of Asian sex workers in Australia (PROS et al 1995). Thai workers in Australia are variously involved with a complex array of big and small operators, such as agents in Bangkok, passport forgers in Kuala Lumpur and travel agents in Singapore, so that they arrive with debts of up to $30,000. However I have shown elsewhere (Brockett and Murray 1994; and see David 1995) that conditions vary greatly, most of these women enter their contracts willingly, and if they can pay off their debt, they may become recruiters or brothel managers themselves.

Because the sex industry is not fully decriminalized and sex workers cannot obtain work visas freely, some of the terms and conditions of contracts are exploitative and working conditions may be poor. Australia's own racist policies contribute to exploitation, since young women from the United Kingdom and

Canada have no problem getting working visas under bilateral agreements, while according to Australian immigration officials, "no young attractive woman, and by that I mean a woman under sixty, is going to get a visa in Bangkok unless she is dripping with gold or has a business background" (David 1995: 25). Through their Operation Paper Tiger, the Australian authorities have deported eighty Thai workers in two years under the 1958 Migration Act, and the continuing crackdown pushes up the cost of the bonds. Attempts by women in detention to claim refugee status have so far been unsuccessful. Workers who are persecuted, arrested and deported before they pay off their debts are left with nothing for their hard work, and since they have to pay for deportation they may end up further indebted. Police and immigration activity depresses business, and means that workers have to hide their activities. This makes it harder for them to be contacted by support organizations providing information, condoms and HIV/AIDS information.

Asian workers who seek employment in the sex industry in Australia do so for the money, just as Australian workers do. Workers should be free to move to seek better pay and conditions just as many Australian workers go to work in Japan and Hong Kong. My experience is that workers are aware of the kind of work they will do when they enter the contract; in the very rare cases when workers have been trapped by false promises, of course this is unacceptable. The Prostitutes Collective of Victoria has argued for working visas to be made available, "thereby publicly diffusing the mythology of the 'coerced innocent'" (PCV 1995), and David (1995) has made a strong case for easier short-term working visas and sponsorship by brothels.

The anti-trafficking campaigns actually have a detrimental effect on workers and increase discrimination as they perpetuate the stereotype of Asian workers as passive and diseased. Clients are encouraged to think of Asian workers as helpless victims who are unable to resist, so they may be more likely to violate the rights of these workers. The campaigns also encourage racism towards Asian workers within the industry (where Australian workers accuse them of undercutting and not using condoms) and in the general community where Asian workers form an ostracized new "underclass" without equal rights (Brockett and Murray 1994).

The movement of sex workers around the region reflects economic differentials and a transnational division of labor: Thai workers head for Australia, Europe and Japan, while Burmese, Chinese and Indo-Chinese enter Thailand. But sex work is not the only job where the prospects vary so much from place to place that people are prepared to take on debts and forged paperwork. There has been a general rapid increase in migration from Asia to the West, and a dramatic reversal of the gender balance so that there are now many more women involved in the largest mass migration in human history (see, for example, Heyzer et al. 1994). The majority are employed on a contractual basis as foreign domestic workers (the "maid trade") in situations which often involve debts, exploitation and sexual abuse—conditions exposed in the media following the 1995 case of Filipina worker Flor Contemplacion, who was hanged in Singapore. Similarly in Indonesia where domestic workers "bring in significant foreign revenue and make rich men and women of those in the body business" (IRIP 1995: 27), there are frequent reports of exploitation and abuse and yet increasing numbers of migrants.

Expectations are raised by the consumer images beamed in by television, and any life is seen as better relative to a poor existence in the village: sex workers are not idealists any more than they are victims, neither have evil procurers and paedophiles created the whole industry. As Tracy Quan puts it, "Anyone who travels to a country, believing that the 'streets are paved with gold' is operating out of some form of greed, desire or ambition. . . . There is a saying among the jaded: 'You can't con someone who isn't trying to get away with something'" (personal communication, September 28, 1995).

Abolitionists Creating and Manipulating Stereotypes

There are now a number of anti-trafficking groups. Not all use an emotive discourse to push an abolitionist, fundamentalist agenda, but some are rooted in the ideology of Catherine MacKinnon (1987) and Kathleen Barry (1981) wherein all sex is prostitution and all prostitution is a violation of human rights—whatever the workers might care to say about it. "Trafficking" is one of the monsters evoked (like sex tourism and child prostitution) since Western sex workers on our own turf have used our own structures of support and advocacy to challenge some of the middle-class feminists who claim to represent us. Abolitionists have created a new "other" by victimizing Asian workers and children to enforce the moral condemnation of prostitution, with broad implications for all sex trade workers, freedom of sexual expression and HIV/AIDS prevention.

The trafficking argument depends on the presence of third parties coercing women into prostitution: if any money is offered to the women or their parents it should be as pitiful as possible, whereas the profits being made from their sexual labor should be as enormous as possible. Media reports also emphasize the involvement of organized crime such as Hong Kong triads in the sex industry (e.g. *Far Eastern Economic Review*, 14 December 1995), making a conceptual leap to assume the prostitutes are forced into the work and their lives ruined. According to the *Bangkok Post* (October 30, 1995) and *ECPAT Bulletin* (November 25, 1995), "Experts [sic] speak of syndicates systematically buying children from families in poor villages all over Asia, of gangs working in cooperation with police and immigration officials to transport their purchases across national borders and of sophisticated networks of paedophiles exchanging information."

It is the prohibition of prostitution and restrictions on travel which attract organized crime and create the possibilities for large profits, as well as creating the prostitutes' need for protection and assistance; it is the erotic-pathetic stereotype of the Asian prostitute which creates the possibility for middle-class women's trafficking hysteria. Logically there is no difference between "debt-bonded" Asian workers and Australian workers choosing to work for Hong Kong triads for more money than they could get in Sydney: it is racism which says that the former are victims and the latter agents. Even the East European workers now being chronically exploited all over the world are rarely con-structed as victims in the same way. In Southeast Asia, middle-class feminist groups still claim to represent sex workers and women's NGOs are involved in the anti-trafficking lobby (see, for example, Sancho and Layador 1993). While there are also splits among women's NGOs, these women are often happy to direct attention onto trafficking and Western/Japanese sex tourism, and away from the local (largest) part of industry. Anti-trafficking groups such as ECPAT and the Global Alliance (GAATW) do not support abolition per se, and are con-cerned with extreme cases of coercion, however the vagueness of definitions and lack of involvement of the workers themselves enabled the Coalition (CATW) to gather support for a radical abolitionist agenda. The Coalition and a number of other NGOs formed a network, supported by UNESCO, called the NGO Coalition Against Exploitation of Women, to take a petition to the Beijing UN Conference on Women in 1995.

Beijing, the UN Convention and Sex Workers' Voices

The Coalition's petition is for a new "Convention Against Sexual Exploitation" to replace the 1949 UN Convention on the Suppression of Trafficking in Persons and the Exploitation of the Prostitution of Others. The 1949 Convention origi-nated with the "exposure" of the White Slave Trade (which was later shown to be negligible) by Jewish feminists and the social purity movement in Europe (Truong 1990; Goldman 1970). It "rests mainly at the conceptual level, i.e. that prostitution is a form of promiscuity which offends public morality, the family and the community" (Truong 1990: 86), and it considers the prostitute as a uni-form category, as a source of evil separate from the socioeconomic environ-ment. Needless to say it ignores the client.

The new Convention Against Sexual Exploitation was previously proposed by Barry at the UN Human Rights Conference in Vienna, 1993. The proposed change would ban prostitution completely, not just forced prostitution: "Legalized prostitution . . . is an open door for traffickers" claims Janice Raymond, an activist with the U.S.-based "Coalition Against Trafficking in Women" (Hornblower 1993: 24). Their petition states,

> It is a fundamental human right to be free of sexual exploitation in all its forms, from prostitution, sex tourism, trafficking in women, mail-order bride selling and pornography to incest, wife abuse, sexual harassment and rape. . . . Sexual exploitation abrogates a person's human right to dignity, equality, autonomy and physical and mental well-being; it preys on women and children made vulnerable by poverty and economic development policies and practices, on refugees and displaced persons, and on women in the migrating process; and serves as a vehicle for racism and Northern domination (NGO Coalition Against Exploitation of Women, 1995).

Sexual exploitation has taken on a life of its own, and everything is conveniently muddled by putting prostitution and pornography in the same sentence as rape and incest so that people's obvious anathema to non-consensual sex is extended by implication to all forms of commercial transactions involving sex. "To equate professional prostitution with domestic violence is to diminish the horror of the helpless; to equate choiceful sex work with the violence of criminal greed is to deny the value and dignity of the work some women choose to do . . . it is the criminalizing of sex work that is partly responsible for society's negative attitudes to ALL women's sexuality" (Helen Vicqua, Scarlet Alliance internal communication, May 19, 1995). Meanwhile, the Network of Sex Work Projects (NWSP) coordinated a sex worker presence at Beijing to counter the anti-trafficking lobby, struggling against a Chinese government which initially did not allow visas for sex workers and prevaricated in every way possible to put people off attending. Most sex worker groups do not currently have resources such as E-mail access, whereas the anti-trafficking lobby is very professional, well organized and au fait with the UN system. However, through perseverance the NWSP did finally receive accreditation for the main UN conference. According to the Network:

> The dominant ideology about prostitution within the United Nations is that prostitution is a form of sexual exploitation which should be abolished. This view has been legitimized and passed into resolutions and laws at conferences such as Beijing with no input at all from sex workers themselves. Many sex workers feel that it is time to demand that we are heard in

such a significant international forum. More than being simply heard it is essential to form some resolutions which reflect our demands for human rights, and have those passed rather than the resolutions which lead to repressive measures to abolish prostitution. To do this sex workers and their supporters need to work to prepare resolutions and to lobby delegates for support at the conference (Doezema 1995).

Abolitionists need to hear that most sex workers, including male and transgender sex workers and men who work with female clients, do the job willingly and do very well out of it relative to other occupations. They need to hear that clients of sex workers come from all walks of life (and include women), they are not monsters, and sex workers as a rule do not hate them. It happens quite frequently that workers and clients develop a personal relationship outside of work, and Asian workers in expatriate bars commonly construct their relationships with clients in emotional, as well as commercial, terms (Law 1996: 80–82).

What can we conclude about the Coalition? Is there an element of titillation in their focus on sex workers, when similar problems are faced by migrant domestic workers and others? Is there an element of self-flagellation due to middle-class white guilt when faced with the rape of Asia by white capitalists? "Where there is an overlay of North-South exploitation—the Western tourist ruining innocent paradise with his credit card and unleashed libido—this version plays easily in certain, well-meaning ears" (Black 1994,12). At the same time the assumptions of passivity, stupidity and silence on the part of the Asian workers underline the inherent racism and class bias in the Coalition's arguments. In the end, the Beijing declaration was largely decided on before the actual conference, and achieved very little in terms of sexual liberation or acknowledgement of women's sexuality due to the strength of Islamic, Catholic and other reactionary groups. Sex work (addressed in terms of trafficking and sexual exploitation) was dealt with in the section on violence against women: existing instruments were recommended to be strengthened and the victims of trafficking supported (UN 1995 Section D). Trafficking is viewed as a global conspiracy which can be dismantled through international co-operation and the paternalistic rehabilitation of victims (assumed female and helpless). The small but staunch sex worker presence at Beijing managed to make a significant impact at the NGO Forum and the UN conference. Some anti-trafficking groups, including GAATW, worked with the sex workers to defeat Section 230(o) of the Draft Platform for Action, and to avoid the creation of the new abolitionist Convention on the Elimination of all Forms of Sexual Exploitation as proposed by the Coalition Against Trafficking in Women.

Summary

In the aftermath of Beijing the hysteria is fading, and the abolitionists, especially the CATW, are again out on a limb. The general interest in the topic has spurred more research and more evidence, which has shown up the predominance of local clients and the relatively small part played by "sex tourists." It is increasingly hard to maintain unsubstantiated rumors, although those who don't believe the hype are placed in a difficult position of proving a negative (JCNCA 1995: 53), while police deficiencies and corruption, the cunning of paedophiles etc., can be conveniently blamed from the other side for the lack of evidence.

Migration of female labor is increasing due to processes of economic globalization and removal of political boundaries, and clearly this process is accompanied by an increasing degree of coercion and exploitation of women due to prevailing systems of sex and gender in sending and receiving countries such as Thailand. The Utrecht conference statement made a valid point that force and not the type of work should be the issue in "trafficking," and goes on:

> . . . the individual right to self-determination includes the ability and the right of the individual to decide to work as a prostitute. In order to reduce the vulnerability of prostitutes and others to trafficking in this context, prostitution and other activities in the informal sphere should be recognized as a form of work. Consequently, prostitutes and other sex workers have the right to safe working conditions through the use of occupational health and safety and other labor ordinances (1994).

Truong argues that the industrial production of sexual services requires a continuous supply of sexual labor: "The effect of this process has been an increase in the use of violence to locate and control sexual labor" (1990: 201). Therefore, boundaries and workable definitions (preferably in line with ages of consent and employment) regarding "underage" sexual labor and controls over the use of force will continue to be necessary. Existing laws and Conventions cover the issues of slavery and similar practices, non-consensual sex and the exploitation of children (Metzenrath 1995), and there is already a Special Rapporteur on the Sale of Children, Child Prostitution and Child Pornography. All states need to ratify and apply (if they have not done so) these conventions, and laws should be introduced or enforced to control the sale of children by their parents, preferably before the sale occurs so that sex workers are not expected to finger their own families to the authorities.

All states need to start decriminalizing prostitution (without creating new categories of good and bad prostitutes), applying occupational health and safety standards to workplaces (including provisions for street workers), and working toward eradicating discrimination. Restrictive immigration policies contribute to the exploitation of migrants and should be reviewed: sex workers should have the right to travel freely and obtain working visas regardless of ethnic background. Governments should follow Australia in funding organizations which provide support and information to Asian workers, and these workers should be supported to form their own groups to achieve greater autonomy (and participate in and strengthen the Asia-Pacific network for sex workers' rights). International networks of sex work projects should aim to inform workers about working conditions and choices. Finally, where sex workers *have* been forced to work against their will they should be offered every support and free transport to their place of origin if they so wish (see also PROS et al 1995).

It is important to distinguish different types of sex trade work using clearly documented participatory research that involves the workers. Blanket statements about prostitution and the exploitation of women are propaganda from a political agenda which seeks to control the way people think and behave. The situations which the anti-traffickers rail against, insofar as they do exist, are a result of economic, political and gender inequalities, and it is those inequalities which should be our central cause for concern. The vast range of sex industries and contexts requires an understanding of diversity and difference and a realization that prohibition and unitary "moral values" are part of the problem, not the solution.

Abbreviations

CATW	The Coalition Against Trafficking in Women
ECPAT	End Child Prostitution in Asian Tourism
GAATW	The Global Alliance Against Traffic in Women
HIV/AIDS	Human Immune-Deficiency Virus/Acquired Immune Deficiency Syndrome
IRIP	Indonesia Resources and Information Project
IWDA	International Women's Development Agency
JCNCA	Joint Committee on the National Crime Authority (Canberra)
JSC	Joint Standing Committee on Foreign Affairs, Defense and Trade (Canberra)
NGO	Non-government organization
PCV	Prostitutes' Collective of Victoria (Melbourne)
PROS	Prostitutes' Rights Organization for Sex Workers (Sydney)
QEWU	Queer and Esoteric Workers' Union (Sydney/Canberra)
SLORC	State Law and Order Restoration Council (Burma)
SWOP	Sex Workers Outreach Project (Sydney)
WISE	Workers in Sex Employment in the ACT (Canberra)

3 An International Perspective on Slavery in the Sex Industry

Jo Bindman

At Anti-Slavery International, we believe that exclusion from society contributes to the worldwide association of the sex industry with slavery-like practices. The major characteristics of slavery are violence with impunity, sometimes to death, loss of freedom of movement and transfer to another owner/master for money or goods without informed consent. It is closely associated with a lack of full citizenship rights.

The designation of prostitution as a special human rights issue emphasizes the distinction between sex work and other forms of female, dangerous and low-status labor, such as domestic or food service work, or work in factories and on the land. It hides the commonality, the shared experience of exploitation, which links people in all such work. The distinction between "the prostitute" and everyone else helps to perpetuate her exclusion from the ordinary rights which society offers to others, such as rights to freedom from violence at work, to a fair share of what she earns, or to leave her employer. An employment or labor perspective, designating prostitution as sex work, can bring this work into the mainstream debate on human, women's and workers' rights. It also allows us to recognize that the sex industry is not always where the worst conditions are to be found.

Since the Convention for the Suppression of the Traffic in Persons and the Exploitation of the Prostitution of Others was published by the United Nations in 1949, our view on women has changed. We can no longer characterize women as the purely passive, and this Convention is no longer appropriate to meeting their needs. Nor has it ever proved successful. We must fight to ensure that women have the same basic rights as everyone else, so that women can take their own decisions.

Let us look at how slavery finds its way into the sex industry. The sex industry exists all over the world and has a huge variety of forms: sex may be sold as striptease or in go-go bars, pick-up bars, night clubs, massage parlors, saunas, truck stops, restaurants and coffee shops, barber shops, in straightforward brothels which provide no other service, via escort agencies, or on the street. Most people who work in these establishments lack formal contracts with the owners or managers but are subject to their control. Those who work in the sex industry are commonly excluded from mainstream society. They are thereby denied whatever international, national or customary protection from abuse is available to others as citizens, women or workers.

The lack of international and local protection renders sex workers vulnerable to exploitation in the workplace and to violence at the hands of management, customers, law enforcement officials and the public. The need for worker protection, to include occupational health and safety provisions, is of particular relevance in the context of HIV/AIDS and other sexually transmitted infections. Sex workers, without their rights in their place of work, are uniquely vulnerable to disease, routinely lacking the full combination of information, materials and authority necessary to protect themselves.

In fact, existing human rights and slavery conventions are in theory sufficient to take the slavery out of the sex industry. The existing conventions outlaw slavery in, for example, the carpet industry in India, in the growing of sugar cane in Haiti, and in domestic service in Indonesia and the United Kingdom. While all of these abuses continue to exist, the existence of conventions means that pressure can be brought to bear on governments to enact them in national law. Once they are part of the law, affected persons, groups and activists can work to ensure the enforcement of the law. This is in essence how Anti-Slavery International works, with our partners on the ground. It can be a slow process, but we believe it can eventually eliminate modern forms of slavery. So in the sex industry too, conventions can be used.

But in the case of the sex industry, the ending of slavery-like practices is held back by the distinction between sex workers or prostitutes, and other workers.

We want to point to the international conventions that protect the rights of children kept in appalling conditions in the carpet industry or of plantation workers trapped in debt-bondage, and which would allow sex workers to claim their rights as full members of local and world society. To do this we first need to identify prostitution as work, as an occupation susceptible like the others to exploitative practices. Then sex workers can be included and protected under the existing instruments which aim to protect all workers from exploitation, and women from discrimination. It is exploitation in every form that Anti-Slavery International exists to fight.

I am sure that most people share my abhorrence of the shocking circumstances in which prostitution often takes place. Many women and girls in the industrialized and developing worlds are brought into the sex industry by deception or find themselves forced to stay within it against their will. There is debt-bondage in which the bonded person effectively becomes the property of the creditor until the debt is paid, rendering the bonded person extremely vulnerable to abuse. It is a system in which an initial payment must be worked off indefinitely on terms set by the creditor and rarely made explicit to the bonded person, who may be passed with their debt from owner to owner. This practice is common in different industries the world over—in plantation agriculture, brick manufacture and carpet weaving. Debt-bonded women in Taiwan's sex industry can be confined in semi-darkness, allowed out rarely and only under armed guard. In Thailand, they may be forced to receive twenty customers per day, powerless to protect themselves with condoms, with the cost of medical treatment and abortion added to their debt, and discarded if they test HIV-positive.

There is trafficking, often combined with debt-bondage, which transports women across national boundaries for various purposes, of which domestic work, "mail-order" marriage and prostitution are most common. Agents in the sex industry bring women and girls from Nepal to India, from the Dominican Republic to Germany, where they are completely dependent upon their traffickers. They have little knowledge of the local language, customs or law, and may not know how to get home even if they have access to their passports. They are threatened with their debt unpaid. At the mercy of the traffickers, they are forced to work long hours in inhumane surroundings.

There is child labor outside the family which deprives millions of children of the future which an education can provide. Long working hours, cramped conditions and lack of care in childhood can damage health for life. Children are often preferred as cheaper and less able to resist poor conditions than adults. They are particularly vulnerable to sexual abuse in the workplace—in the case of child domestic workers, it is almost commonplace. Thousands of girls in their early teens are in brothels or on the streets, their youth rendering them especially vulnerable to intimidation.

Exacerbating these problems and creating others in countries where welfare and education provisions protect citizens from debt-bondage, trafficking and child labor, are laws aimed at suppressing the sex industry which criminalize women. Criminalization in the United Kingdom deprives women in the sex industry of civil rights. It means that women can be arrested, locked up and fined on the evidence of the condoms that they must carry to protect their lives. Women can be beaten, raped or even murdered without recourse to police protection.

The examples I give here are of slavery in the sex industry. However, slavery is not inherent to the sex industry. Many women all over the world go to courageous lengths to enter the sex industry. In our world today, people in general and women in particular are often faced with limited opportunities to provide for themselves and their families. These are women considering all the dangers to which social exclusion will expose them, and the economic exploitation that they may face, and still calculating that this is their best available option.

Can we tell such people what they may or may not do? Do they deserve anything less than the best possible conditions sought for other workers? Can we tell them that we would take away their power to choose this occupation, maybe condemning them to worse conditions in another field? Work, for example, in a glass factory in India, where the heat, fumes, noise and constant risk of terrifying injuries from the furnaces creates a hell for its workers and where life expectancy is said to be reduced by ten to fifteen years. Or back-breaking toil in subsistence agriculture all day, followed by a load of domestic duties, just to scrape together the bare minimum for survival. Closer to our homes, it can be better than cleaning lavatories or enduring monotonous hours for very low pay on the production line. And it could be the only job available where a mother can be around to collect her children from school.

We in the human rights field must work alongside efforts towards economic justice, towards viable economic alternatives for everyone, ending vulnerability to slavery-like practices. Let us at the same time fight debt-bondage, trafficking, child labor and the inhumane conditions, violence and intimidation which they incorporate. Let us fight laws which exclude women in the sex industry from society and which deprive them of the rights that everyone else enjoys, at least on paper. Let us fight exploitation in every form.

4   Women, Labor, and Migration

The Position of Trafficked Women and Strategies for Support

Marjan Wijers

Introduction

"Traffic in women" is a broad category covering various forms of exploitation and violence within a range of (informal) labor sectors that migrant women work in, including prostitution, entertainment industries and domestic work. Trafficking is not limited to prostitution, although this is a popular belief, and not all prostitution involves trafficking. We can define trafficking in the narrow sense as the process in which migrant women are brought into prostitution through the use of coercion, deceit, abuse or violence and in which they are denied fundamental human rights and freedoms such as the right to decide to work as a prostitute or not, the right to decide on the conditions of work, the right to enter and leave the sex industry, the right to refuse certain customers, the right to refuse certain sexual acts, the right to freedom of movement, the right not to be exploited, and so forth. If trafficking is defined in a broader sense it can apply not only to prostitution, but also to other forms of labor such as those mentioned above.

Since 1987, the Foundation Against Trafficking in Women (STV), based in the Netherlands, has been working professionally and has given assistance to more than 900 women. This is just a small fraction of the number of women that is estimated to have been in one way or another trafficked to the Netherlands. Social workers, health care workers and police estimate that this number is between 1,000 and 2,000 per year. As STV and Dutch policies have concentrated primarily on the traffic in women for the purpose of prostitution, this essay focuses mainly upon this form of trafficking.

Principles for Support

The first step in supporting victims of trafficking is to gain at least some understanding of their position, their needs, dilemmas, motivations, and of the problems they face in the process of trafficking. Searching for ways to support trafficked women means starting from the reality of migrant women and the recognition of the right of trafficked women to survival and self-determination. This assumes that their own needs and aspirations are taken as a starting point for any action. •

To understand the reality of trafficked women we need to look at, at least, five factors through which their situation is determined. These are a) their position as women who migrate from one country to the other, regulated by migration laws; b) their position as women who migrate for work, regulated by policies and laws dealing with migrant workers; c) their position as women who work or worked in prostitution, regulated by prostitution laws; d) their position as victims of (internationally organized) crime, regulated by criminal policies on trafficking; and e) their position as women in their home countries and in the receiving countries, which is reflected in the first four areas. Existing policies to combat trafficking mainly build on prostitution and migration laws.

Position as Migrants and Migrant Workers

Looking at trafficking from the perspective of the majority of the women we are concerned with, it is clear that most women come to Western Europe because they are looking for a better way to make a living. In this sense, they should be seen as labor migrants. Migration is an age-old survival strategy for men as well as for women. It implies courage and initiative to try to change one's own or the family's situation. Certainly, women who have become victims of trafficking can not be classified as passive or stupid victims. This may seem self-evident, but ten years of daily work on the issue of trafficking proves it is still not the case for many people involved in the whole process, such as police officers and the judiciary.

The growing gap between the rich and poor countries particularly affects the situation of women and children. The breakdown of national economic and political systems, as in the Central and Eastern European countries, brings hardship and confusion to the general populace, but women are particularly vulnerable in such situations. They are often in the paradoxical situation of being responsible for the family income, while not having access to well-paid jobs nor the same opportunities for legal labor migration as men. As a consequence, the number of women migrating is increasing dramatically. Nearly half of the migrants worldwide today are women, although in official policies women are almost exclusively seen as dependents of male labor migrants.

Women have few opportunities of getting work in formal labor sectors, either in their home countries or in the more developed countries. They are relegated to the informal and unregulated labor market—without rights and without protection. Over the last fifteen years new, more dubious and unprotected labor markets have developed internationally, such as the market for female domestic workers, for marriage partners and for the sex and entertainment industry. Simultaneously, numerous multi-national recruiting agencies, impresarios and marriage bureaus have mushroomed, that actively—and usually dishonestly—recruit young girls and women who are looking for the opportunity to make a living elsewhere.

This labor division is also reflected in migration patterns. There are few legal and independent ways for women to migrate within the informal sector. Owing to the nature of the work and the forms of migration open to them, they are forced to make use of the services of untrustworthy organizations and middlemen. This places migrating women in extremely vulnerable situations, subject to abuse by procurers, employment agencies, artist agencies, marriage agencies and all other kinds of middlemen, who intervene in the beginning, somewhere in the middle or at the end of the process.

On the European side, Western European countries all claim they are not immigration countries. For this reason labor migration into the European Union is very restricted. Shamefully, it seems that the richer the country, the harder they try to keep migrants from poor countries out. Though official policies hold that Europe should not allow more immigrants, these official statements can hardly be maintained if we realize that apparently a demand does exist, to put it in economic terms, for certain types of workers and that these workers, often immigrant, keep our economies going. The group of migrant women we are concerned with works cheaply, does not lay claim to legal and social protection—because their legal situation is too precarious—and generates significant state, private and criminal revenue.

Official policies of the receiving countries in Western Europe, however, forbid labor migration from so-called Third World countries and, recently, from Central and Eastern European countries. The majority also prohibit migrants from working as prostitutes, even if they permit nationals to do so. In reality, almost the only work migrant women are allowed to do is in the entertainment sector or sex industry, whether this is the official policy, as in Switzerland, or just everyday practice, as in the Netherlands. At the same time these sectors are the most marginalized, if not criminalized, in society. Moreover prostitution is not even recognized as labor by most, if not all, countries. This creates a considerable gap between official policies and day-to-day experiences of prostitutes, mail-order brides and domestic workers. And this is where organized crime comes in: filling the gap that official policies leave open.

Migrant women who are trafficked do not have access to legal resources in order to bring their traffickers to justice. In the majority of the receiving countries those with an illegal status will be immediately deported. They are not protected legally by national or inter-State policies. On the contrary, most state policies regarding "aliens" effectively turn these women into criminals instead of victims. Employment agencies, entertainment agencies, procurers for prostitution and other middlemen operate in the countries of origin without any effective government control. They take advantage of the women's vulnerable situation and their wish to migrate. Since there are practically no possibilities for poor, unskilled women to travel independently and to work legally in these countries, they are almost totally dependent on recruiting agencies and brokers, and thus in imminent danger of falling victim to criminal networks. In receiving countries the increasingly restrictive immigration laws resulting from European unification have clearly negative effects for women who attempt to migrate. The laws appear to benefit the traffickers, who will always find ways to circumvent laws, while simultaneously working to the disadvantage of migrant women, increasing their dependence on third parties.

The overall picture is that trafficked women are considered, above all, as undesirable aliens. The fact that they may be a victim of sexual violence and exploitation is completely subordinate or even irrelevant to their immigration status in the context of current immigration policies of European countries. In this situation it is almost impossible for migrant women to ask for protection if exploitation, violence and forced prostitution occur.

Position as Women Working in Prostitution

States have different policies on prostitution. All policies have in common that prostitutes are denied basic human rights, held in contempt, isolated, marginalized and sometimes criminalized. Some countries, such as the United States, have a *prohibitionist system*. All prostitution is declared to be unacceptable, and most or all aspects of prostitution are prohibited and criminalized. Not only the procurer but also the prostitute is liable for punishment, as is any third party. In most cases the primary target for law enforcement, however, is the female prostitute, not those who profit from her income. This law denies the reality of prostitution and the fact that for various reasons women work as prostitutes to earn an income. Illegality renders prostitutes completely dependent upon others, such as pimps, procurers, police officers. Corruption and blackmail are everyday practices. Trafficked women are completely at the mercy of pimps and brothel keepers, as there is not one authority they can, even theoretically, turn to.

In the second type of system, as in Germany, the existence of prostitution is more or less recognized. Prostitution is either 'legalized' or regulated by the State (through different forms of registration and other forms of State control) in the interest of public order, public health and tax generation. Usually prostitutes are required to register with the police and to have regular STD (Sexually Transmitted Disease) tests, with penalties for women working without a license or "health certificate." This *regulatory system* creates a difference between legal and illegal forms of prostitution. Many women do not want to register because they fear the stigmatizing effects. Other women cannot register because of their illegal status. In both cases women end up in an illegal sector with all the negative consequences this entails.

The third system, *abolitionism,* emphasizes the moral and ethical arguments against regulation and the involvement of the State or any other third party. Prostitution is seen as a moral evil, undermining the family and family values and involvement of the authorities is thought to encourage moral decay. According to this view the prostitute should not be penalized—she is the victim—but all other aspects of prostitution are considered criminal activities. No distinction is made between forced and consensual prostitution. Prostitutes are basically seen as passive victims of the social and economic system that need to be rescued. This view negates individual choice and denies women the status of subjects capable of assuming agency and responsibility. However, many cases are known where no legal proceedings have been initiated against traffickers under an abolitionist system because the women did not reflect the stereotyped image of a victim of trafficking, for instance because she agreed to work as a prostitute.

The majority of the European countries have adopted a system based on the abolitionist view. For example, laws in the Netherlands, Belgium and Great Britain and the 1949 *Convention on the Suppression of the Traffic in Persons and the Exploitation of the Prostitution of Others* are predominantly based on this view. This leads to a rather confusing and paradoxical situation. On the one hand, working as a prostitute is not punishable, but any involvement of a third party is illegal, be it a brothel keeper or a friend, independent of the consent of the women and whether or not they exploit the women involved. One the other hand, registration and payment of taxes are enforced in many countries with an abolitionist system. Although unintentional, in practice abolitionism leads to isolation and criminalization of prostitutes. Moreover any third party is forced to operate illegally, which puts the women concerned at greater risk of violence and exploitation.

Lastly there is the *system of decriminalization*. As far as I know, the State of New South Wales, Australia, is the only place where decriminalization not only of prostitutes but of the prostitution business itself is a starting point for prostitution policy. The basic principle is the right of independent adult women to determine their lives by themselves. Elsewhere, this view is mostly favored by prostitutes' organizations and women's organizations that support prostitutes' rights. According to this view, any policy should be based on the rights of the women to self-determination and the protection of their rights as workers. Criminalizing the sex industry creates ideal conditions for rampant exploitation and abuse of sex workers. Prostitutes in this system are not treated as victims or denied responsibility and accountability for their decisions and actions, as is done in all the systems mentioned above. Moral judgement against prostitution is not the principle motivation in drafting policies, because of the danger of marginalizing and stigmatizing prostitutes. Rather it is believed that trafficking in women, coercion and exploitation can only be stopped if the existence of prostitution is recognized and the legal and social rights of prostitutes are guaranteed. It is not considered realistic to attack prostitution, but instead, appropriate to fight violence and exploitation through existing laws, such as labor regulations and civil rights laws. Traffic in women could and should then be prosecuted as a severe violation of several laws.

Position of Women as a Victim of Organized Crime

Traffic in women mostly takes place in a network-like structure and is based on violence. This has many consequences. Even if existing policies allow women to report to the police, only few women will do so, for various reasons.

Confidence in the Police System

Most women have no trust whatsoever in the police or any other authorities. Corruption and abuse of power are frequent in many of their home countries, but many migrant women also have bad experiences with the (immigration) police in receiving countries. As we have seen, in many countries prostitution is prohibited or illegal. Migrant prostitutes (whether they are forced or not) are continually at risk of deportation, imprisonment, harassment and abuse. In most of the home countries of migrant women, protection by the law is the privilege of the rich and powerful. To have the law work in your favor, you need money and connections, things that are at the disposal of the traffickers but not of the women. Moreover, most women are illegal in the country of residence. This implies that any contact with authorities puts them directly at risk of deportation.

Fear of Deportation

Although at first glance, deportation could appear as a way of escaping the trafficking situation, the reality is far more complicated. Many women consider deportation an even worse prospect than accepting the situation in which they find themselves, and try to survive in the hope that at some point they will succeed in realizing their original aims for migration. Women accept the offers made by recruiters, because they do not accept the confinements of their situation at home. The offer for work abroad represents one of the few avenues to a better future. Often, they borrow money to pay for the costs of middlemen. They can be indebted to their own family, but also to the recruiters. In many cases the family relies on the women's income. If they are deported, they return home with empty hands, with no money and with debts that will never be paid off. If it becomes known that a woman has worked as a prostitute, this can have serious social consequences. Not only has she to worry about the effect this can have for her family, she also has to face the possibility that her family will not accept her anymore. Surviving without family can be extremely difficult. Moreover, it is questionable whether deportation means an escape from the criminal circuit. Many cases are known of women who, after deportation, were awaited the recruiters and taken back immediately. There are many ways to keep a woman under control: debts that must be paid, threats to inform her family about her prostitution activities, threats to harass or harm herself, her family or children if the woman does not comply to their demands. Deportation certainly does not put an end to the fear for reprisals, whereby the woman is not only risking her own safety but also the safety of her family.

Fear of Reprisals

If the woman reports the case to the police—either voluntarily or because she is arrested as an illegal alien—she takes a tremendous risk. Even in the Netherlands, where a woman is entitled to a temporary residence permit if she is willing to testify in court, she loses the right to stay the moment the case is settled and she is not needed anymore as a witness. Expulsion means that she will be at the mercy of traffickers again, without anybody to protect her. Pressing charges also means a higher risk that her history will get known at home, for instance when the criminal investigation involves the gathering of information in her home country. During the time that a woman is under control of her traffickers, in most cases she is continuously told what they would do to her if she dared to escape or go to the police. These threats are no jokes. They do not lose their effect when the police get involved, even if the police are understanding and motivated to support her. Family and children at home are also an easy target for reprisals. Trafficking in women is an internationally organized crime. Women realize very clearly that the power of the national police stops at the border, but the power of trafficking networks does not.

Network-Like Structure

Often trafficking in women finds place in a network-like structure. In general, the women are only familiar with a part of the criminal network. It is possible that several women are in the same network without knowing each other, or without dealing with the same members of the network. However, they are aware of the fact that the people who are controlling them form part of a larger network. This is a very frightening thing. As was said to one woman after a vain attempt to escape: "Remember, there is no use in trying to escape. I have people everywhere to watch you. You don't know them, but they know you." Sometimes women are used against each other. One woman, for instance, is used to instruct or control other women in exchange for privileges, such as a bit more freedom of movement or the possibility of sending money home. Women are given false information about each other or played against each other. In this way a web of disinformation, insecurity and fear is woven around them. They are not in the position to freely exchange information with women trapped in the same network. Through this system of disinformation women can imagine a completely false notion of the position of other women involved. In the case of a criminal investigation, this can lead to the dismissal of the case for reason of contradictory statements.

Survival Strategies

The situation of extreme dependency in which victims of trafficking often find themselves is comparable to situations in which people are kept hostage. One survival strategy in such a situation is to try to protect yourself by trying to appease the persons who control you, to adapt or to anticipate their wishes. Survival strategies of women will then be directed towards influencing individuals in the network instead of trying to escape. Most women learn very quickly that open resistance is not the wisest course to follow.

Position as Prostitute

All women involved in sex work are very aware of the prevailing attitudes towards prostitutes. This is one of the reasons why they do not want other people to know that they work or have worked as prostitutes. At STV, we have become very aware of these kind of prejudices, for instance through the distinction that is made between "innocent" and "guilty" victims. People, including police officers, prosecutors and judges, can easily identify with women who comply to the stereotype of the naive and innocent victim, unwittingly forced into prostitution. But the moment a women has worked as prostitute or wants to continue to do so, or even when she just stands up for herself, compassion turns into indifference or outright hostility. Common opinion holds that once a prostitute, a woman looses all her rights and is no longer entitled to protection against violence, exploitation, abuse, blackmail, and being held prisoner. Unfortunately, these attitudes are all too familiar for the women involved. In addition to the reasons mentioned above, this also explains their lack of motivation to report to the police. A decision to report to the authorities is always based on the conviction that you have certain rights and that you have a claim to protection in case of violation of these rights. There is no need to say that these attitudes towards prostitutes work clearly in favor of the criminal networks and very much against the women.

Conclusions and Strategies

If we want to develop policies to combat trafficking and to support victims it is essential to be aware of the fact that we are dealing with women who have many good reasons to be scared and who are under massive pressure. They find themselves in a very vulnerable situation and have to survive in unpredictable and insecure circumstances. They will and have to continually consider which strategy renders them the best chance to survive. This does not mean they are weak, stupid or passive victims. On the contrary, a great many of the women who become a victim of trafficking end up in this position because they do not want to accept the limitations of their situation, because they are enterprising, courageous and willing to take initiatives to improve their living conditions and those of their families. But somewhere in this process they get trapped.

We can distinguish between two types of strategies to combat trafficking in women. On the one hand there are repressive strategies, including more restrictive immigration policies, more penalization and stronger and more effective prosecution. Repressive strategies have a strong tendency to end up working against women instead of in their favor, for example, by restricting women's freedom of movement or by using women as witnesses for combatting organized crime in the interest of the State without allowing them the corresponding protection. At the same time, these repressive measures are the most attractive for governments. They fit very nicely with state interests and supply them with a tidy set of arguments: "Close the borders and deport illegal women, and the trafficking in women will end." A noble intention that nobody would dare to contradict, yet for all the reasons presented above, it is highly problematic.

On the other hand there are strategies that aim to strengthen the rights of the women involved, as women, as female migrants, as female migrant workers and as female migrant sex workers. To prevent trafficking, to offer trafficked women genuine support and to improve their position and that of women in general the interests of the women concerned should form the basis for advocacy work and political campaigning. Support strategies will have to be directed towards empowering women at all stages of the trafficking process. Action should be directed towards enabling them to take back control over their lives and towards facilitating their ability to speak up for their own rights. All the strategies must be based on the recognition of women's right to self-determination and to choose—on non-stigmatization and non-victimization. This approach clearly starts at the other end, to strengthen the rights of the women involved, as women, as female migrants and as female migrant sex workers. It does not support any repressive measures if the rights of the women involved are not at the same time defined and protected, whether it be as witnesses or as workers. This is the hard and slow way, but I am deeply convinced that it is the only way that will work in the end.

5 Discourses of Prostitution
The Case of Cuba

Amalia Lucía Cabezas

During the past five years, Cuba's re-entry into tourism and the resurgence of sex work have been regularly featured in U.S. popular media. Beginning with the *Playboy* pictorial on Cuban women in 1990, periodic articles in the mainstream media have used Cuban women's bodies to chronicle the current economic crisis (Cohen 1991; Darling 1995; Passell 1993). While these reports employ low-intensity warfare to undermine socialism in Cuba, they have inadvertently placed Cuban women at the center of analysis. Certainly, the gains Cuban women have made in the areas of education, reproductive rights, and the struggle against gender discrimination were not featured in glossy magazine articles during the past thirty-seven years. But, as they say on Madison Avenue, "sex sells," and Cuban women selling sex have captured the imagination of the U.S. mainstream media, as well as that of scholars in Cuba and the United States. For some scholars, the glaring ideological contradictions indicated by the reappearance in Cuba of sex for sale point to the failure of socialism. For them, the sexuality of Cuban women is a sign of defiled nationhood, exploitation, and tourist imperialism.

Other scholars valorize the independence, self-esteem, and entrepreneurial skills of *jineteras*, the name given to Cuban sex workers. Sexuality in this case is valorized for economic and social purposes. Both arguments focus, albeit not explicitly, on the sexuality of Cuban women and reject the separation between sex and economics.

My concerns in this chapter center on the way scholars theoretically frame the issue of sex work. I am interested in the discourse on prostitution, and, particularly, the power dynamics and relations constituted by this discourse. I propose to examine the ideological articulations that inform this field of knowledge and, hence, the knowledge created on the topic of Cuban women and sex work.

Information disseminated about Cuban women and sex workers in popular U.S. media, as well as in scholarly publications, replicate the dominant discourse on prostitution, ignore the points of resistance of the sexual revolution, and fail to contextualize these studies within an historical and economic framework. What informs these studies is the continuing construction of prostitutes as pathological, deviant subjects; a similar conceptualization was used to construct "the prostitute" in nineteenth-century Europe.

I begin by examining the ways in which prostitutes have been constructed in Western European thought, because this discourse continues to dominate both popular and scholarly writings on sex workers. I use Foucault's writings on the *History of Sexuality* to elucidate the emergence in nineteenth-century Europe of a modernistic "science of sexuality" (Foucault 1978). It is at this point that in Western history sex was inscribed as an issue for public scrutiny through regulation, categorization, and organization. Foucault tells us that sexual relations outside of marriage were identified as the principal area of perilous sexual activity and that new sexual identities were created, such as the heterosexual, to better isolate and focus attention on certain forms of human sexuality labeled as "perverse." Sex became a nexus of power and knowledge through religious and ideological discourses in which the collective understanding of sexuality was exercised. Sexuality became, Foucault claims, a "pivot of the two axes along which developed the entire political technology of life. On the one hand, it was tied to the disciplines of the body: the harnessing, intensification, and distribution of forces, the adjustment and economy of energies. On the other hand, it was applied to the regulation of populations, through all the far-reaching effects of its activity" (1981:145). The imposition of a regime of heterosexual conjugality, to reproduce the laboring classes, served the functions and interests of modern industrialism. To enforce heterosexuality further, prostitutes were given the social function of maintaining the virtue of "respectable wives" and of sexually and emotionally servicing the laboring classes and the military. Saint

Thomas Aquinas makes this point clear: "Prostitution in the towns is like the cesspool in the palace: take away the cesspool and the palace will become an unclean and evil-smelling place" (Henriques 1963:45).

The sexuality of working-class women, and in particular the sexuality of women who sold sexual services, came under the direct examination, interrogation, and regulation of the scientific establishment and the state. Prostitutes were identified, classified, surveyed, and registered by the police, the state, and medical authorities. They were separated from their working-class communities and criminalized (Walkowitz 1980). As part of the rise of genetics and sociobiology, prostitutes' brains, genitals, and hands were measured, and observations that distinguished and/or categorized them as somatically different from "normal," heterosexual women and "somatically closer to the criminal" were recorded (Bell 1994). This so-called scholarship concluded that prostitution was a genetically transmitted disease. Genetics, scholars argued, explained the incidence of various family members working in the sex trade. Other findings along these lines claimed that prostitutes were nymphomaniacs and vectors of disease, lacked moral standards, and were pathological, unintelligent, emotionally immature, lazy, vain, and childlike (Gomezjara and Barrera 1992). Under the scrutiny of the doctor, social scientist, policeman, lawyer, the judge, and the administrator, a new social, economic, and sexual identity was created, one that targeted and made suspect all working-class women (Corbin 1990; Goldman 1981; Stansell 1986; Walkowitz 1980).

Christian religious mores, which constructed human sexuality as consisting of opposed male and female categories, conceptualized female sexuality as either passive or nonexistent. Male sexuality, in contrast, was conceived as driven by natural forces that predetermined aggression and the fulfillment of biological desire. The prostitute was constructed in relation to the bourgeois female ideals of the passive, virtuous wife who lacked sexual desire and the virginal daughter. It is the prostitute's role, as well as that of the sexual victim, to accommodate the overpowering sexual drive of the male. The prostitute's clients acted on "natural desire" and were exempt from examination, persecution, confinement, and social stigma. Thus, the role of the state and of the client was effectively excluded from this discourse.

Although these views were modified over time, it was not until the twentieth century that a major change occurred in the conceptualization of the role of women in society and of the part that their sexuality played in that regard. Despite challenges to the dominant paradigm in the first half of the century, it was the influence of the New Left and the Civil Rights Movement that finally created major points of resistance to the dominant discourse on sexuality. Oppositional discourses around issues of sexuality and sex work gained prominence when sexual minorities, feminists, lesbians and gays, and prostitutes in their own struggle for civil rights and self-determination sought to counter the prevalent knowledge constructed about them. For example, along with prostitute unions, the International Congresses of Whores (1985 and 1986), the International Committee for Prostitute Rights (1985), the World Whores Summit (1989), The National Conference of Prostitutes in Brazil (1987), and the World Charter for Prostitutes' Rights (1985) articulated a new political subjectivity that sits on the border between sex and work and that seeks to transform the identity of the prostitute. The prostitutes rights movement has been challenged to include transgender, Third World, lesbian, gay, bisexual and heterosexual, migrant men and women. Sex worker organizations have emerged throughout Latin America and the Caribbean. Organizations such as La Unión Unica in Mexico City, Maxi Linder in Surinam, and Movimiento de Mujeres Unidas (MODEMU) in the Dominican Republic promote changes in the political, social, and judicial system. They advocate the decriminalization of prostitution, the recognition of prostitution as legitimate work, and the acceptance of prostitutes as working women.

The prostitutes' rights movement helps us to understand that criminalization of prostitution serves to drive this business into a hidden economy that makes sex workers vulnerable to further marginalization and exploitation that leave them without recourse to legal and medical protection. Freedom of occupational choice, protection of health and safety, and prosecution of those who commit acts of violence against sex workers are central to the struggle.

Jan Strout, in recent publications of *Cuba Update* and the *Socialist Review*, discusses the politics of sexuality in Cuba's economic crisis (Strout 1995; 1996). Her articles are based on the findings and conclusions of studies done by the Federación de Mujeres Cubanas, the National Center for Sex Education, and La Asociación de Mujeres Comunicadoras. According to Strout, these studies argue that prostitution in Cuba today is radically different than it was prior to 1959. An important distinction is that today the majority of the *jineteras* are dark-skinned women who do not have relatives in the United States sending them dollars. In contrast to pre-Revolutionary Cuba, the vast majority of clients are foreigners, not Cubans. The practice of prostitution is no longer characterized by "slave-like conditions" and coercive pimps; instead, "today's young women practice *jineterismo* for the 'freedom' to go out dancing, dining, going to concerts, visiting Varadero Beach or other resorts, and shopping in dollar stores" (Strout 1996:10). Young Cuban women trade their bodies for dollars not out of economic necessity but by choice, "for consumer goods and recreational opportunities." In contrast to pre-Revolutionary times, today women are offered economic and educational opportunities. The social and cultural climate has also changed: prior to

1959 "there were strong social taboos [against prostitution], upheld by families, religious leaders, and even by the male client;" today "most of the women who practice *jineterismo* are not ashamed of their activities" (Strout 1996: 10).

According to Strout, these investigations show that Cuban women are "motivated by the desire to go out, to enjoy themselves, to go places where Cubans are not allowed to go, and to have fancy clothes." Moreover, *jineteras*

> reject work as a way to earn a living; they don't study for career prepara-
> tion; they don't link love with sexual relations; they are influenced by
> other people, mainly peers; and they are not aware of the risks associated
> with prostitution such as violence, drugs, AIDS, pornography, and crime
> (Strout 1996: 11).

Furthermore, these young women are charged with having "limited social values" (Strout 1996: 11).

These claims operate from within a conceptual framework that addresses the "problem" of prostitution as one of moral turpitude. Operating in these claims are assumptions about the sexuality of women in Cuba, in particular that of Mulatas and Afro-Cubanas. The knowledge created in these studies about women of color replicates a historical trajectory and ideological constructs of Mulatas as the sexually available, exotic, erotic Other. This model of analysis, using morality and ignoring women's agency, constructs working-class women, and specifically women of color, as pathological, vain, greedy, and lacking morality, social values, emotional maturity, and ultimately, revolutionary consciousness. Mulatas and Black Cubans are once again relegated to their historical trajectory of promiscuity and licentiousness while White Cubans are implicitly constructed as their opposite.[1]

Furthermore, implied herein is that the growth of sexual commerce is due to a lack of morality, or perhaps even revolutionary consciousness, and not of economics, lack of viable opportunities, and women's determination to control their bodies. A return to the repressive social climate of the 1950s, when men, whether as religious leaders, as clients, or as patriarchal figures, disciplined women through the social mechanisms of shame and stigmatization will not erase the fact of sex work.

The Cuban Revolution has addressed many of the inequities of the sex-gender system by promoting women's equal participation in educational and occupational opportunities. The ratio of female doctors, technicians, and scientists in Cuba, for example, is one of the highest in the world and testifies to a commitment to gender equity (Díaz, Fernández and Caram 1996). Nevertheless, since 1990 Cubans have witnessed the worse economic crisis in their history. Economic indicators describe declining levels of production, consumption, and earnings and the massive reduction of imports of medicine, food products, petroleum, spare parts, and commodity goods. This economic crisis has disproportionately affected women, who are primarily responsible for the maintenance and reproduction of families. Their daily struggles to find food, cook, shop, and maintain a home are heroic. In a crisis characterized by shortages in all basic necessities, including food, oil, soap, kerosene, and medicines, and at the same time exacerbated by power outages, lack of transportation, long lines, and rationing, women are overly burdened by the difficulties of daily life (Lutjens 1995). Opportunities for education and work have been curtailed, restricted, and limited. Additionally, the power of the almighty dollar makes a state-employed surgeon earn less than a hotel parking attendant. Most people who do not receive remittances from abroad have to invent ways to make do.

It is interesting to note that when speaking of the massive exodus of rafters in 1994, Strout characterizes the young men as "leaving to seek economic opportunities in the U.S. more than for any explicitly political reason" (1996:84). No stigma is attached to, nor judgments made about, their moral values and desires for commodity goods, recreation, fancy clothes, or "to go places where Cubans are not allowed to go" (1996:84). Nor is there mention of the rejection of educational and work opportunities that Cuba has offered them. This large space of tolerance is not offered women who participate in sexual commerce. Their motivations may vary from travel, entertainment, and clothes to meals, consumer goods, and the vital daily necessities that make survival in this period of crisis possible. These are some of the same reasons why most people work in boring, hazardous, and exploitative jobs, and why people choose to improve their economic circumstances through strategies that include marriage and migration. In the early 1990s, many even risked their lives crossing the shark-infested ocean in makeshift rafts.

The Cuban studies focus their attention primarily on *jineteras*, and not on *jineteros*, who sexually service men and women. In the absence of a discussion of the foreign clients, the state, and the tourism industry, responsibility for the existence of prostitution is implicitly assigned to Cuban women of color. Strout critiques the studies by pointing out that they target female sex workers, without scrutinizing male sex workers and foreign clients. However, she makes no attempt to analyze the way in which prostitutes are discussed nor the dialectic between structural conditions and the agency of Cuban women. Furthermore, she analyzes the situation in Cuba in a contextual vacuum without regard for the political and economic situation that creates a market for sex work in Cuba as well as other parts of the Caribbean region.

In contrast, the emerging body of scholarship on sex workers, and the practices of the sex industry in the Caribbean region and other parts of the world, is contextualized within the international and sexual division of labor, the dynamics of global economic integration, and local, sexual, and racial cultural formations (Bolles 1992; Kempadoo 1994; Troung 1990; Sturvedant and Stolzfus 1992). Scholars are advancing our understanding of sex work by examining sex work within global, historical, and cultural processes (Guy 1995; Kempadoo 1994, 1996; Allison 1994; White 1990). They incorporate an analysis of systems of gender, sexuality, race, culture, color, nationalism, and economy to create nuanced understandings of the practices that take place within the sex industry.[2] Implicit in these studies is the recognition of sex work as a form of labor and livelihood for many men and women around the world. In the late twentieth century, the study of prostitution is finally beginning to shift from the investigation of deviant, pathological subjects that require scrutiny and surveillance to a critique of social science, patriarchal control of female labor and sexuality, and the social construction of sexuality. Further, although women's work in domestic, sexual, and reproductive functions is invisible to economists and considered an extension of women's biological nature, feminist scholars argue that it produces accumulation and added value to the circulation of capital (Waring 1988; MacDonald 1996; Troung 1990). Therefore, some of these studies take into account the process of internationalization of production in the areas of leisure and entertainment and examine how these processes incorporate surplus extraction from women's bodies and sexual labor (Allison 1994; Troung 1990). They connect the practices of the local sexual trade, as facilitated by state and capital intervention, to the transnational sex industry linking various regions of the globe. Under global economic restructuring, sex work is organized within the service sector and operates within formal and informal economies. Studies of the tourism industry consistently point to increases in prostitution in the Third World (Lea 1988). They also indicate that tourism as a strategy for economic development extracts social and cultural costs (Pattullo 1996). Moreover, global economic integration as seen in export manufacturing plants and free trade zones in Asia, the Mexico-U.S. border and the Caribbean is driving low-wage female laborers to moonlight as prostitutes (Ong 1991). Sex work appears, therefore, as a strategy for many women to cope with the painful economic consequences of global capitalism.

In assessing the status of sex work in Cuba we need to shift the level of analysis from the pathological model to the numerous and complex forces that inform sex work. We need to ask how the sex industry in Cuba is organized in both the formal and informal economy. Who benefits from the wages of sex workers? What are the specific social processes that create conditions of exploitation? What are the forms of resistance and the possibilities for organizing sex workers? At another level, we need to understand how global capitalism creates conditions for women to sell sexual services at far better rates of pay than the sale of other forms of labor.

Finally, a structural analysis of the situation would reveal that prostitution is not a unique development in Cuba. Waring (1988) and other feminist scholars tell us that capitalist accumulation takes place at the level of women's bodies on a global scale, from household reproduction to export manufacturing and the tourism and sex industries. We need to recognize that women's work and transnational capitalism are inherently intertwined. Therefore, policies and studies must aim to create the most advantageous conditions for women workers to sell their labor with the recognition that women's sexual labor is their own. It does not belong to the capitalist patriarchy or the state.

Race, class, and geographical location make some women automatically suspect of being prostitutes. The label "puta" or "prostituta" goes beyond the actual sex worker to characterize any sexually active woman. In fact, in societies that objectify and commodify women, it is dangerous for a woman to proclaim her sexuality without "confirming" that she is in fact a prostitute. Women traveling without a male companion, single women, single mothers, women with multiple sexual partners, women who dress a certain way, all fall under the suspect category of being whores. Challenges to male domination can bring women accusations of being *boconas, atrevidas, descaradas, putas,* and more. Deviations from the narrow definition of what counts as a "good woman" can bring us verbal and physical punishment. The stigma attached to sex workers can be hurled against any woman at any time. Therefore, the discourse on prostitutes fits within a binary system that seeks to divide women, control them, and ultimately benefit from their labor.

Notes

1. For discussions of racial dynamics in sex tourism, see Fusco's chapter in this book; for an examination of current race relations in Cuba, see Fernández (1996).
2. For an excellent development of the concept of sexual labor for the Caribbean region, see Kempadoo (1994, 1996).

6 Prostitution, Stigma, and the Law in Japan
A Feminist Roundtable Discussion

Group Sisterhood: *Junko Kuninobu,*
Rie Okamura, Natsumi Takeuchi, Mari Yamamoto,
Masumi Yoneda and Midori Wada

Translated by Kyoko Saegusa and George M. Landon

Introduction

Yamamoto: We have been meeting as Group Sisterhood[1] for a year now and today
we would like to discuss "prostitution." What got us all
started was Ms. Tsuboi's report called "What's Wrong With
Being a Loose Woman?" In the course of talking about my
experience and feelings, I have come to think that sexuality
and the problem of prostitution overlap. Society considers
prostitution bad, and people generally approach the problem of prostitution from the perspective that "prostitution
is a violation of women's rights." Here, though, we would
like to reexamine the assumptions that underlie such discussions of prostitution.

Tsuboi: I have been interested in issues concerning sexuality,
and was involved with a survey on men's sexual awareness in a sub-committee of the Women's Studies Study
Group. I am currently part of a movement to eradicate
child prostitution within Asian tourism. All along I have
questioned the existence of the Prostitution Prevention
Law. Is this law really for the women who practice prostitution (or who are forced to)? The Law hasn't eliminated
prostitution. To the contrary, the many who practice

prostitution now have to remain clandestine, and are left with no rights, only societal stigma. I have had a hard time accepting this situation.

The Problem of "Specificity"

Tsuboi: There are three elements in the definition of prostitution according to the Prostitution Prevention Law: "unspecificity,"[2] money, and sexual intercourse. It is not considered prostitution when one's sexual relationship involves a "specific" partner and money, or when one has sex with "unspecific" men but no money is involved, however is it considered prostitution if partners are "unspecific" but of the same sex and if money is involved?

Yamamoto: It depends on how one defines sexual intercourse. One may say that sexual intercourse can also involve a penis and a penis, and a vagina and a vagina, but the actual enforcement of the law seems to be limited in scope to only a penis and a vagina.

Tsuboi: Conventionally, the reasoning against prostitution has been that it is bad to buy and sell sex and it is the existence of money in sexual activities that is thought to be the problem. However, prostitution is not the only form of sex for which men with financial power have paid money (and which women have sold for money). I wonder if marriage and dating haven't been some others. The true problem with prostitution, therefore, is not so much the selling and buying of sex with money. I have come to think that prostitution is considered bad because of people's sense of filth and revulsion toward women who have sex with "unspecific" men. So far women activists, maintaining that there should be no women who sleep with "unspecific" men for money, have been trying to rescue such women from this predicament. Monetary compensation is considered okay, as long as a woman has sex with a "specific" man, because they are presumed to love each other. Women prostitutes are not the only women who are disgraced by this notion. Society will stigmatize a woman as "loose" once she sleeps with "unspecific" men. My feeling is that unless we correct this situation women's problems won't be solved.

Wada: The Prostitution Prevention Law says in the first clause that prostitution degrades human dignity. I can't swallow the expression. It sounds to me as if it implies that women who practice prostitution violate the human rights of those women who support monogamy.

Yoneda: The same is true with the Preamble to the *Convention for the Suppression of the Traffic in Persons and of the Exploitation of the Prostitution for Others.* It states that prostitution goes against the dignity and values of people. My feeling is that I wouldn't want others to force such a notion upon me. My vagina is important to me, but it bothers me when it is equated with my personhood. It is strictly an individual matter how one relates her vagina to her personhood, isn't it? It is wrong to regard the vagina as something sacred and to tie it indiscriminately with the person's character. Even when one has sex with someone one really likes, at times one wants the act to be over quickly.

Tsuboi: So far in feminist movements, we have said that prostitution is bad because it involves money, that it is wrong to turn sex into a commodity. That, in effect, supports a viewpoint that equates women's sexuality with their chastity and personhood. Inadvertently, feminism has supported the division between prostitutes who deal with multiple partners and women who deal with specific partners. In other words, at the beginning, feminist protest was against men, but in the course of time it has been replaced by protest against women who sell sex and against women who approve of the deed.

The Prostitution Prevention Law

Yoneda: The Law defines prostitution more narrowly than we do in our discussion of prostitution in general. Critics of prostitution say that it is bad to sell sex for money, but selling sex for money includes not just sexual intercourse but stripping for money, and offering other sexual services. Why is only selling sexual intercourse illegal?

Tsuboi: Good point. Recent sex industries keep coming up with all kinds of services that do not involve sexual intercourse, such as "image clubs"[3] videos, and virtual reality programs. Things that evoke images and stir imaginations are getting much more popular than those that give direct and physical stimuli. When we think of the current situation in which sex industries have become this diversified, the definition of prostitution that hangs on to reproduction and copulation is out of date. In fact, the Prostitution Prevention Law can cover only a part of today's sex industries and those parts covered by the Act are getting fewer and fewer. What is even more problematic is, however, that many Asian women are brought to Japan to practice what the law defines as prostitution.

Yamamoto: The problem of women who come over from developing countries to practice prostitution is entwined with the problem of how to draw a line between forced prostitution and voluntary prostitution, and we would like to discuss it a bit later. First of all, how did the Prostitution Prevention Law come about?

Yoneda: The Prostitution Prevention Law was passed in 1956. In 1958, a year after it came into force, Japan ratified the *Convention for the Suppression of the Traffic in Per-*

sons and of the Exploitation of the Prostitution for Others (adopted at the UN General Assembly in 1949). One factor involved here is that they needed the Prostitution Prevention Law to pave the way domestically to ratify the Convention. After Japan lost the war, the international community was of the opinion that a democratic Japan and a Japan which allowed prostitution were not compatible. Japan was working toward coming back into the international community, and it couldn't afford to ignore this opinion.

Japan abolished licensed prostitution after the war, in 1946. The order to abolish this system came from the occupation forces. The order says that maintaining licensed prostitution would go against the ideal of democracy, and that it would be incompatible with the development of individual freedom within the nation. Japan's licensed prostitution was a target of criticism at every international conference. It is true that there had been a home-grown anti-prostitution movement, but I don't think that it alone could have eliminated red-light districts, since Japan is a male-dominated society. I would think that international pressures were a big contributing factor. Here is a parallel situation: international circumstances were that as one of the advanced economies, Japan had to ratify the Convention on the Elimination of All Forms of Discrimination Against Women within the UN Decade of Women. In order to do that, the government had to pass the Equal Employment Opportunity Law, which it never wanted to create.

Okamura: What was the purpose of passing the Prostitution Prevention Law?

Tsuboi: I think there were two purposes: One was to help those who were traded or forced into prostitution; the other was to punish those "loose" and "evil" women who willingly sleep with "unspecific" partners. The women on the Committee to Promote the Enactment of the Prostitution Prevention Law began their action saying that "they rose up in order to protect women's chastity and build a sound society."

Wada: No way! Did you say "chastity" just now? The women who promoted the enactment of the Prostitution Prevention Law were those who were securely built into institutionalized marriage, that is, who had internalized the moral code that men had established. They criticized women who were outside institutionalized marriage for their sexual activities.

Tsuboi: The core people who were involved in the promotion of the Law had a basic idea of one man and one woman as a couple. In the enactment of the Prostitution Prevention Law, they seemed to aim at establishing "a healthy one-husband-one-wife system." I think that the law ended up legalizing discrimination against female prostitutes.

Distinguishing Forced and Voluntary Prostitution

Kuninobu: If we argue that it is okay to earn money from selling sex, or if it's okay to be remunerated, or to have actual insertion of the penis into the vagina, or to have sex with multiple partners, or if it's okay to have sex with someone whom you don't love, then what it comes down to in the problem of prostitution is to what degree the person in question does it, based on her own decision, does it not?

Wada: I don't think it is a stretch of the imagination to think that there are women who can choose between sex for pleasure and sex for reproduction, and who decide to make it their work. I would imagine, though, that such women would be threats to men. Remember, men were so scared when women declared that "it's a woman's decision to have babies or not." They would pee in their pants if they read *Women at Point Zero* by Nawal El Saadawi, don't you think? The book is about a proud and confident prostitute. The idea that they can prevent prostitution and moral decay by stigmatizing prostitutes underestimates the power of women!

Tsuboi: But prostitution has been considered to be "a result of some sort of coercion, even if it looks as if the person has chosen it of her own free will."

Kuninobu: And, that is reality in Asia.

Yamamoto: Isn't it because we have looked at Asia only in that light?

Kuninobu: No, that isn't so. In reality, there are a lot of young women in developing countries who are forced into a situation where they don't have a choice but to go into prostitution. Also, I wonder if it is true that coeds sell sex casually, as the mass media report. They all say they would rather not sell sex if they could be clerical workers or computer engineers who make enough money. Prostitution really is an easier way to make a lot of money than any other choice available to them. It is a lie that there are women who willingly sell sex and enjoy it. In particular, it is a problem that women who come to Japan from Thailand and the Philippines have no choice.

Yoneda: But that is not limited to prostitution. Anyone would rather earn money by doing what she wants to do. There is also a limit to individual abilities, so one chooses a job that is most efficiently carried out within the limits of her own abilities. The difference is whether to choose to be a clerical assistant or a prostitute. We can put it that way.

Kuninobu: But then, people gravitate toward prostitution because it carries an economic value that is overwhelmingly higher. Besides, young women are assigned a commercial value according to inherent attributes such as their figures and body shapes. And mass media create an illusion that there can be individual choice. That's how I see it. If it's not others' business to interfere with someone selling sex and earning money, then there's no need for the law. However, it is problematic to boil this down to a matter of individual choice. The problem won't be solved by explaining it away as a matter of individualism. That won't leave any room for judgement. We will end up leaving things as they are. That's precisely what this male-dominant society wants to see.

Yoneda: I think that, to the contrary, there is also a problem in not resolving this issue as a matter of individual choice. If a woman says that she has chosen prostitution of her own will, why can't we accept her claim as it is? Isn't it because we ulteriorly think, "One could not possibly choose prostitution of one's own will, nor should one. I would rather die than choose prostitution"? I think this issue has been discussed without involving the prostitutes themselves for too long. A woman should be able to make decisions concerning her own sexuality, right? Then, doesn't she have the ability and right to decide whether to use her vagina as a tool of trade, or whatever? The question of whether one is coerced or one does it of just one's own will is similar to the question of whether a sexual activity is rape or whether it is done with consent. I believe that we must first hear the involved parties' claims and believe their words. We must start from there.

Kuninobu: Are the involved parties the only people who are allowed to talk? If one considers "selling-sex labor" as between-the-legs labor, it doesn't differ much from brain labor or muscle labor. For example, it is common that working for wages within one's capacities is turned into forced labor against one's own will, which becomes labor exploitation. It's just that it's hard to believe that there are many women who would actively and willingly sell sex, which is considered to be "closely connected with one's personhood." I would like to focus on the social structure in which other options are closed to women. Of course, I would like to make sure that we don't simply dismiss sex labor merely as morally evil. What I have begun to see, through relating to women who are from the Philippines and Thailand, and who are struggling to earn a living, is that it is important yet difficult to communicate to those women that "not selling sex" is part of defending their human rights. There are parents in Thailand who close their eyes to the reality of their daughters selling sex. Having seen that, I have great misgivings about supporting a movement to recognize prostitution as a woman's right to work.

Prostitution as Work

Takeuchi: I think that we should separate the issue of prostitution itself and the issue of coercion. Let's take the victimization of Asian women who come to Japan. When these women have been deceived and locked up, the issue for them is rape and trafficking even if the objective of the middlemen is prostitution.

Kuninobu: Prostitution has a very high commercial value, and the market is expanding.

Tsuboi: I think that the reason prostitution has such a high commercial value is because it is illegal. Because it is illegal, ordinary people cannot get into it; Yakuza[4] and organized crime thrive by it. Because of the risk of being arrested at any time, it is expensive. If it is legalized, we can discuss the working conditions as an issue for the Labor Standards Act, for example. If more and more ordinary women practice prostitution because it is legal, an evil sort of business will be eliminated, which in turn will bring the prices down. The current Prostitution Prevention Law has the kind of ill effects that the prohibition law used to have in the United States.

In 1991, the three Thai women who stabbed a female Thai manager of a prostitution business were indicted for burglary and murder (the Shimodate Case, Mito Local Court decision, 1995). The women had come to Japan on a false promise, and they were locked up and were ordered to repay nonexistent debts by practicing prostitution. Their daily work was nothing but forced labor. The civil court decided that while the women were entitled to claim wages for working as barmaids, they were not entitled to claim wages for prostitution because prostitution is not recognized as labor and is illegal. They were also entitled to a small monetary compensation as a consolation.

Takeuchi: Once prostitution is recognized as labor, one would be able to sue someone for breech of contract. But given the current situation, even if the Prostitution Prevention Law was eliminated, the court would rule that such a contract (for example, between a sex worker and an employer) is void, since prostitution still violates what Clause 90 of the Civil Code calls "the public order and decent conduct." The defense would not be given a chance because the women would have been engaged in an "unacceptable activity."

Wada: The public order and decent conduct! It comes down to moral regulation. I can't swallow it. The moral code is, after all, defined by men; one that is convenient for men. Who gains by saying that prostitution is bad? I think women ought to question that. The moral code is forced upon women only; there are different moral standards on sex for men and women. Also, is it appropriate to legally regulate morals? I would think that we should take up these two issues.

Okamura: I hear that prostitutes are demanding that prostitution be recognized as labor.

Kuninobu: There are labor unions for prostitutes in the U.S. and elsewhere. There certainly is a movement to claim labor rights for prostitutes. I wonder, though, what are they claiming as rights?

Yoneda: You are referring to the so-called "right to" movement. When I talk about this movement (in Japan), people tell me this will work only in the United States and Europe, but it won't work in Asia. It is true that the majority of Asian women go into prostitution out of economic necessity, and, in a way they are forced into it. Still, or rather because of that situation, I think it is all the more necessary to recognize prostitution as work and improve working conditions for these women. Isn't it our job to secure a livable environment where they won't be exploited illegally, to create a situation where they can network among themselves, and where they can voice their demands, and to help them build up the power to get out of prostitution when they want to? They are not going to accept us as long as we work on the premise that they are victims who are forced into prostitution, something that humans shouldn't practice, that our mission is to protect and rehabilitate them, that we should abolish prostitution from the face of the earth! That's simply a nuisance to them. If I were a prostitute I would say to hell with do-gooders. The situation that forces women into prostitution won't go away by telling them that they were forced into it, that they are victims.

The Customers

Yamamoto: I get angry every time I discuss prostitution with men. They talk only about the women, the sellers, and not the men, the buyers.

Okamura: I participated in a tour to Korea by chartered boat. Men on the boat were talking about buying prostitutes in Korea. They would say, "City women are costly, but women get cheaper as you go to rural areas." I felt nauseated. One recent trend is to talk about the buying side of prostitution. For example, there is a movement that demands the insertion of a clause into the Prostitution Prevention Law punishing the customers.

Yoneda: However, Japan's Prostitution Prevention Law says that, in principle, selling sex is illegal, but the seller doesn't get punished unless she promotes it publicly. I wonder if it's possible to punish the buyer but not the seller. True, it is a big problem that the buying side hasn't been questioned, and it makes me angry too. Still, won't it be kind of short-circuited thinking to propose to punish the buying side to correct that omission?

Tsuboi: In meetings where we discuss the eradication of child prostitution in Asian tourism, I occasionally encounter men who say things like, "I have watched a porno movie in which adults have sexual intercourse with children, but the children didn't seem to dislike it," and "we should establish licensed child prostitution." They don't think they are saying anything atrocious. Such men make me think that we should do something about the buying side. I realize that I live in a society where men do not have any ethical philosophy or standards in the area of sex. I don't think we solve problems by punishing everything by law. That will force people underground, and violate the rights of women and children. That won't be the solution.

Okamura: Once we recognize prostitution as work, prostitutes' work conditions can be guaranteed. The Prostitution Prevention Law is not helping them, and prostitution is not being prevented. I think we should abolish the law.

Kuninobu: So we won't punish either the seller or the buyer?

Takeuchi: Of course it is absolutely necessary to keep protesting against those men who only look upon women as objects with which to satiate their sexual desire, and to tell those men that we question their humanity. I don't think the kind of problems we have discussed will be solved by inserting a clause in the current Prostitution Prevention Law punishing the buying side. We need to dig deeper and examine the implications of regulating prostitution by law and consider what grounds there are for doing so, and examine the advantages and disadvantages of such an approach.

Kuninobu: So, what do we have to do?

Toward a New Law

Yoneda: The Prostitution Prevention Law doesn't solve anything. We have to abolish this law and establish something in place of it.

Tsuboi: I think what is needed is a law to punish sexual violence such as molestation, sexual harassment, rape and forced prostitution, the kinds of acts that disregard the person's intentions and feelings.

Yamamoto: If women speak up and say they didn't do it with consent, that it was a rape, men would probably get scared and would ask if it would really be okay to buy sex. If that happens, the situation will change for the better, won't it?

Wada: Men have been making the law for the most part. Women have been silenced so far. Especially concerning sex, it has been a taboo for women to look at their own genitals themselves. It has been out of the question to discuss sex. Next time they create a law, women's thoughts and ideas ought to be at the basis of it. Especially the voices of those who are the active participants. What do women working in sex industries want? Women own vaginas. Why do men make decisions for them?

Yoneda: The Ikebukuro case[5] suggests that prostitutes have no human rights. The court decision says that she shouldn't have killed the customer even when she was endangered by the unexpected sadistic acts being done to her at the hotel. They say it was excessive defense. There are many instances where prostitutes are killed at hotels, and such murders make very little news. The court says that she wouldn't have been killed had she obeyed him, that she was to blame because she killed the man by reacting excessively. She isn't even allowed to deny the customer's acts while she was terrified of the possibility of being killed. A prostitute puts up with the customer, but cannot claim the remuneration from the customer if he flees after the transaction. If a prostitute sues for forced obscene acts and rape when she was forced to perform them or to have sexual intercourse because the customer threatened her with a knife, the prosecutor wouldn't act on it. Why should she be left in such a state where she has no rights whatsoever? Is it because she's a prostitute? This is wrong, isn't it? There has to be a law which entitles a prostitute to sue if she was forced to do something against her will.

Tsuboi: It would mean that we have to aim at establishing a law prohibiting sexual violence which bases itself on women's rights to sexual freedom and self determination on sexual matters.

Yamamoto: We held this roundtable with the intention of thinking about the issue of women who are practicing prostitution as our own problem, no matter what the circumstances of those women may be. Women working not only in prostitution but also in sex industries find it hard to speak up and to be heard. We think that if we could undo such social stigmatization, it would lead to true liberation for women.

Notes

1. Group Sisterhood has met monthly, starting in January 1993, at Messena Hirakata in Hirakata City. It started as a study group on the Convention on the Elimination of All Forms of Discrimination Against Women. Discussions deal with a range of women's issues including laws that effect women.

2. Translators' Note: The Japanese Prostitution Prevention Law of 1956 uses the term *futokutei* in Clause 2. This Japanese word is customarily translated into English as "unspecified" or "unspecific." In addition, some relatives of this word are used in the discussion of the Prostitution Prevention Law by Group Sisterhood. In translating these key Japanese terms, we sought not to deconstruct them by rendering them in various contexts by one or another of their well-known entailed connotations; rather, we used the key terms themselves and ask the reader to keep this in mind. We recognize that this keystone technical terminology is sometimes awkward, but it is the terminology of both the Law and Group Sisterhood's discussion of it. As such, it serves to illuminate the problem of both the Law and its applications.

3. An image club is a store where a (male) customer assumes the role of a pervert or molester

and touches the (female) partner who assumes the role of a coed or nurse. The woman dresses as such and the man excites himself through tactile stimuli, and eventually ejaculates.

4. Organized criminal syndicates.

5. In the Ikebukuro case a prostitute killed her customer in a hotel room where she worked, and was indicted for murder. The defense claimed self-defense, but the court ruled excessive defense. Tokyo Local Court decision, 1987; Tokyo Higher Court decision, 1988.

Part Two

Migrations and Tourism

Introduction

Transnational movements for work, business and leisure characterize the late twentieth century. And in the new global arrangements, it is no longer simply a question of movement between the industrialized North and developing South, but a complex picture that includes border crossings within and between developing nations that is heavily dependent upon female labor. In the first three chapters in this section, we examine the migration of women for sex work in West Africa, Asia, and the Caribbean and in the latter two, sex tourism in Thailand and Cuba. Each chapter explores sex workers' agency, irrespective of age or gender, within the context of structural factors that underpin the transnational movements. The dichotomy between voluntary and forced prostitution is shown to be quite unwieldy and inappropriate for describing sex workers' experiences as neither explanations separately do justice to the complexity of the various situations. The writings also all illuminate points of resistance among sex workers and conscious strategies they employ to shape and control aspects of the sex industry.

Defining prostitution in an African context is complicated, John Anarfi explains in his chapter "Ghanian Women and Prostitution in Cote d'Ivoire," due to the wide range of relationships in West Africa that involve an exchange of sex for material benefits and goods. Nevertheless, research shows that since the mid-1980s, Ghanian women have migrated to the neighboring Cote d'Ivoire for prostitution in its narrowest sense, to sell sex for money. Anarfi points out that the migration has been spurred by several factors, among them the failure of the Ghanian economy in the 1970s, government and international "stabilization" programs, the growth of a large informal sector and the lack of educational and employment options for women. Through his own and other research, he establishes that the migration occurs primarily on an individual basis through networks of friends and family, with the majority knowing they will work in the sex industry. Often entering Cote d'Ivoire without documents, the women are likely to be assisted by Malian smugglers and Ghanian intermediaries, some of whom charge exorbitant rates for their services causing, in some instances, situations of debt-bondage. In the sex industry older women organize and run the businesses on the day-to-day basis. Prostitution, while illegal in Cote d'Ivoire, is condoned by the State and considered by many to be inevitable due to the large number of male migrants in the country. The women's migration is circulatory in that they maintain regular contact with family and friends, through visits, correspondence and remittances, and ultimately return home. Prostitution, Anarfi concludes, is a transient phase in the women's lives, and sex work primarily a means to support themselves, children and kin or to acquire capital to start their own businesses. Economic independence and female agency remain thus, central themes that emerge from the research.

Satoko Watenabe, in the second chapter in this section, explores experiences of five Thai migrant sex workers in Japan through research she conducted in 1995–96. She describes how the women experience a great deal of control over their migration, even though they may arrive in Japan with restrictive contracts and large debts. Once at work, the conditions, Watenabe explains, are quite variable, depending upon whether the migrants are in snack-bars, on the street, or in "special eating places." Each site has its own specific type of organization, clientele and prices for sex. The majority of the women, the author found, worked as free-lance bar hostesses, yet like many other sex workers, had to pay a "security fee" for protection and were heavily supervised by a bar owner or manager. Sex work, even though considered immoral by the women, was seen as the quicker way to earn a large sum of money in comparison to the other options open to migrant women in Japan. They were thus able to send home substantial sums of money for their family, often for the purpose of building a new home, buying consumer goods or to pay for their sibling's education. Being undocumented migrant sex workers in Japan, Watenabe points out, means that they are in a vulnerable position. The women described a continual fear of raids of their workplaces by police or immigration officers and deportation, and knew that if they were to visit their family, they may not be allowed to re-enter Japan. Despite this fragile position Watenabe shows that a strong network exists between Thai sex workers in Japan, providing support, information and friendship.

In my own contribution, "The Migrant Tightrope: Experiences in the Caribbean," I discuss the relevance of migration for prostitution for working Caribbean women, arguing that sex work is one of the many sources of livelihood that women in this region rely on to sustain themselves and families, and that migration is often an avenue through which they can effectively engage in sex work. My chapter is based on research I carried out in the Dutch Caribbean island, Curaçao, where the government has regulated and institutionalized prostitution by migrant women since 1944. The research points out that the majority of the women who travelled to the island over the past fifty years to work in the main brothel were not duped, but instead were very conscious about the type of work they would be involved in. It was the working conditions, laws and social stigmas around prostitution that formed the greatest obstacles. Furthermore, for the Curaçaoan situation, it was not always abject poverty that carried women into sex work, but rather the broader gendered divisions of labor they were faced with, the particular income-generating traditions and job opportunities that exist in Caribbean countries for women, and the increasing responsibility that Caribbean women carry to provide for their families. And although the majority of the women in my study worked independently, situations where they became indebted and dependent on middle-men, criminal organizations and the government did exist. Beside stigmas towards prostitution, sex workers in Curaçao were also positioned according to racialized ideologies and structures. The "light-skinned Latina" represented the ideal of the erotic, sensual woman, and it is this racialized group that was both desired and over-represented in the sex industry. Despite the legality of prostitution on the island, the reliance of the Curaçaoan sex industry on, almost exclusively, migrant women, severely inhibited the development of any consistent organization among brothel workers. The Curaçaoan arrangement has also led to deep-rooted divisions between women and a state system that extracts profit from, and highly controls, migrant female sexual labor but denies the women worker's rights and protections.

Heather Montgomery's chapter, "Children, Prostitution and Identity," is based on anthropological research she conducted in a slum community in Thailand. The subject of child prostitution, she argues, is one that easily evokes passions, moral outrage and sensationalism as it seems to be a metaphor for all the social, economic and moral evils of our world. Nevertheless, she proposes we need to put aside moral issues and biases and examine child prostitution in the context of not only the political economy but also the meanings children give to their own activities and identities, if we wish to construct objective studies of prostitution. She therefore places emphasis on understanding the agency of the children. In her research she found that the children felt a strong sense of obligation to support or help their families financially, and that it was this sense of obligation that took many into the sex industry in the absence of other, or well-paid, income-generating activities. The children formed their own ethical system to cope with prostitution that allowed them to sell sex and at the same time to preserve a private sense of humanity and virtue. They did not identify with the term "prostitute," regarding it to be insulting and derogatory, but instead described their activities in terms of "having guests," with the money they received for sex being defined as "gifts." Furthermore, sexuality was not experienced as something integral to their personality or identified with personal pleasure or fulfillment. The children, Montgomery concludes, used their work and activities as a basis from which they could develop strategies, exploit their situation and construct power within the constraints of the broader social and economic context.

Cuba has recently seen a rapid growth in the sector of the sex industry directed at tourists and has gained much international attention because of the emergence of *jineteras* (young female sex workers). In her chapter "Hustling for Dollars," Coco Fusco traces some of the historical and contemporary race, class and gender factors that shape this new form of sex work, discussing some of the contradictions and hypocrisies surrounding the issue. She points out that while it is generally considered that prostitution in Cuba was completely eradicated after the revolution due to government actions and rehabilitation projects for prostitutes, it did not completely disappear, subtly continuing under state supervision. The economic crisis in the 1990s and Cuba's turn to tourism, however, has created a new group of sex workers, drawing in young women and men as "escorts," "temporary partners" and "potential wives of foreigners." And even though the revolution has brought about greater sexual freedom for women, the emergence of a younger generation who easily engages in sex work is widely seen as an indicator of the failure of the revolution. Fusco describes the racialized arena in which prostitution in Cuba plays out, one that is shaped by the historical, ideological location of the Mulata as the sex object. She contends that this stereotype continues to thrive particularly in the view outsiders hold of Cuban women and in deeply rooted Cuban attitudes towards sex between black women and white men. The image of the exotic, erotic Mulata is, she points out, also becoming a self-conscious identity among the women themselves, a strategy to enhance their position in the sex industry. Since the mid-1990s, the Cuban government has introduced new crusades against prostitution. This renewed clampdown, Fusco suggests, should be understood in the context of a government attempting to gain some control over the flourishing underground economy that has emerged around the sale of sex to tourists. And while economic hardship for Cuban women is a major reason for entering into sex work, Fusco also reminds us that their move is also shaped by the national promotion of non-productive leisure activities and pleasurable consumerism, which has fostered new aspirations and dreams among the younger generations. She concludes by proposing that what is needed is a less repressive and more culturally appropriate way of understanding Cuban women's involvement in sex work. Her chapter draws from interviews with *jineteras* in Cuba, illuminating some of the young women's experiences, dilemmas and strategies.

Kamala Kempadoo

7 Ghanaian Women and Prostitution in Cote d'Ivoire[1]

John K. Anarfi

Ghanaian Women and Migration

Until the 1970s, migration studies in Ghana (and for that matter in all of West Africa) focused on the movement of men (see, for example, Rouch 1956, Hill 1963, Caldwell 1969). Any mention of women was as wives left behind in the rural areas to tend to farm plots and care for children and village property. In situations where migration was longer-term or even permanent, there was some movement of the women from the "home" areas to join husbands working abroad, or to remarry a parentally approved co-ethnic (Brydon 1992). Women appear to have been neglected in the earlier studies because they were regarded as mere passive participants in the migration process, and because it was thought that their motives might not be different from those of the primary migrants they followed. With the increasing number of independent women joining the emigration process in recent times, however, the need to know who they are, why and how they migrate, and where they go has become very compelling. Since the mid-1970s, therefore, there have been studies of the movement of women and an examination of the causes and consequences of their moves (Anarfi 1990; Brydon 1977, 1979, 1985a, 1985b, 1992; Dinan 1983, Sudarkasa 1977).

The pattern of population movement in West Africa has generally been determined by economic conditions prevailing in the various countries of the sub-region, and by the time. Geographical conditions have led to what has become known as the traditional pattern of movement from the economically less favorable Sahelian north to the more favorable forest south. Until the 1960s, Ghana was the leading immigration country in the sub-region. Since that period it has been overtaken by Cote d'Ivoire. Although Cote d'Ivoire, like almost every country in Africa, has been experiencing economic problems in recent times, it is still an important destination for many migrants from countries in West Africa, including Ghana. As far as Ghanaians are concerned, Nigeria emerged as an important destination country from around the middle of the 1970s to the early 1980s. The Ghana-Nigeria migration was dominated by males unlike the Ghana-Cote d'Ivoire stream which is predominately female (Anarfi 1982, 1990; Painter 1992).

The questions of what migrant women do has received a fair measure of attention in the literature. Until the early 1970s, the dominant impression was that they were prostitutes (Nadel 1952, Little 1973). This attitude has been blamed on the misapplication of patriarchal ideology rather than hard evidence (Brydon 1992). Kenneth Little (1973) is seen by Brydon (1992) as the worst offender in this respect, with his publication *African Women in Towns*. In this book, Little portrays the urban women as antithetical to expressed ideals of female behavior. He is severely criticized by Sanjeck (1976) for stating. "Scratch an African urban woman and you find a prostitute."

Since the mid-1970s there has been an increasing number of studies bearing on women's role in the urban areas, mostly by women, which have considerably modified the latter stereotypical view. Both Sudarkasa (1977) and Brydon (1987) found that the number of migrant women in their studies who were prostitutes was very small. Dinan's work (1977, 1983) corroborated by Brydon's (1987), brings into focus the thorny issue of who is a prostitute in the African context. They contend that rather than being able to pigeonhole sexual relationships neatly into two types, marriage and prostitution, one can discern a range of relationships. There are indeed prostitutes in Ghana' s towns, defined as women who sell sex on a regular basis to a number of different clients and without any emotional or long-term basis to the relationships (Brydon 1992). These may be contrasted with married women and with a whole range of premarital and/or extramarital relationships extending from boyfriend/girlfriend romances (called *mpena* in the local language) to relationships involving those characterized by

Dinan (1983) as "sugar-daddies" and "gold-diggers." These relationships differ from prostitution in that they are often long-term, sometimes producing a child or children, and may also contain a domestic component.

Why Do They Choose Cote d'Ivoire?

Our 1986–87 detailed survey in Abidjan showed that the vast majority, eighty-six percent, of women moved for economic reasons (Anarfi 1990). Akosua Ado-mako-Ampofo (1993), touching on the factors which push Ghanaian women to neighboring countries, particularly Cote d'Ivoire, also explains that as a result of a combination of internal and external factors, Ghana's economy gradually began to grind to a halt by the mid- to late 1970s, culminating in the drawing up of the Economic Recovery Program (ERP) in 1983. This in turn led to implemen-tation of the International Monetary Fund's Structural Adjustment Program (SAP) which involved "stabilization measures" and structural reforms. Agricul-ture and the informal sector were and still are expected to absorb the bulk of the large numbers of unemployed workers displaced from the public and private sectors. This must be viewed in light of the fact that the so-called informal sec-tor already counted for over fifty percent of the total labor force (over ninety percent in the case of women). Many Ghanaians, especially women because of their lower education and lack of marketable skills, suddenly found themselves without any regular income-generating opportunities. Increasingly, some of these women moved into prostitution, a significant number in neighboring Cote d'Ivoire.

Adomako-Ampofo (1993) laments over the general lack of appreciation of the factors which push Ghanaian women into international prostitution, quot-ing as a typical example an excerpt from an editorial in *The Weekly Spectator* (December 14, 1991), one of the government-run newspapers:

> There is also a problem of stopping those (greedy and avaricious) women who go . . . to earn money the immoral way. Ghanaians must find a way of keeping these women in the country to learn profitable trades or to engage in farming to earn a decent living instead of allowing them to cross borders to lose their lives in a most shameful manner. . . . It must be noted that if even they do not lose their lives, they come back to infect others in the country.

Sadly, these calls for "clean-up campaigns" make no attempt to analyze the underlying economic factors which propel women into prostitution. Adomako-Ampofo (1993) adds that labelling women as the blackguards fails to recognize their culturally prescribed obligation to provide for their households in a setting where the majority have had little access to education or resources, and few alternative employment openings other than petty trading. For example, by 1988, although the gap between male and female school attendance had narrowed considerably among the lower age group (primary levels), almost four times as many young men as women aged nineteen to twenty-four years were attending school. Government and private enterprise employed three point seven percent of the female labor force in 1960 and by 1984 this had only increased to seven point four percent. During the same period, the proportion of the female labor force that was self-employed declined from ninety-six point three percent to ninety-two point five percent (Ghana census reports, 1960 and 1984).

Adomako-Ampofo's (1993) observations about the negative effects of Structural Adjustment Programs on women, especially small scale farmers, have been documented by other writers also (Anker et al. 1988; Palmer 1991; Clark and Manuh 1991). Work done by Clark and Manuh and corroborated by Abayie-Boateng (1992) indicates the worsening economic position of many Ghanaian female traders and farmers. Traders stated that people "don't buy" since "there is no money." This "no money" syndrome also referred to the traders' own lack of capital. Clark and Manuh found that those who remained in the markets were vulnerable to bankruptcy. The majority of the traders interviewed by Abayie-Boateng in July 1992 felt that the government policies had adversely affected their work since the mid-eighties. Almost all the women claimed that household budgets had gone up without a corresponding increase in incomes, and that the quality of life generally had declined. The study revealed that women found themselves in a state of unparalleled poverty as a result of certain government policies.

How is the Migration Organized?

As a result of the factors listed above, large numbers of young Ghanaian girls are migrating to Cote d'Ivoire to work as prostitutes. This migration is not a recent development (Arhin 1981). An important feature of the movement is that it is largely an individual migration (Anarfi 1990). Other important features of the migration of Ghanaian women to Abidjan that we observed in the research are as follows:

—Relatives and friends have acted as the main sources of information on Abidjan for the migrants. However, institutionalization of the migration means that the relative importance of relatives as sources of information is waning over time;

—Migration decision-making is mainly an individual affair;

—Possibly as a result of the language barrier (Ghana being Anglophone and Cote d'Ivoire Francophone), education does not play any significant role in the decision to migrate;

—The Ghana-Abidjan migration stream is highly urban-selective. Female migrants are more likely to originate from an urban locality in Ghana than are males. However, there is a trend of more and more women leaving for Abidjan from rural areas.

Most of the emigrants enter Cote d'Ivoire by land. The most important entry points are Elubo, Gonokrom, Kwameseikrom, Sampa, Kofi Badukrom and Osei-Kojokrom. Next in popularity come the water routes, with Half-Assini and Jehwi-Wharf as the most important ports of entry. Entry by air is not very important because of the largely illegal status of the migrants.[2] Furthermore, the successful entry of the large number of Ghanaians into Cote d'Ivoire was the result of an institutionalized system of support involving drivers, the migrants, immigration officials, other law enforcement agents of the two countries, and some agents of these officials. Quite often the drivers act as mediators between the migrants and the law enforcement agents. To dodge harassment by immigration officials and police at the entry checkpoints, some immigrants decide to cross the border on foot. This is often done under the expert guidance of smugglers, mainly Malians, who do a brisk trade between the neighboring countries and Cote d'Ivoire. Foot crossing used to be a popular means of entry into Cote d'Ivoire prior to the Economic Community of West African States (ECOWAS) free-movement protocol. The only problem then and now is that sometimes the guides demand extra payments from the emigrants while they are still deep inside the bush, threatening to give them up to authorities if they fail to pay. In recent times, as a way of getting over the problems associated with entry by land, entry via boats has been assuming increasing importance. Although the journey by boat is slower and takes longer, it brings the migrants to the heart of Abidjan without harassment by immigration officials and the police.

As part of the institutionalized system of support for illegal entrants into Cote d'Ivoire, there are agents at the points of embarkation in Ghana, ready to aid intending emigrants unable to finance their trips. These agents sponsor the journeys and at the point of disembarkation in Abidjan negotiate with people who pay the costs quoted by the agents and take the hard-pressed immigrants into their employ. Some agents, mainly Ghanaians, visit towns in Ghana and lure girls to Abidjan with promises of lucrative jobs; Adomako-Ampofo (1993) adds that some of the girls are actually kidnapped from their families. Often such migrants are made to work for months without pay to cover the amount paid to release or transport them. It must be added, of course, that some women, perhaps the majority, go to Abidjan knowing they will work in the sex industry (Adomako-Ampofo 1993).

The Choice of Profession

Writing on the vulnerability to AIDS of some groups of Ghanaian woman, including sex workers, Adomako-Ampofo stresses that "women's disadvantaged positions have a direct influence on the kind of sexual relationships they enter and their clout to negotiate within these relationships" (1993: 1). She adds that "for the most part poor and disadvantaged young women service the sexual needs of relatively better-off older males. . . ." Citing Ankomah (1992), Adomako-Ampofo writes that "reciprocal transaction," rather than exploitation, would seem to be a more accurate description or modern urban relationships. She explains that people attempt to maximize rewards and minimize losses, with social interaction viewed as an exchange of mutually rewarding activities. In the transaction, the partners attempt to maximize the resources they possess by manipulating the opportunities they perceive in their environment. In the case of Ghanaian women, "the only economic capital some or them possess to trade with . . . is their sex organs" (Assimeng 1981).

Of the sample of 1,456 Ghanaian women interviewed in Abidjan, almost all claimed to have left Ghana in the hope of attaining economic independence, and a little over seventy-five percent were working in prostitution. In his study of male migrants from Niger and Mali to Cote d'Ivoire, Painter (1991) notes that "in terms of the number of times their origins were mentioned by men in our groups, Ghanaian women are the most frequent source of sex contact. . . ." Painter (1992) adds that Ghanaian women were most frequently identified by the men with easy and cheap sex, and that the men were most likely to describe Ghanaian women in negative terms, often stating with emphasis that women from Ghana are the most notorious for their far flung commercial sexual activities. However, he regrets that "fewer of the men seemed to appreciate the economic necessity and hardship that drives Ghanaian—and other—women to sell their sexual services." An earlier study among 103 prostitutes in the Krobo area of the Eastern Region of Ghana Kusi, indicates that the major motivating force for entry into this kind of work was financial. Some needed to support children and kin, others had been neglected by their husbands, and still others felt that this was the only way they could acquire capital to start their own business.

Conditions in Cote d'Ivoire seem to provide a fertile ground for commercial sex to thrive. From the late 1960s, Cote d'Ivoire replaced Ghana as a major destination for migrants in the West African sub-region. As a result, more than twenty-five percent of Cote d'Ivoire's population is foreign-born (Painter 1994). Men account for the vast majority of migrants from the Sahel to the coastal countries of West Africa, including Cote d'Ivoire. Married or not, they rarely travel with female companions. The result is a serious sex imbalance (i.e. a preponderance of men) in certain parts of Cote d'Ivoire, especially the capital, Abidjan.[3]

Konotey-Ahulu (1989) reports that Cote d'Ivoire seems to make no secret of the fact that it caters comprehensively to international prostitution. He remarks that Ivorians themselves appear to be certain that European visitors subscribe substantially to the prostitution industry. A Western seafarer quoted by a local paper as saying: "I have visited many ports and cities around the world. but Abidjan is unique when it comes to women. They are hot, cheap and ready!" (quoted in Adomako-Ampofo, 1993: 11). Despite official denials, prostitution is big business. Officially regarded as illegal, it is nonetheless condoned by officialdom and brothels operate without hindrance.

Other conditions in Abidjan make entry into prostitution relatively easy (Anarfi 1993). For one thing, the sex industry is highly institutionalized, with older women initiating newcomers by seeking out clients for them. To facilitate this, almost every brothel has one or two rooms reserved ostensibly for visitors. The older migrants deliberately withdraw their hospitality after the first two days, to compel the newcomer to look for money to fend for herself. It must be added that job opportunities are very limited for the immigrant woman with very little or no formal education or workable skills. The few who find work in bars or restaurants find the long hours and backbreaking activities less rewarding, and soon opt for prostitution which is more leisurely and pays better. The migrants advertise their lucrative business when they return home from their sojourn abroad with rich clothes, jewelry and a well-kept appearance that speak of success. This attracts other, younger women in the towns and villages, most of whom happen to be unemployed (Kofi 1986).

Social Organization

One kind of social organization among the Ghanaians, particularly the women, is closely linked to the sex industry in which the majority are employed. This is a purely informal type or association and is highly decentralized. In Abidjan, whole blocks or houses, some having over fifty tenants, are occupied by Ghanaian women. To maintain order in the house, one of the women, usually the oldest who also happens to be the caretaker, is regarded as the head of the tenants. All the women in the house refer to her as "mother." She is the first to receive all their complaints and together with the other older women in the house tries to settle cases. If that fails, she refers them to the community chief. Each house has its own unwritten code of conduct. This usually regulates the payment or bills (rent, light and water), inter-tenant relationships, maintenance of sanitation in the house, the receiving of visitors, the handling of sickness and bereavement among the migrants, and the general conduct of their profession. It is at this level that the women operate a kind of rotating credit system known in Ghana as *susu*. The main benefit from this kind of association, therefore, is financial.

Religion can be a potent factor in rallying people because of its universal appeal. Most of the migrants in Abidjan were not practicing their religion. Not only did the women in prostitution regard themselves as deviants, they also saw themselves as sinners unworthy to go to church. When asked why they did not go to church in Abidjan, many replied, "How can you go to Church when you are in this kind of business?" (Anarfi 1990: 157). Some Ghanaian men were exploiting the situation by establishing kinds of free-for-all churches to satisfy the psychological needs of the migrant women. The names of such churches and their approach to worship appeal especially to the woman who feels despised.

Family and Community Ties

The Ghana-Cote d'Ivoire migration, like others elsewhere in Africa, is mainly circulatory, meaning that the migrants do not break away permanently from their places of origin. Until they finally come home, they maintain continuous contact with their families and communities by correspondence and through regular visits. Our 1990 survey in Abidjan established that relatives and friends were influential factors in the migration process as sources of information about Abidjan. In the African context, including Ghana, an individual is likely to migrate when the break with family and village does not need to be complete, and when it is possible to retain ties by remittances and contributions to religious rites and family well-being. Caldwell (1968) found that nearly two-thirds of Ghanaian migrants intended to return to their village. Similarly, an overwhelming majority (ninety-eight percent) of Ghanaian immigrants in Abidjan stated that they would return home one day (Anarfi 1990).

The Abidjan immigrants also maintain family and community ties by making regular visits home (Anarfi 1990). When asked, more than half of the Ghanaian women in Abidjan said they visited home regularly (at least once in twenty-four months). In fact, over forty-two percent visited home at least once in twelve months. Most of the migrants who had never visited home had lived in Abidjan for less than twenty-four months, and were victims of a serious riot in September 1985 when Cote d'Ivoire nationals attacked Ghanaians in the country following a football match between the two countries in Ghana. Many of the Ghanaian immigrants postponed their visits home when they lost their property in the riot. Visits are usually planned to coincide with festive occasions such as Christmas, Easter and other local festivals.

Remittances have become accepted as an integral factor in studies of both internal and international migration in developing countries. In Ghana, as elsewhere, they are seen as an important link between the migrant and the home community (Caldwell 1969; Nabila 1974; Anarfi 1982, 1990). In our 1990 study, most of the migrants were found to remit money regularly at least once every twelve months. The bulk of the migrants' remittances went to the upkeep of the family back home. Apart from this, a significant proportion or the money sent back went into other ventures such as savings, renovating or building a house, or investing in profit-making ventures. Thus, by their behavior, the Ghanaian immigrants in Abidjan maintain strong ties with their areas of origin.

Hopes and Aims

From the information given so far in this review, the aim of the Ghanaian women emigrants in Cote d'Ivoire is obvious: economic motives predominate. The women go to Cote d'Ivoire to work and get money. A recent study of prostitutes in Nigeria (Orubuloye et. al. 1994) asserts that the women who engage in prostitution regard it as a transient phase in their lives. The study notes that in order to ensure a later life of marriage, business ownership and respectability in one's area of origin, it is necessary that the transient period as a prostitute be spent far away. In an earlier study on Ghanaian immigrants in Lagos, almost all expressed the intention of coming home one day and only five percent had plans to take up salaried jobs (Anarfi 1982). The implication is that because of the migrants' feeling of inadequacy in the economic sphere of social life at home, their hope was to amass a fortune before returning home, to get themselves established economically.

A similar observation could be made about the Ghanaian women immigrants in Cote d'Ivoire. Apart from stating that their main motive for emigrating was economic, they demonstrated their willingness to enhance their location-specific capital by remitting home, saving and/or investing in commercial venture. Parallel work in the Krobo area in the eastern region of Ghana, shows that in relative terms the women migrants attain a certain measure of economic success (Anarfi 1990). Several had returned to their home areas with money to build houses and establish themselves as traders (Kofi 1986). However, the success tend to be short-lived. Only one returnee in the study had maintained her economic success. In the majority of cases, even if the women returned from

Cote d'Ivoire with money to build or set up business, their money and other capital and other capital resources soon dwindled. As a result repeat migration is very common among the Ghanaian women emigrants.

Conclusion

Unable to adequately fend for themselves in their home country because of their inability to compete with men for the few available jobs in the formal sector, further worsened by deteriorating economic conditions, many Ghanaian women have fled to Abidjan, Cote d'Ivoire, for greener pastures. Their extremely low educational status and lack of skills bar them from entry into the formal job market of the Abidjan economy. Almost all the women are forced into the informal sector where they have created jobs for themselves. A serious sex imbalance in the city under conditions of limited job openings for immigrant women in particular, have compelled many of the Ghanaian women to go into the sex trade. The operation of the sex trade in Abidjan is such that the profession has become the pivot around which other social and economic activities of most of the Ghanaian women spins.

It may be rightly assumed that the movement of Ghanaian women to Abidjan will cease when Ghana's economy improves. Nonetheless, a conscious effort should be made to improve the economic lot of women in the country through the improvement of skills and the formalization of the commercial activities and small-scale farming in which the majority of Ghanaian women are engaged. This is necessary if the dignity of the Ghanaian woman is to be maintained by keeping more of them in Ghana and enabling returned women migrants to invest their income properly, thereby preventing them from repeating the migration.

Notes

1. Excerpted from "Female Migration and Prostitution in West Africa: The Case of Ghanaian Women in Cote d'Ivoire" in the *Studies in Sexual Health* Series, published by the Regional AIDS Program for West and Central Africa of the Deutsche Gesellschaft für Technische Zusammenarbeit (German Technical Co-operation GTZ), 1995.

2. A very large majority of the migrants in our study, eighty-four percent of the females and nearly sixty-seven percent of the males, did not have passports. This means that, notwithstanding the ECOWAS protocol of free movement for West African nationals, they had entered Cote d'Ivoire illegally.

3. The 1975 Cote d'Ivoire population census gave the sex ratio of the country's nationals as 105 males to 100 females. This is added to by an immigrant sex ration of 163 to 100.

8

From Thailand to Japan
Migrant Sex Workers as
Autonomous Subjects

Satoko Watenabe

I could speak about my work to those Japanese women who
protest against prostitution. If they said "Quit the work and go
back home," I'd reply, "I'll go back if you give me enough money."
What should I do back in Thailand? There is no good work for a
woman like me.

—Meow

Introduction

The following is a summary of my research on Thai sex workers in Japan conducted through interviews in Yokohama, Tokyo and Chiba,
between December 17, 1995 and March 31, 1996. The five Thai
women interviewed were Lak, Sai, Meow, Pet, and Nok. The
ages of the five women fall into the category of twenty
to thirty-four, the largest age group of Thai women appre-
hended for violating the immigration control act in 1989
(the latest available figures). In this summary, the interviewed women are given fictitious nicknames, names common among Thai women, in order to maintain anonymity
due to the nature of this study.

Because of problems in approaching Thai sex workers, I
worked as a "hostess," though unpaid, for a week at a snack
bar that employed undocumented migrant women. The bar
owner, a Japanese man married to a former Filipina dancer,
understood my intentions and was very helpful. Since he
introduced me to the six hostesses with a brief explanation
of my purpose, all the women were friendly and cooperative. Participant observation greatly helped me to gain
knowledge of their work and the bar system as well as the

experience of working as a bar hostess. I also believe that it has enhanced the quality of information obtained through interviewing Thai sex workers. Above all, the experience in the bar has convinced me that entertaining a male client is nothing but work, which is quite tiring and stressful to the woman entertainer. This is in contrast to the prevailing view that merely "sitting with a man and pouring drinks" is not something deserving of a high wage.

Migration to Japan

None of the five women had visited Japan before. Each entered the country three to four years before the time of the interview on a "temporary visitor" visa, which permitted a stay up to ninety days. Accordingly, all of them over-stayed their visas. All of them said that they obtained some information on prospective jobs and general working conditions in Japan before they made a decision about the migration. However, the quantity, as well as the quality, of information they had prior to their migration varied. The extent and quality of information a woman had access to before migration seemed to have deter-mined the manner in which she migrated and found work in Japan, and there-fore, the degree to which she would be exploited in both Thailand and Japan.

It is widely reported that many Thai women who migrate to work in Japan make a verbal contract with recruiters or brokers. This contract gives little detail of the actual terms of employment, working conditions, and the repayment of charges for recruitment, travel, and placement within an establishment. Thus women under contract may find themselves in debt upon arrival. Meow, for example, knew what kind of work she was going to do in Japan and took the job because of its high pay. But her first job, as a hostess-cum-prostitute in a snack bar in Shinjuku, Tokyo, was harder than expected. She had a debt of 3.7 million yen (approximately $37,000), which she paid back within three months. Nok was told by the recruiter that her work in Japan would be as a bar hostess when she agreed to the contract in Thailand. It was only after she arrived at the first work-place in Itako, Ibaraki, a local town fifty miles northeast of downtown Tokyo, that she found that she had to go out with a customer to a hotel in the vicinity of the bar. She was forced to see three to four men a day. At first she was shocked and cried with grief and misery everyday. She had to pay back a total of 4.5 mil-lion yen, including 0.7 million yen for accommodation, meals, costumes, etc., which she completed within seven months. In both cases, the women received no wages until they paid back their contracted debt.

Three of the women interviewed knew through their friends and/or the mass media that they would end up heavily indebted and in a situation in which they had little control over their work if they went to Japan under this type of contract. Lak, advised by her friend who was already working in Japan, turned down the offer of a Thai broker, who said, "You don't need even 100 yen ($1) to go to Japan. We'll get you everything necessary." Instead, she borrowed 300,000 yen ($3,000) from the friend and obtained a passport and a visa with the help of another friend. Sai paid 1.5 million yen ($15,000) to a broker in Chiang Mai for the acquisition of a passport and a visa, an air-ticket, and the introduction to an "old Japanese lady" who would accompany her to the first workplace in Hiroshima. She borrowed the money from her father in Thoeng, Chiang Rai, who obtained a loan from a bank by using his land as collateral. Pet obtained the passport and the visa by herself and bought an air-ticket to Tokyo, which altogether cost her about 100,000 yen ($1,000). Having booked a hotel in Tokyo, she flew there with the 300,000 yen ($3,000) from her own savings. English learned through a department store job helped her to make these arrangements on her own.

The recruiter and the broker in Thailand may or may not be the same person. Women are recruited in cities or rural areas in Thailand, sold to brokers who have contacts in Japan, and brought, usually by the brokers, to their first workplaces in Japan. Recruiters and brokers in Thailand include various kinds of people such as members of organized crime syndicates, travel agents, small business owners, and Japanese businessmen. Even when they are aware of the disadvantage of such a deal, many Thai women depend on recruiters and brokers to obtain their passports and visas because they do not know what to do with the paperwork. Migrant women, as well as the recruiters, are usually unaware of the involvement of international organized crime syndicates in their migration.

None of the women reported that they were forced by anybody to migrate. Pet, however, was under pressure from her mother who had repeatedly "asked" her to go since she was 17 years old. None had learned Japanese prior to their migration to Japan. They learned the language mainly from their Thai colleagues and friends, and partially from their clients, employers and language textbooks, after arrival in Japan.

Working Conditions in Japan

Sai, Pet, and Lak were bar hostesses, while Meow and Nok were "authentic" sex workers, i.e., specialized in having sex. "Hostess" is the term used in Japan for a female worker who entertains a customer by chatting, pouring drinks, singing, dancing, hugging, etc. in bars and nightclubs. The work of bar hostesses ranges from menial service through intellectual entertainment to providing physical and emotional comfort. Sexual intercourse is not unusual, though it usually takes place outside the establishment. What kind of work is actually required of a hostess depends on the client and the establishment. A high-class bar expects its hostesses to be not only attractive and elegant but also intelligent and knowledgeable about various things from art to economy and politics, since its clientele often include corporate executives and high-ranking officials. There are more casual bars that welcome working-class customers and make them feel at home, there are also bars that force hostesses to have sex with the customers. "Bar hostesses" are far from being an homogeneous group in terms of work they do and pay they receive. It is equally true that not all migrant women who work as bar hostess are engaged in prostitution or forced into prostitution.

Sai spent five months in Hiroshima working at a snack bar before she moved to Yokohama about three years ago. Having a contact in Yokohama, she left Hiroshima because she could not earn sufficient money to send to her family in Thailand. Since then she worked in several snack bars in and around Isezaki-cho, Yokohama. During this period, she acquired quite a few regular clients who continued to visit her even after she changed her workplace. Thus, she had enhanced her power vis-à-vis her employer wherever she worked. Pet spent her first six months in Japan acquainting herself to the life, studying job availability, and working briefly in Tokyo. Having almost run out of money, she moved to Yokohama and found a job in a snack bar in Isezaki-cho with the help of one of her Thai friends. She left the bar two months later because she did not like the Taiwanese *mamasan* [madam] and the work was underpaid. At the time of the interviews, she had been working in the same bar for more than two years.

Having heard from a friend about the higher income opportunity, Lak started working in a prostitution bar between Shimodate and Shimozuma. Including herself, eighteen Thai women were working in the bar. At the inception of the job, she was offered a loan of one million yen ($10,000) by the Thai *mamasan* of the snack bar on the conditions that she should repay 1.8 million yen ($18,000) within four months and that the debt would become two million yen ($20,000) after that date. Accommodation and meals were to be provided during the contract. She accepted the offer as she wanted to send home a good sum of money quickly, but she later regretted the loan not only because she noticed that the interest rate was too high even with free accommodation and meals but also because all the money she received from her clients was taken away by the *mamasan* based on her dubious calculations. She was quite sure that she could have earned more if she had not borrowed the money.

Prostitute bars where Meow and Nok worked were situated under and along Keihin Kyuko Line, a railway that connects the bed-towns of Yokohama to the office-towns of Tokyo, forming a belt between Hinode-cho Station and Kogane-cho Station. This kind of establishment is called a "special eating place" in Japanese but is better known among the customers as a "fucking place." Each bar has some space in front where a customer can have a drink at a counter or a table, with a room behind or above it, where the woman provides a sexual service. When the sex worker is busy with a client, the front door is closed, usually with a lit pink fluorescent lamp above it, which indicates that the woman is at work. Normally only one worker is on duty in the bar. The woman charges a customer 10,000 yen ($100) per ten minutes for having sex in the bar. The time limit may be twenty minutes, depending on the management and the worker's bargaining power. Another 10,000 yen will be charged for an extension of ten minutes (or twenty minutes). Since the 1970s the major work force of these "eating places" has been composed of women from other Asian countries, e.g., Taiwan, Korea, China, the Philippines, and Thailand. In recent years, Thai women have become the most conspicuous, thus probably the largest, group of sex workers on the belt, judging from media reports, information obtained from police officers, and my own observations. Thai women working in bars on the belt are mostly free-lance sex workers, i.e., those who are not under contract or who have worked off their contract debt. There are some sex workers who are still under contract and are paying back to their creditors, usually *yakuzas* (members of Japanese crime syndicates). Their immediate supervisors are often migrant women from other Asian countries, but mainly from Taiwan. The customers include not only Japanese men but also migrant male workers from various countries, such as China, Taiwan, Korea, Malaysia, Indonesia, Thailand, India, Iran, Brazil, and Peru.

Nok, who came to Japan under contract, started working in a snack bar that employed more than ten Thai women as prostitutes in Itako, Ibaraki. After spending seven months "dating" with three to four clients a day to pay off her debt, she moved to Chiba, where she worked for a few months. When she went to Yokohama in late 1993 with the help of a Thai friend, she chose to work in a prostitute bar. She was still working there in 1996. During this period she sought not only a higher paying job but also a better place to live.

A bar hostess usually works six hours a day and six days a week in the bar. Sunday is a holiday at most establishments. In order to maintain a certain number of clients, however, she has to spend much of her free time calling her clients and/or having meals with them. Moreover, a bar hostess has to "work" to prepare herself for the bar work for at least an hour. This includes make-up, hairdressing, and changing clothes. Therefore, on average their actual working hours are longer than six hours a day. The more clients a hostess has, the more power she has vis-a-vis the management. Among migrant women, however, only experienced or skillful workers can establish a steady clientele.

Sai usually started work around 8:00 P.M., when she would meet one of her regular clients somewhere outside and take him to the bar. If she had such company, they would enter the bar around 8:30 P.M., and the client would have to pay an extra 3,000 yen to the bar, of which she would get 2,000 yen. The charge differs by establishment. This system, called *dohan* in Japanese, is used by most hostess bars that employ Japanese women in order to bring more clients in and thus increase the sales. The working hours of sex workers on the Hinode-Kogane belt differ by worker since the bars are usually open twenty-four hours a day, seven days a week. Each establishment employs two or three women and they work six to twelve hours in two to three shifts. The women working in a bar usually change their shifts because almost everyone wants to work during the busiest time, i.e., from 6:00 P.M. to midnight. Some have one or two days off every week but others work seven days a week.

At the time of the interview, Nok was working from 6:00 P.M. to 4:00 A.M. seven days a week. She did not take time off unless she felt too tired to work. The conditions when she was working off her contract debt were far more severe than in this other job, because she was forced to see clients even during a menstruation. Meow used to work from 6:00 P.M. to midnight or from 6:00 P.M. to 6:00 A.M. She did not work on Sundays and sometimes took a leave.

Women working in the bars on the belt, as well as street prostitutes in the Isezaki-cho area, cannot work safely without paying a "security fee," the term used by *yakuzas*. If they do not pay it, on one hand, they will be harassed by the *yakuza* to whom they are supposed to pay the fee. On the other, they will have no protection against harassment (e.g., abusive acts, rape, murder, theft, nonpayment, etc.) by their clients. Clearly, they would not have to pay the fee if their work and overstay were not criminalized. Some of their immediate supervisors, usually called the *mamasan* or "mama" in a bar, are migrant workers themselves. Thai women often called their *mamasan* the "boss." But in some cases the boss designates an overseer who loans contracted women to establishments, supervises their work, and collects their earnings as a payment for the debt. This was the case of the Thai woman boss who was murdered in Shimodate in 1991 by her three Thai workers who had been coerced into prostitution and repeatedly and harshly punished by her for their refusal to work. The five women I interviewed did not have this kind of serious trouble with their mamasans and bar owners mainly because they were not working on contract. If they had, they said, they would change their workplace. Sai, for example, had a conflict about her pay with the bar owner, who reduced her daily wage from 10,000 yen to 8,000 yen because of stagnant sales of the bar. However, he agreed to pay her at the previous rate when he learned that she was about to quit and move to another bar.

The three bar hostesses reported that they had no serious problems with their clients in their bars, apart from the troublesome work of entertaining clients who were *yakuza* members. The men, according to the women, were rude and demanding. A hostess may be harassed by a *yakuza* client for the reasons that she is not providing a service that is satisfactory to him and/or that she does not pay enough respect to him. There is also the possibility of getting involved in a fight between conflicting *yakuza* groups. Thai sex workers are also exposed to the risk of STD infections. Judging from their experiences, Thai sex workers without a contract seem to have more power to practice safe sex than women under contract.

Meow and Pet reported that some Thai sex workers have sex for pleasure with Thai "hosts," a Japanese term for male sex workers working in "host clubs" whose customers are mainly women, female sex workers in particular. The price for such a sex service ranges from a few hundred dollars to $1,000 per night or per "session," depending on their relationships and/or the need of both the woman (for sexual and emotional care) and the man (for economic gain). If a woman wishes to "rent" such a male sex worker, she has to pay him 500,000 to 700,000 yen ($5,000–7,000) per month.

All the five women considered sex work immoral, whether they were practicing it or not, and felt that society viewed sex work as immoral. But they engaged in sex work because it was the quickest way to earn a large sum of money out of the jobs available to them in Japan. Their ideas seem to stem from the Thai morals that despise prostitution (and yet allow men the right to commercial sex). According to Lak, Sai, and Meow, sex work assured them of freedom from marriage and men. Meow contradicted the general view that a prostitute sells not only her sexual service but also her personality. To her, the "sale of sexual access" was not the same as the "sale of self." Her view was similar to that of an "ordinary" worker, i.e., "I sell my time but not myself."

Home Links

Once or twice a week or whenever necessary, the Thai women called their families in Thailand. They were more likely to call than write a letter because they were busy and did not have much time to write. On average they spent 10,000–20,000 yen ($100–200) per month on telephone calls to their families. In their calls and letters, they talked about life in Japan and their families' life in Thailand. Those with new houses under construction in Thailand (Sai, Meow, Pet, and Nok) often talked with their parents about the new house and the additional money needed for its construction. Their parents also asked them to send money for buying various goods, siblings' school expenses, and/or festivals. The money they sent home ranged from 10,000 yen ($100) to 400,000 yen ($4,000) monthly, depending on the type of work they did, its ups and downs, and how they lived. But they had all sent a considerably large sum of money to their families. Nok had remitted about 5 million yen ($50,000) in two years. Sai, Pet, and Meow had sent "more than 3 million yen ($30,000)" and Lak "more than 2 million yen ($20,000)," since she had been in Japan.

None of the women had visited their families since their arrival in Japan. It was clear that they would have liked to be able to visit their families in Thailand and then to return to work in Japan, but it was simply not possible. As they had overstayed their visas, they would first have to "surrender" to an immigration office and then, most probably, be deported if they wished to go back home. The women reported that it had become impossible for ordinary Thai people like them to obtain a tourist visa for Japan. According to them, the Japanese Embassy in Thailand granted tourist visas only to "rich" Thais who could present required documents such as a proof of property ownership and an income certificate. Before issuing a visa to her/him, the Embassy had to be convinced that the applicant was wealthy enough to go to Japan as a tourist, but not as a worker. "Imagine that you can't go back home when you want to. It's so hard for me," Sai lamented.

What they wished to have most in their life in Japan was a "visa," more precisely, a work permit. They feared being caught by the police or the immigration control and being deported back to Thailand before their savings hit the target or before they felt it was time to return. Meow had even stopped going to the bar, having seen almost every day two or three Thai workers being caught in police and immigration raids on the Hinode-Kogane belt. She was seriously checking the possibility of forged marriage to a Japanese so that she would not have to fear immigration raids, though she would have to pay the "husband" probably 1.2 million yen or more every year.

Each of the five Thai women interviewed, as well as most Thai women I met during the fieldwork, had developed some form of social network through which they shared support and information. Such networks were formed primarily among Thai workers themselves who came to know each other through work, by meeting and/or by telephone. In some cases, as Sai did, older or more experienced workers took care of younger or new workers, providing accommodation, taking them to clinics, finding them jobs, introducing prospective clients to them, etc. Lak said it was difficult to develop such peer support for women working under contract but they still helped each other, hiding from their bosses. Unlike the general view that Thai women are the most vulnerable group among migrant workers in Japan due to a lack of social networks, these women have a network of friends, though it may be less overt compared to such formal networks as churches and women's organizations (e.g. the Filipino Wives of Japanese Associations).

Conclusion

The five women, as well as most of the Thai migrant women I met during the fieldwork, spent a significant part of their earnings on purchasing houses, often of western-style, and other goods, notably automobiles, for their families and themselves. This suggests that working-class Thai people's demand for consumption far exceeds the income domestically available to them, particularly in rural areas. By migrating to work in Japan for higher wages instead of working in factories or agricultural fields in Thailand, they reject the existing international division of labor and the international wage hierarchy. As illustrated in the experiences of the Thai women, migrant workers partially contributed to creating new consumption habits, but the rapid economic expansion since the 1980s has had a larger impact on consumption patterns. While the surge of the urban economy has swelled the size of professional and skilled white-collar workforce and enabled them a higher level of consumption, workers in rural areas and lower-waged urban sectors have become increasingly dissatisfied with the lower level of consumption and thus demand higher wages.

The case studies indicate that Thai migrant workers find more favorable class conditions in Japan even though they have to endure the undocumented, thus often exploitative, circumstances. In becoming accustomed to the work and life in Japan, the migrant women achieve a higher level of bargaining power vis-à-vis their employers. They may be creating a new wage division within Japan's sex industry as well as in the sector of women in general, but they can also be understood as multinational workers who, by moving across the artificial barriers of nation-state borders, are, at least to some extent, breaking down the international wage hierarchy and recomposing the structure and distribution of power within the working class against capital's control.

While regarding sex work as immoral, the five women did the work because it was far better paid than any other job available to them in Japan as well as in Thailand and, for some, it provided independence from marriage and men. The money they earned in Japan expanded the choices available to them, to educate themselves or their children for other types of work and to begin their own businesses upon returning home. They differentiated between the sex they had for money from sex for their own emotional and physical satisfaction. They may not have thought of themselves as rebels against male power and social control, but, at the same time, they did not view themselves as sexual slaves, either. As one of the bar prostitutes clearly described it, they sell sexual access to their bodies but not themselves. Even for the sexual access, they tried to minimize it for maximum gain and to reduce the chances of being exploited and abused by their customers. The sex workers were all subject to disease, injury, mistreatment, indignity, physical and psychological abuse, and coercion but these conditions are not unique to sex work. Other types of work also involve at least some of them, if not all. Significant to autonomist Marxist analysis on which my entire study on international migration is based, is that the Thai migrant women choose sex work of particular forms despite the unfavorable conditions.

Since mainstream feminists in Japan view all forms of female migration from other Asian countries into the sex industry as traffic in women, sexual exploitation and abuse, their campaigns tend to reinforce the police and immigration control over the migrant women and thus further endanger and limit the choices of those whose lives they aim to protect. Unless they have no other choice (e.g., being sent by the Thai Embassy), the Thai sex workers would not approach Japanese women's organizations, knowing they would only be told to quit the job and go home immediately. They also assumed that Japanese women did not welcome them because their work was related to sex. From the sex workers' experiences, the best way to "protect" their lives from exploitation and abuse would be to support the decriminalization of sex work and legitimize the migration for such employment.

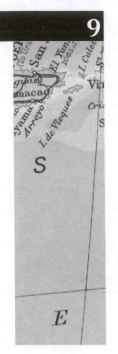

9   The Migrant Tightrope Experiences from the Caribbean

Kamala Kempadoo

Third World prostitution is often considered by non-practitioners as an activity that young women are lured into under false pretenses, that is caused by depraved western men, and as something that a woman would never consciously enter into. Nevertheless various accounts suggest that the sale of sexual labor is an integral part of many working Third World women's lives and strategies. This is also the case for the Caribbean, a region of the world where I have been doing research on the subject since the late eighties.

There are of course many variations in the sex trade in the region, as the essays on Cuba, Suriname and the Dominican Republic elsewhere in this book illustrate. This chapter focuses on the Dutch Caribbean and in particular, on a small island, Curaçao. In 1944 this island was established by the colonial government as a center in the region for prostitution by migrant women and it continues to exist as such today. Annually approximately 500 women, mainly from the Dominican Republic and Colombia, travel to the island to work in the government-regulated brothel, *Campo Alegre/Mirage,* for a maximum period of three months. Their presence on the island is regulated by the Immigration, Health and Police Departments, tolerated by the Catholic Church, appreciated by local men, yet reviled by local women. Some of the complexities of women's movement to the island and their stay in the brothel are described here, alongside more general trends for migrant prostitution in the Caribbean.

Entering the Sex Trade

The following experiences told by women whom I interviewed in Curaçao in 1993 illustrate the heterogeneity in the ways in which Caribbean and Latin American women become involved in prostitution.

> Ana was a thirty-one year old woman of Chinese descent, who was childless and single at the time of the interview and came from a town in Columbia. She "began to train as a prostitute in Columbia" and knew she was applying for sex work before arriving in Curaçao. She could no longer pay for her study (Biochemistry), could find no other employment and consequently had cast around to find a way to support herself and to help provide financially for her aunt and mother.
>
> She had heard about work at the brothel via a girlfriend, and at the time of the interview, was there for the first time. She enthusiastically stated that she earned "good money," and during her first month had not encountered any major problems. Her idea was to save enough to buy a house for the family.

> Rubia had heard about *Campo* from a girlfriend who had previously worked in the night-life on another Dutch Caribbean island, Aruba. She had borrowed money to pay for the trip and had gone through "a lot of trouble" to get to the Curaçao. Until her arrival however, she had no knowledge of the type of work she had applied for. A *Campo* representative stationed in the Dominican Republic was the agent through whom she had made the arrangements.
>
> Rubia was under the impression that she stood to make a large sum of money in a short period of time, but found a different reality. Lodging, food and medical fees were expensive, and clientele scarce. She felt that almost everything she earned went back to *Campo*, that she was actually working for the brothel, instead of for herself. She had heard that conditions and money were better in Holland and thought she would like to go there. She was bored in the brothel, having nothing to do during the day,

and having to be back by 6 P.M. During trips to town, she met with much hostility from Curaçaoans and resented the discrimination and prejudice.

Rubia was married, twenty-four years old, and had five children. She had not told her husband about the kind of work she was doing in Curaçao. Although at home in the Dominican Republic she ran her own small business in which two women worked for her as prostitutes, Rubia had not expected to take up sex work herself and disliked the life at *Campo*. Given the debts she had incurred to make the trip, she had little choice but to stay for the three-month period. She was quite resigned to the situation.

Gloria was an Afro-Colombian woman, in her mid-twenties, and extremely angry about having to do sex work. She had given up her previous job to travel to Curaçao yet did not know beforehand about the precise nature of the job. A friend had told her about well-paid casino work on the island, and she was under the impression that *Campo* was strictly a gambling house. She was extremely shocked on arrival and cried for days. During her first week she was beaten and bruised by a client and consequently refused to work for several days.

Gloria complained of the high living costs and realized that much of what she was earning was actually remaining in Curaçao. Her assessment was that she had little option but to stay since she had no other job to fall back on, needed the money, and had to pay off debts. She estimated that she would be taking home between $800–$900, a meager amount in her eyes, for the type of work.

Gloria was a married woman, had done various jobs previously, including that of an auxiliary nurse, and had no children. At *Campo* she kept pretty much to herself, confiding only in one girlfriend. She was emphatic about never recommending *Campo* and despised the situation she was in. She planned to return home, find another job, and study.

Alicia was an experienced sex worker, but this was her first visit to Curaçao. She came from a small town in Columbia, was twenty-five years old, and had one child. Although she held a high-school diploma, she could find no other employment. She found that prostitution at home was also difficult given the kind of discretion needed. Alicia had heard about *Campo* from another woman, had applied to work there directly through the Immigration Service in Curaçao and had mortgaged her parents' home in order to pay for the trip. On arrival in the brothel she realized that it was not what she had expected or been told about—even after two months, she found it difficult to save much of her earnings.

She planned to return again to the brothel, although at a time of the year when, she had been told by other women, it would be busier, and declared that she would continue with this work until she had enough to buy a home and settle. She looked forward to making it one day to Europe.

The situations of the four women clearly describe a fluidity and porousness in boundaries of "forced" and "voluntary" participation in sex work. Ana and Alicia, for example, were well aware of the nature of the work and applied to *Campo* with that knowledge. The type of employment in Curaçao was clear to them, and was an extension of activities in their countries of origin or elsewhere in the region. Sex work was one activity they were either familiar with or were prepared for, and although the conditions in the brothel were not exactly what they were led to expect, they consciously employed their sexual labor to make a living. Others, such as Gloria were drawn by the idea of a short-term, well-paying job in Curaçao, couched in terms of "night-club" or "entertainment" work. They became entrapped in *Campo* due to loans they had to repay. The brothel was incorrectly represented in the networks into which they were linked, and hence they were not aware beforehand of the type of work that was expected. In other cases, women reported to know of the character of the job, yet refused to stay due to the abhorrent working conditions in the brothel, particularly the restrictions on their movements and the isolation of the brothel from the city and the rest of island life. With the police files and records showing that around half of the women arriving in *Campo* each month had previously visited, there is some ground to assume that at least fifty percent of the women working in the brothel at any one time are consciously involved in prostitution (Police reports 1944–1993; personal interviews).

None of the women I interviewed in 1993 specifically expressed the idea that sex work was their life-long profession or for that matter an activity around which their identity revolved. They all had engaged in a number of other income-generating activities, such as sewing, textile, factory, domestic and secretarial work, selling food, teaching and nursing. There was no indication that prostitution was their only means of survival, rather just a temporary one. Some were prepared to continue in it for a while longer, but others were ready to find something else after their three-month stay on the island. This part-time incorporation of sex work into their lives reinforces insights voiced by nurses and police officers who worked closely with migrant prostitutes in Curaçao whom I also interviewed in 1993, as well as findings from studies and surveys of women's activities in the broader Caribbean region (Azize et al. 1996). The concept of "sources of livelihood," of which sexual labor is just one element, best captures the notion of the multiple and varied resources that Caribbean working women tap into to sustain themselves and their families (Senior 1991).

Survival in a capitalist global economy is clearly an underlying principle of all the women's actions. However, it is not always clear that it is due to abject poverty, or lack of other skills and possibilities that women turn to this particular income-generating activity. Indeed, it is difficult, from the situations described by women in prostitution in Curaçao and in other countries, to simply state that the sex trade in the Caribbean involves extremely poor, illiterate, ignorant women, drawn from the rural underclass in the region. A woman may run into a specific financial problem, and the idea that she can accumulate a large sum of money in a relatively short period through sex work may undergird her move into the sex trade. Research and testimonies suggest that the sale of sex is considered viable for women of different backgrounds and is subject to as much "choice" as any other income-generating activity for women in gendered labor markets (Kane 1993, Bolles 1992). In Cuba, in the 1990s, sex work is clearly an activity of well-educated young women, many of whom are professionals in other areas (Diaz et al. 1996). Combining sex work with activities in other informal sectors is also a well established phenomenon in the region. Haitian women, for example, increasingly use sex work to build up initial capital in order to begin a trading career in household goods or other items; women from the Dominican Republic may engage in sex work while buying goods in the Free Trade Zone in Curaçao (Interview with the Haitian Consul in Curaçao 1993; Lagro and Plotkin 1990). Sex work, in this perspective, is another resource that women rely on to support and shelter themselves and families, to acquire a few desirable luxury items, to buy a plot of land, to develop some other kind of business or to more generally improve the quality of life for themselves and kin. The amount they can potentially earn in the sex trade on a temporary short-term basis may be an initial pull, and can be a retaining force. In the light of a decline in well-paid jobs in formal sectors for both men and women, and the increasing pressure on women to be an important if not the sole breadwinner for the household and family, sex work for many Caribbean women may seem a very real option. The notion of prostitution as a way for women to get by or "make do," is also reflected in the new terms that are emerging in the region for these activities, such as *trabajadoras sexuales* in the Dominican Republic, *sekswerkers* in Suriname, and *jineteras* in Cuba (see chapters on Cuba, Suriname and the Dominican Republic elsewhere in this book).

Migration

Curaçao is not the only place in the Caribbean region that hosts a sex industry that is dependent upon migrant workers. A survey made in 1996 of the situation for the Latin American and Caribbean region shows that women travel for prostitution from Brazil to Suriname, from Cuba to Mexico, from the Dominican Republic to Panama, Antigua, Haiti as well as the Dutch Caribbean, from Colombia to Trinidad, from Guyana to Trinidad and Suriname, and from Trinidad to Colombia (Azize et al., 1996). These particular trends appear to be linked with women's movements around the region for purposes of informal commercial trading, otherwise known as suitcase trading (Lagro and Plotkin 1990), domestic work and marriage (Azize et al. 1996), yet due to the underground or informal nature of these activities, the extent of the connections are unknown and the links may in some instances be quite tenuous. It is generally assumed however, by researchers and activists in the region that due to the restructuring that Caribbean economies have been subjected to, particularly since the mid-1980s under pressure of the World Bank and the IMF, and due to shifts in global patterns of production and accumulation, women are increasingly more active in informal economies, which includes sex industries (Safa 1995, Senior 1991, Bolles 1992). This trend is coupled with a large number of female-headed households—the Caribbean having one of the highest rates world-wide at thirty-five percent in 1990—and thus a high level of responsibility for women to provide for their households (UN 1995). Migration to a wealthier part of the world in order to generate income for the family's survival takes on greater significance in the overall picture of declining income-generating opportunities for women at home.

Gloria's and Rubia's experiences demonstrate however that migration for sex work is not always an independent action on the part of the women. These two women for example, were recruited for work in Curaçao through an opaque process involving middle-men. Others were flown to the island directly by hotel or night-club managers, both male and female, or in the cases of the escort service and in some situations outside the central brothel, the women worked under the immediate supervision of a manager. Involvement in sex work and amount earned was, in these examples, controlled and managed directly by others.

But even for those who are not directly accountable to an ever-present manager, sex workers in the Caribbean operate in a sector that attempts to feed off their earnings. Husbands, partners, security guards, handymen, taxi drivers, customs officers, immigration and police officers, and politicians (all predominantly male) take advantage of the women's informal or pseudo-legal status as sex workers. In addition to pay-offs exacted by these individuals, a profitable business has emerged around the provision of loans for the airfare and documents for travel. Few women can afford to pay these costs on their own, and thus money is borrowed. In the case of Curaçao, money was loaned to the women either in their country of origin by a local broker, or by a "hotel" manager in Curaçao in order to acquire a round trip ticket to the island. The initial period in sex work becomes for the women, a struggle to ensure that this debt, with interest, is paid off. Extras also add up considerably, such as "assistance" with the application process from Colombia which can cost up to US$100, transport to and from airports, costs for health certificates, visas, birth certificates and passports as well as for false papers, and the women may become indebted for large sums to men both at home and in Curaçao. These financial obligations, bribes, pressures, false promises, or direct management ensures that even though the majority of sex workers in Curaçao are technically self-employed, independent persons they are situated in a relationship of dependency vis-a-vis individual men, criminal organizations, and the government. The situation for women in Curaçao appears to be mirrored elsewhere in the region (*Juntarnos* 1996, Kalm 1975, Azize et al. 1996. See also Fusco elsewhere in this section).

Migration for any kind of work enhances a person's vulnerability to exploitation, extortion and other malpractices due to factors such as the migrants' unfamiliarity with the institutions and discourse in the new context, her lack of citizen rights, dependency on the recruiting agent and/or xenophobia and racism in the "host" societies. In the sex trade, these situations are commonly exacerbated by the outlawed status of prostitution, the quasi-documented position of the migrant, and the intensity of moral condemnation of commercial sex and female sexual activity. Thus even in a place such as Curaçao where the government suspended its own legal prohibitions on brothel-keeping and pimping in order to accommodate the sex house *Campo Alegre*, international laws and hegemonic patriarchal-religious ideologies and moralities have shaped the local situation, placing women who sell sex in a physically unsafe, and economically insecure zone. Migrant sex workers in the Caribbean, like many of their counterparts elsewhere in the world, stand at the nexus of oppressions and exploitations around gender, sex, class, nationality, and race, constituting prime targets for those out to make a quick profit.

Race and Sex Work

While it remains true that women of all cultures and ethnicities are active in prostitution, there is nevertheless a trend evident throughout the Caribbean, that racialized hierarchies are structured into the sex trade. In Curaçao, for example, women who command the better working conditions and pay on the island work as escorts for "VIP's" and are more often than not white European women, mainly Dutch (Personal interview with an escort business owner, 1993). Migrant sex workers from Colombia and the Dominican Republic are predominantly "light-skinned," mulatto (mixed African-European) women, while "local" prostitutes who invariably work the streets and ill-paid sectors, are far more likely to be of Afro-Caribbean descent. Formal and informal regulations in Curaçao furthermore not only exclude Haitian (synonymous for Black) women from the *Campo* brothel, but favor "light-skinned" Latin American women. As one man simply put it, "if she's light-colored, then she is sexually attractive to this population" (Interview 1993 with a former *Campo* client).

Reports from other countries signal a similar trend. In Haiti, for instance, women from the Dominican Republic are considered by the men to be more exotic and professional than Haitian women and, in the words of one man, are preferable because "they more closely approximate to Western standards of beauty" (Chanel 1994). In a similar vein, a tourist to Cuba states "The girls that are the easiest to find are usually black and from Oriente. I think the girls in the Dominican Republic, who are all mixed race, are more beautiful than these Cuban girls." (World Sex Guide 1995). Elsewhere, the Cuban racial-sexual hierarchy is described as one where "fair-skinned, fine-featured, 'shopping girls'," are the highest priced sex workers, with "mulatto" and black women in the lower echelons of the sex trade (Cooper 1995, see also Diaz 1996, and Fusco elsewhere in this book). In Belize "brothels tend to hire exclusively young 'Spanish,' 'clear-skinned' women . . . who come from the neighboring Central American Republics" to work for British soldiers, male tourists and Belizean men (Kane 1993: 971–2).

Colonial racist hierarchies, embedded in Caribbean societies for several centuries, are reasserted through this structuring of the inferiority/undesirability of "blackness" and superiority/privilege of "whiteness." The patterning has produced a situation where on the one hand a specific category of Caribbean womanhood is targeted to sustain local economies and businesses, and on the other hand color and "race" define a woman's sexual capital. In keeping with Frantz Fanon's analysis of colonialism which he saw as producing the "Black Skin, White Masks" phenomenon in the Caribbean (1979), the notion of "Black Bodies, White Faces" seems to capture the post-colonial Caribbean ideology of female sexual attractiveness. It revolves around a synthesis of racialized stereotypes of a heightened sensuality, uninhibited sexual passion and physical desirability of the Black African female body and fine or "delicate" facial features and silky hair of the White Euro-American woman. The "brown-skinned girl" constitutes a mainstay of the Caribbean sex trade.

Family Matters

"The family" may also condition and help structure sex work. In the region where working-class women are traditionally breadwinners and often sole providers for their children, and where older women in the family are important for the care and upbringing of small children, economic responsibility for the household is a central concern for many women. Feeding, clothing and educating children is also a common reason given by women for entering the trade. Or, as in Ana's case, the earnings were to support adult family members. Some women working in Curaçao decided to engage in sex work while their children were very young, simply to prevent a situation where a child would begin to enquire about the mother's activities (personal interviews 1993). While women were in Curaçao, it was often their mothers who cared for the children left at home. Although this scenario may suggest that most of the women were single parents, from all accounts the majority of sex workers had a steady partner. Sex work then provided part of a larger household income.

Shared or full responsibility for the economic welfare of the household may not be the only way in which the family influences a woman to begin with sex work. Some follow in a mother's footsteps: the role model in their lives includes prostitution as a source of livelihood, and daughters are socialized to view sex work as a potential income-generating activity. In yet other instances, the broader family may be a direct source of manipulable, cheap labor: nieces, sisters and female cousins are recruited for a family member's business such as in the following case:

> At the age of twenty-one, Joanna was the mother of six children. Her aunt, who ran a guesthouse in Curaçao, convinced her that she could easily make money in Curaçao to support her family, and arranged for her to move to the island and to marry. Joanna was pressured both by her sense of responsibility to her children and mother and by her aunt's insistence, but was horrified at the situation she found herself in once in Curaçao. She spent her first years in fear of her aunt and her clients.

> Five years later, the aunt moved the operation to the Netherlands. By that time Joanna had become quite independent and had decided to stay in the trade. She opted to move with the rest of the house to Europe.

The other side of the coin is that members—male partners, mothers, aunts and children—become dependent on the woman's earnings and remittances home, and expectations and pressures for her to continue this financial support weigh heavily. Once having started to make a reasonable living from her overseas work and improving the living conditions and life-style of the family, she may have to continue in the trade in order to maintain the situation. Also, the prestige of having a daughter for example, who has "made it" overseas raises the social status of the family at home. That the woman's job is not selling flowers or hamburgers, or working as an "artiste" in an exclusive club, but rather selling her sexual labor, is not necessarily known or acknowledged by the family. Reliance by mothers, aunts, children, husbands and other family members on the steady financial support in such a scenario takes precedence over concern for her welfare and actual activities, and can pressure her into prostitution indefinitely. The family then can be a factor that compels women into, and occasionally out of, sex work.

Marriage

The status of Curaçao as a part of the Kingdom of the Netherlands is another dimension which affects migrant women's lives. Marriage to a Dutch citizen can provide a step towards better work opportunities, living conditions and a quality of life believed to be available in the Netherlands and its colonies, and is often perceived by women in the wider Caribbean as a way to get away from hustling and poverty-stricken conditions. Three distinct scenarios in the relationship between sex work and marriage are evident in Curaçao.

First, benefits accruing from marriage in the Dutch Caribbean colonies are sometimes used by men to encourage women to leave their home countries and return with them to Curaçao. Young women are plied with promises of a better life and, in the hope of finding a loving, secure partnership, they may accept. Once in Curaçao, the promised life may turn out to be a dream. Perhaps the man is already married and houses his new sexual partner elsewhere, demanding her fidelity. She could find herself living with a mother-in-law or other family members. She may be continually confronted with stereotypes of the Latin American woman as "whore." As the story goes:

> The men talk so sweetly, you just fall in love—they tell you so many nice things, of how beautiful life is in Curaçao, and you marry. You think you're in Paradise. You come to Curaçao and find you have to live with the mother, or sister. And everyday you're cursed as a Sandom whore. . . .

In some instances these relationships disintegrate and turn hostile, and the women are subjected to brutal physical violence, sexual abuse and intimidation. Having little financial resources of her own and being economically dependent on the husband, the woman may be battered into docility and silence. Alternatively, she may be forced to turn to prostitution by her "husband" or she may consciously take up sex work as a means to escape from her dependent situation.

Payment for marriage by a woman to acquire Dutch citizenship for sex work is a second scenario. Such an arrangement means that a migrant woman can stay and work legally as a prostitute in Curaçao or travel to Europe without restrictions. In 1993, the sum for the marriage ran for around Nag2000–3000 (approximately $1,000–$1,500) and could include a trip to the Netherlands. Such marriages are often arranged through third persons, not always with the woman's full consent. The marriage partners are often described as being mentally or physically handicapped, or senior men (Kempadoo 1994). Marriage for legitimate sex work status is organized and linked to an underground market of forged and false documents—birth certificates, travel permits, passports and health certificates—as well as to more organized operations (de Stoop 1992; van Ammelrooy 1989). Usually in such a case there is no intention for the couple to live together; the marriage is merely one of convenience for sex work, whereby the woman is able to operate as a documented worker in the Dutch context. In cases where the woman is tricked into such a marriage for prostitution in either the Caribbean or the Netherlands, she is made to buy her freedom through paying costs for marriage, travel, documents and so forth. Since these costs far exceed the actual amounts, the "debts" trap her in sex work for several years, paralleling a situation of indentureship. The transactions and relationships are commonly referred to as "schijnhuwelijken" or "bogus" marriages.

Third, while working in Curaçao, perhaps in *Campo,* or downtown on a tourist visa, close and intimate relationships between a prostitute and client may develop, leading to marriage between the two. The woman retires from her work, and after five years she is able to petition to be removed from the prostitutes register at the KZP office (police records 1944–1993). Such a marriage is defined by the authorities as "real," as opposed to the "bogus" marriages constituted by the second type of arrangement, and the partners, it is claimed, may stay together for many years.

Silences

As the four experiences presented at the beginning of this chapter suggest, a great deal of ambiguity exists around migration for sex work. Many women come to know about a place to make money via other women, and female networks appear to be the most important element in the transmission of knowledge. Alicia's account for Curaçao describe, for example, how another woman may give the initial prompt to pursue a lead for work on the island. In a survey in the Dominican Republic in 1993 among 288 *trabajadoras sexuales,* twenty-nine percent of women who had experienced migration declared to have been assisted by family and friends (COIN 1995). However, as illustrated in Gloria's and Rubia's stories, there was an unspoken element between women about the nature of the activity in the country of destiny: sex work was not always talked about openly by women between themselves. Nor is it always made explicit through the recruitment and selection process. Even with the "legality" of sex work, as in a place like Curaçao with a forty-five year old government-regulated brothel, the nature of the activities for the women is concealed by government, police and immigration officials. Applications to work in *Campo*, for example, do not have to mention the nature of the work the woman is hoping to engage in, nor is the word "prostitution" mentioned in the correspondence or forms issued by the Immigration and Police departments in Curaçao. According to the criteria used by the police for selecting candidates for work at the brothel, simply stating an interest in *Campo* is sufficient. Sexual activities for women, such as sex work, sexual labor, and prostitution, despite the extent to which they are practiced, thus remain virtually invisible in everyday discourse. This discursive shroud reinforces broader social stigmas around both commercial sex and female sexuality in various Caribbean societies (Wekker 1994, Clemencia 1995, Alberts 1992).

The extent to which silence on the subject of sex can influence a Caribbean migrant sex worker's life is partially visible through their experiences in Curaçao. Gloria, for example, was physically and psychologically hurt due to misinformation. Other interviewees in Curaçao did not necessarily define their activities as "wrong" or something to be personally ashamed of—they were defiant and proud. Nevertheless, they would often not tell family members about the work they were doing. In the Dominican Republic, around fifty percent of the women declared their family knew about their sexual work (Personal interviews 1995, COIN 1994). In Suriname, secrecy is of utmost importance to a street-prostitutes' survival (see the Maxi Linder interview elsewhere in this book).

Migration to another country or island offers some relief from familial and community condemnation of prostitution in that it allows women to work anonymously in a new environment, far away from their home context. Yet another way in which women attempt to fend off any stigma and conceal their activities is, after a stint of sex work elsewhere in the region, to exchange their earnings for goods in the free-trade zone and to travel back home with goods to trade (Kempadoo 1994). In relation to Curaçao, immigration officials and police may take advantage of the reputation of the island as a "whorehouse" in its negative yet titillating sense, and demand sexual services in lieu of payments for duty on the goods on the woman's return to her home country. Away from home in Curaçao, women have also to deal with local prejudices and hostilities. The island, in its colonized mode dominated by a middle-class European orientation and steeped in Catholicism, reflects perceptions of prostitution that rely heavily on notions of degradation, evil, and immorality. Nineteenth-century European morality and struggles to regulate or abolish prostitution have the upper hand on the island. Here also, aside from the general stigma of "puta" which is used to denigrate sex workers, the association between women from Santo Domingo in the Dominican Republic and prostitution has led to the denigrating term "Sandom." Latin American women—Spanish speakers from any part of the Caribbean, Central or South America—are often collectively labelled in this way.

Interviewed migrant sex workers in Curaçao all stressed some aspect of the negative social attitudes towards them. Several held the impression that they were viewed by the larger society purely as sexual objects or drug addicts who were lacking dignity and self-respect. An apprehension about leaving the brothel or visiting other parts of the island was common due to the hostility they would encounter. Curaçaoan women were included for criticism by the prostitutes, with comments such as "They don't have a good opinion of us, they often think we will take their men away from them," or "Curaçaoan women think badly of us, look down on us."

Migrant women who are registered with the police authorities in Curaçao are known, defined, name themselves and are seen explicitly as prostitutes, but many more are involved in sex work outside *Campo/Mirage* who do not admit to their activities. As far as one woman was concerned, "if women accept money, jewelry or clothes in exchange for sex, they are prostitutes." Many local women deny being involved in sex work, will not register, refuse to go for medical checks, and see themselves as superior to licensed migrant women. *Campo* sex workers commented on this hypocrisy: "We are here to sell sex for money. Local women do it, but they say it's for love." "There is the problem of the 'elite ladies' in Curaçao who won't dare to put a put a foot in *Campo*, even if they work as call girls. They don't want to know about it." An awareness of the hypocrisy, clandestine sex work, supercilious attitudes of other women, and moral condemnation of licensed prostitution, can result in defiance and anger among self-conscious prostitutes.

The social condemnation of female sexual activity and prostitution is not limited to migrant sex workers, but extends to include settings and locations frequented by prostitutes as well as to non-sex workers associated with prostitutes. In turn, avoidance of sex work establishments and of contact with licensed migrant prostitutes maintains the separation between notions of "whores" and "women" and continues to support the separation between local and foreign women. Sex work, it is safe to say, is still defined by many on the island as a "nasty business," from which "decent" women should stay far away.

Constantly being defined as outside of the realm of "womanhood," and being isolated in their workplace, migrant female sex workers in Curaçao are confronted with a wall of disrespect. There is little interaction with the island life during the day. The night time is theirs, and it is hoped by many Curaçaoan men and women alike, that they will stay in the dark. For non-registered women, there is the underlying fear of being "discovered" and identified as a "puta" whether one works as a "crack"-prostitute, an escort-girl or lives as a "sponsored" woman. Secrecy and hypocrisy dominate many women's lives, for apart from the registered migrant women, many local women are engaged in the business. The dominant notions of sex work as dirty, degrading and immoral are still very pervasive and contribute to women's silence and isolation.

Movements for Change

Even though migrant sex workers in Curaçao may operate relatively independently, their position remains fragile. Many are vulnerable to physical violence and abuse from police and clients, poor working conditions and societal condemnation which forces them into dependency relations, forms of indentureship or debt-bondage, isolation, or underground trafficking businesses. Government regulations, such as the ban on the licensing of local sex workers, and the stipulations of a limited stay for migrant women, furthermore undermine any long-term association or solidarity among sex workers. Migration ensures that women have no firm basis or commitment in their place of work. Migration to even further sites outside the Caribbean compounds a sex worker's vulnerability given the distance from home, family and community and the wide cultural gap.

Collective action and resistance among migrant sex workers is not very visible to those outside the sex trade. In Curaçao some organization occurs in the workplaces or during working hours, on a sporadic or spontaneous basis. These activities include group defense against physically abusive or violent clients, protests in 1990 against a rent increase for rooms in the brothel, and resistance against attempts by the *Campo* management to keep the women's passports. Undoubtedly there are other events. The geographical and social isolation however that surrounds prostitution, means that such activities are undocumented and concealed from general knowledge. Conditions on the island are also not conducive to building a sex workers' or prostitutes' organization or movement: temporary migrant worker's status prevents any long-term commitment to the place of work or to each other, the hostility from local women towards migrant prostitutes hinders any feminist or women's solidarity for addressing the issue of sex work and the lack of a local organization that supports prostitutes' rights means a lack of continuity in addressing pertinent issues.

Nevertheless there are initiatives elsewhere in the region. In Suriname, we are beginning to see the organization of sex workers that is partially spearheaded by a migrant woman (former sex worker) from Guyana, although this initiative primarily concerns "local" street workers and has not as yet mobilized Brazilian migrant sex workers in the more exclusive clubs (see Maxi Linder interview in this book). In the Dominican Republic, the COIN organization, set up for AIDS prevention created a network of out-reach "Messengers of Health," which in turn led to the formation of MODEMU—as autonomous sex workers organization. Similar organizations and initiatives advocated by Caribbean sex workers for the empowerment of working women and for changes in prostitution relations, may emerge with the increasing attention to the sex trade and women's health issues as well as with the increasing visibility of young women turning to sex work in the region. Whether it come from concerned activists, health care practitioners, feminists or prostitutes themselves, it seems likely that women's voices on sex work in the Caribbean will be increasingly heard.

Children, Prostitution, and Identity
A Case Study from a Tourist Resort in Thailand

Heather Montgomery

Introduction

Every few years an issue relating to children attracts the attention of the media and is quickly turned into an international cause célèbre. In the 1970s, it was malnourished and starving children in Africa. During the early 1980s, it was child labor in Asia, which was followed by street children in South America. Now it is child prostitution. It is often seen as *the* problem of the nineties, leading to new laws being passed in some countries enabling that country to prosecute its own citizens for abuses committed against children abroad.[1] The increase in awareness about incest and child abuse in Western countries has sensitized people to abuse in other countries and the suspicion that some Western men are perpetuating this abuse has created a climate of absolute intolerance to child prostitution in all circumstances (La Fontaine 1990; Jenkins 1992).

Child prostitution is viewed as an evil which must be eradicated by all means possible. This is a perfectly understandable response and one with which few people, except possibly pedophiles or others with obvious ulterior motives, would disagree. However will all the concern about child prostitution, individual children who sell sex have been largely overlooked. The stereotypical image that is portrayed by the media and by NGOs campaigning to end this prostitution concerns a passive, helpless victim awaiting rescue by some "good" adult (Scheper-Hughes and Stein 1989). What is noticeable is that children themselves are rarely allowed to speak. In all the information received from the media about child prostitution, there is little about the children themselves. The unvoiced implications are always that only adults can represent children, that only adults can fully understand the situation, and that children may be prostitutes but they cannot understand it and certainly cannot analyze it. There is therefore little for them to say. As knowledge of the extent and nature of child abuse in the West grows, there is even greater confidence in speaking on behalf of child prostitutes: the effects of prostitution on them are stated with conviction.

My contention in this chapter is not that child prostitution is acceptable or that it is in any way beneficial to the children concerned in the long term. What was apparent, however, from my own fieldwork was how very differently campaigners against child prostitution and the children who actually sold sex conceptualized prostitution. The children in my study had very different means of seeing themselves and what they did and they constructed their social and personal identities in various ways. Prostitution was how they earned money but it said little about more pertinent issues such as loyalty, filial duty and private morality. It is these qualities that were important to the children and prostitution, far from negating them, actually reinforced them.

Attitudes to Prostitution

Attitudes to prostitution in general, and child prostitution in particular, are never neutral and inevitably the latter is viewed as a problem. Although the source of the problem is differently located for child prostitutes abroad and child prostitutes at home, the image of children selling their bodies for profit arouses indignation and outrage. It is a powerful metaphor for many things; societal decay, moral degeneracy, capitalism and patriarchy in its extreme form and the exploitation of Third World peoples by Westerners, in the form of both business and tourism. To study child prostitution in developing countries therefore, especially from the supposedly dispassionate and neutral standpoint of the observer anthropologist, is extremely difficult because there is a great deal of pressure to examine it as a prelude to stopping it. It is very hard to disassociate research from policy and therefore child prostitution must always be cast in terms of being a problem needing a solution, either the problem of how to stop Westerners going abroad and buying sex or how to stop children in overseas countries becoming prostitutes. There is a tendency to perceive prostitution as a moral issue, set apart from the wider political economy. It is seen as an aberration which demands immediate action and quick solutions. Prostitutes themselves, both adults and children, are viewed in a particular light which either regards them as depraved individuals in a functioning society or oppressed characters in a base world. Either way, the effects of economics on their lives and the amount of control over what they do are glossed over and ignored. Certain elements of academic feminism in particular seem unable to come to terms with prostitution of any sort, unless it is set entirely in the context of male exploitation of women. The war of words that has broken out between women who write from a sex worker's perspective (Bell 1987; Delacoste and Alexander 1988; Ryan 1992) and other women who claim to speak for them (Barry 1984) is the consequence of this and an exposure of the intrinsic biases that researchers bring to prostitution. There is a moral bias inherent in most studies of prostitution so that even those who want to study prostitution sympathetically come to it with a set of expectations that are fulfilled because they are looking for them. One academic, Cleo Odzer, who studied prostitution in Thailand, quotes two other researchers, who write of their sample group of prostitutes,

> It is a story of tortured, twisted people. It is a story of blatant degradation. It is, if you will, a sordid, shocking, gruesome story, and it has little trace of hope or uplift or joy. Sordidness and ugliness are the concomitants of prostitutes' commonplace, everyday routines of living. Here are people narcotized to accept hurts, humiliations, abasements as their daily portions. Here are people who know little or nothing of hope or joy or uplift (1990: 3).

The same biases shown in the above quote apply equally to any study of child prostitution. It is extremely difficult to study the children's lives objectively and to say that children do know something of "hope or joy or uplift" without accusations of condoning child abuse which is automatically equated with child prostitution. I was once roundly condemned by one activist over a paper I had written in which I suggested that the children I knew love their families and find security and happiness in them. She wrote to me, "Personally, I think that your conclusion may lead to misunderstanding . . . there is the suspicion at the end that [you say] despite everything that these children go through, they still come up smiling, so that's fine."[2] The desire for information is for stories which emphasize the degradation and abuse of children, not the mundane aspects of their lives or even the areas of their lives away from prostitution. Maggie Black has written, "There is, for good or bad, a public appetite for information particularly of the most sensational kind which confers a special commodity status on

the subject of 'child' sex" (1995:6). Although sex with children is widely condemned, it is still an issue which causes great, if appalled, curiosity. There is a
continuing fascination with it which is fed by the media and the NGOs and it is
clearly an issue which both repels and allures. While newspaper articles often
claim to be raising awareness, they can also titillate. This public interest in child
sex undoubtedly exists but it is not the straightforward reflection of outrage that
it claims to be. It rarely raises awareness and frequently has the affect of harnessing prurient horror for political ends which often substitute understanding for
sensationalism and moral outrage. Child prostitution is cast as a clear cut case of
good and evil while ignoring the wider political economy that allows child prostitution to flourish. La Fontaine in the "Introduction" to *Child Sexual Abuse*, writes
that social scientists lay themselves open to charges of "academic voyeurism
[which are] no substitute for more action on behalf of the victims" (1990: 17)
when they attempt to write about any issues involving the sexual abuse of children but this voyeurism is inherent in all accounts of child prostitution. A call
for action at the end of a newspaper article or an NGO fund raising leaflet, does
not obviate the suppressed excitement of many stories.

A Case Study of Child Prostitution

During 1993 and 1994, I was based in a small community in a tourist resort town
in Thailand which earned its income through the prostitution of the children
that lived there. It was a small community of less than one hundred and fifty
people and it was situated on the edge of a tourist town. It was a poor community without running water and only intermittent electricity but the people
there rented land and had built up their own houses. There is a stereotype of
child prostitution that claims that they are tricked into leaving home, or sold by
impoverished parents into a brothel where they are repeatedly raped and ter-
rorized into servicing up to twenty clients a night. There is certainly good evidence for some of this. Children have been kidnapped from neighboring countries, especially China and Burma, and kept in appalling conditions (Center for
the Protection of Children's Rights 1991; Asia Watch 1993). Others have been sold
or debt-bonded by their parents (Heyzer 1986; ISIS 1990; Lee Wright 1990; Koompraphant n.d.; Muecke 1992). There have also been horrific cases of young girls
and women imprisoned in brothels and unable to escape when the brothel has
caught fire.[3] It is undeniable that child prostitution is risky and dangerous in
Thailand and many children are caught in situations which present a great
threat. The children with whom I worked were not in any of these categories
however, and they present a different, but rarely acknowledged model of child

prostitution. They were technically "free" in that they were not debt-bonded or kept in brothels and they lived with their parents. They were perhaps not typical of all child prostitutes in Thailand but they are an important group whose lives and identities challenge many of the expected stereotypes of child prostitution.

There were sixty-five children under the age of fifteen in this slum and at least forty had worked as prostitutes at some point. These children worked because they felt a strong obligation towards their families and believed that it was their duty to support their parents financially. Income generating opportunities were extremely limited in the slum and outside it: there was little regulated, legal work available. The land on which they lived was poor and would not support raising crops and they did not have the education or training to take on even menial jobs in the resort. In these circumstances, prostitution, especially with foreign clients, was the only job which brought in enough money and many children turned to prostitution as a way of fulfilling their perceived obligations. Poverty is an often-cited cause of prostitution and in this community it certainly played a part. However, poverty and prostitution should not be linked too simplistically. Most children from poor families are not prostitutes and poverty is not necessarily the root cause of all child prostitution. In the case of the children in this community, it is far more pertinent to examine obligation and its effect on prostitution. The most powerful mitigating circumstance for many children was not that they were earning money because they were poor but that they were earning money to help their parents.

To outsiders, the lifestyle of the villagers looked extremely unpleasant and squalid and certainly the villagers themselves never romanticized it but there was an internal dynamic to the life of the community that enabled the people there to continue with their own logic and set of ethics. None of the children liked prostitution but they did have strategies for rationalizing it and coming to terms with it. They had found an ethical system whereby the public selling of their bodies did not affect their private sense of humanity and virtues. When I asked one thirteen-year-old about selling her body, she replied "it's only my body" but when I asked about the difference between adultery and prostitution, she would tell me that adultery was very wrong. In her eyes, adultery was a betrayal of a private relationship whereas prostitution was simply done for money. She could make a clear conceptual difference between her body and what happened to it and what she perceived to be her innermost "self." In a similar way to the prostitutes in Sophie Day's study (1994), these children could delineate clear boundaries between what happened to their bodies and what affected their personal sense of identity and morality. Selling sex was not immoral because it violated no ethical codes. Betraying family members, failing to provide for parents or cheating on spouses or boyfriends was roundly condemned but exchanging sex for money especially when that money was used for moral ends, carried no stigma.

Prostitution and Identity

Within this community it was relatively easy to find out who had sex for money and who did not, but the children's perceptions of what they did were much more complex. It quickly became obvious that categories and labels were not simply academic nit-picking but fundamentally important to the children's images of themselves. I had set out to study child prostitutes but almost immediately became aware of what an arbitrary and limiting classification this was. As de Zalduondo, correctly argues, it is wrong to "address prostitution as if it were a trait (like height or religiosity) rather than as a response to perceived needs and constraints. Sex work is an occupation, engaged in by choice or perceived necessity: it is not an orientation or property of the individual" (1991: 237). I soon discovered that "prostitute" was not a definition that the children ever used about themselves and that it had nothing to do with their sense of identity.[4] While it was common for children or their parents to say they *pay thiaw kap farang* (go out for fun with foreigners), *jap farang* (catch foreigners) or even *mii kheek* (have guests) I never heard anyone refer to themselves as a child prostitute (*sopheni dek*) or even a *ying borikan* (business woman—a common slang term for prostitute).

For the children themselves, to be called a child prostitute was a great insult and deeply hurtful and it is a phrase that they threw out at each other when they wanted to be particularly hurtful.[5] In one instance, I once deeply upset a nine year old boy called Nong by asking if he ever *jap farang* (caught foreigners). He burst into tears of rage and frustration and would not talk to me for two days. Eventually he told me "I never went with foreigners, why won't anyone believe me?" All along he was telling the truth; while he pimped for other children and introduced them to foreigners, he never went himself. In his own terms he was not a prostitute and hated to think that others saw him in this role. He pimped for others and was in charge of their finances. He could exert patronage and control over others and was very proud of this role. Yet, aspects such as this, children pimping for others are overlooked and it is common for journalists and NGO workers to ignore this side of their lives completely and to write stories about child prostitutes, ignoring the reality of the rest of their lives away from prostitution and labeling them with names that their 'subjects' neither use nor understand. As Maggie Black writes, "Neither their work, nor their self-image, nor their aspirations are confined to sex work. The prostitute label has been stuck on them by the beholder" (1994: 12).

The children's attitudes towards prostitution were often contradictory. They would readily say that they "had guests" or were "supported by foreigners" or they would use other phrases suggesting prostitution but that they disliked the term "prostitution" (*sopheni*). They would rather use words that conveyed an ambiguity and a conceptual distance between selling sex and working. Their reactions to the term prostitution suggest they knew of the stigma involved with it and were keen to downplay its importance for them. They continually emphasized that they did not "sell sex" but that they "went out for fun with foreigner." While some clients simply bought sex, these sorts of relationships were disliked and rarely talked about. What they preferred to discuss were the men who were "friends" and who consequently had reciprocal obligations with the children and their families. The children were more comfortable talking about love and romance than they were about commercial transactions and preferred to stress relationships above money. They consciously downplayed the importance of money to them. They never set a price for sexual acts: money that was given to them after sex was referred to as a gift or as a token of appreciation. Money was not the end point of the exchange but a way of expressing affection. Sometimes a client would not leave cash for the children but would pay in kind, such as through rebuilding or refurbishing a girl's house. Given this, it is easy for the children to deny prostitution. The men who visit them are not clients but friends who help out whenever the children need it.

This attitude contrasted with some of the older adult prostitutes who viewed what they did in terms of economics and commodities rather than romance. They would sometimes say simply that they "sell cunt" (*kai hee*) or "sell ass" (*kai dut*). However, like the children, this attitude was not consistent and many adult women also hoped that prostitution might lead to romance. If they had a client who returned more than once, he very quickly became classified as a friend rather than a client. They were then girlfriends rather than prostitutes and like their younger sisters or daughters, they clung on to other identities, even while acknowledging the economic basis for what they did. They still saw themselves as "having friends" or "going out for fun with foreigners." To believe in a reality where prostitution meant only "selling cunt" or "selling ass" would mean giving up the conviction that their foreign customers respect them as "friends" and would one day take them away from their current life. That some of the older prostitutes sometimes became disillusioned was not surprising considering that some had been working for many years without having married or been supported by a rich foreign friend, but the children were still quite idealistic about the chances of one of their "friends" buying them and their families a big house and helping them to escape from slum life. For these children, the length of time that the men had been coming to them and the help they had given them meant that they could be classified as friends or even fictive kin rather than as clients. Almost all the children steadfastly refused to characterize the relationships with long-term clients as prostitution, abuse or exploitation. Another long-term client gave money to a couple of the girls if they asked for it and his most favored partner always denied that he abused her. She said "he is so good to me, he gives me and my family money whenever we need it, how can he be bad?"

It is easy to claim that the children are misguided or that they suffer from a form of false consciousness. Simply because a child does not recognize exploitation, it does not necessarily mean that it has not occurred. Poor Thai children are extremely vulnerable to abuse from richer, Western men and there is an obvious sense in which these children are exploited. They were also aware that prostitution was considered unacceptable by others in their society and they have good reasons to deny its importance and place in their lives. However, these children do explicitly reject the status of victims. They actively try to form reciprocal arrangements with their clients and the rejection of labels such as prostitution is not simply a denial of reality but a way of manipulating that reality. They recognize the structural power their clients have over them and do their best to direct it to their benefit.

For campaigners against prostitution, labels are difficult and there has been much debate on what to call children who sell sex. Kevin Ireland for example writes in *Wish You Weren't Here*:

> Child prostitution is where the person selling or hiring their sexuality is under eighteen years of age, although, wherever possible the terms "child prostitute" and "child prostitution" have been avoided, as they imply a sense of decision and control on behalf of the child. All children under the age of eighteen who are in prostitution are considered, *de facto*, to be sexually exploited (1993:3).

Therefore, phrases such as "prostituted children" or "children exploited by the sex industry" have come into use among some campaigners. Yet while these may sound less offensive to Western ears, they also deny some of the reality of the children's lives and ignore the strategies that are employed. The children that I knew did have "a sense of decision and control" and to deny them this is to deny the skillful way that they use what very small amount of control that they do have. The search for victims of child abuse sometimes obscures the acknowledgement of children's agency. In the context of child abuse in Britain, Jenny

Kitzinger writes, "Children are constantly acting to preempt, evade or modify sexual violence. However 'adult-centric' discourses ignore such strategies: children are not seen as agents in their own lives. They are only visible as they relate (literally or theoretically) to 'the adult world'" (1990: 165).

For the children that I knew, however, neither prostitution nor sexuality were the focus of their identity. Identity was so bound up in status, prestige and hierarchy that sexuality was a means to those ends rather than an end in itself. Identity was also based around belonging to a community and they would very fiercely defend themselves against comments or threats from children in neighboring villages. Although the level of violence was high within the slum, as soon as the children were threatened by outsiders, they banded together in an inseparable group and fought the other children. If slurs were ever made about prostitution or poverty, revenge was swift and the children would go en masse to the other village in a show of unity and strength.

The straightforward links between identity and sexuality that have often been assumed in the post-Freudian West were not apparent in this community. Sexuality was never identified with personal fulfillment or individual pleasure. As selling sex was rationalized as having guests or friends, the children did not identify with prostitution and many of the negative connotations that it has. Prostitution was an incidental way of constructing their identities. It brought in enough money to look after parents or pay for a family house, and a child could view herself as a good, dutiful daughter. Prostitution was the means to this end but it was no end in itself. It was a way of paying back debts to parents and fulfilling filial obligations. For the campaigners against child prostitution, however, the conflation of sexual and personal identity is key. Prostitution, they argue, damages children, not necessarily because of its physical risks but because it damages their identity. If sexuality is abused, the child is "ruined" and often unable to be rehabilitated into society. One campaigner, for example, claimed:

> When boys and girls have been forced to receive several customers a night seven days a week, they will be so traumatized that very little can be done to help them resume anything like a normal life. The solution is not in rehabilitation but in ending the trade altogether (O'Grady 1992: 1).

I would certainly never try to suggest that the children were not damaged by prostitution either physically, mentally or emotionally. The effects were often very obvious in the forms of bruises, STDs or drug use. However, I do not believe that Western models of psychology can always be applied directly to children in other countries and still be useful. I also believe that it is vital to look at children's own perceptions and explanations of what they do before anyone can try to help them and that we must acknowledge the importance of children's strategies and forms of control if we are to fully understand what enables them to continue to find meaning in their own lives

Stratagems and Control

The conditions that the children lived in were extremely difficult. Their lack of education, their poverty and ill health all made them vulnerable to abuse and exploitation by those with more power. Yet, prostitution is always seen as the ultimate indignity and one which is far beyond all others. It is also always seen as one which they passively accept. In all the accounts of child prostitution that I have read in Thailand and overseas (admittedly by journalists or campaigning NGO groups) the children's passivity is always emphasized. They are weak, helpless and have no control at all over their own lives. Yet, as Scott has shown, resistance, even in the harshest circumstances, is possible and does occur (1985). What is seen as passivity by outsiders may in fact be a form of protest. While direct confrontation is rarely in the interests of the weak and powerless, an unwilling compliance is not a sign that they have given up or that they passively accept what is happening. Rather it is an acceptance that their options are limited and their position weak, but even within those limits, they do not have to believe in what they have to do. They do not have to accept the dominant ideology that identifies them and stigmatizes them as prostitutes when, in their own terms, they are dutiful and much-loved family members.

The children that I knew did not passively accept this abuse and having a sense of control over some aspects of their lives was fundamental to them. For some, prostitution was a bad option with better pay than other bad options while others complied with their family's wishes that they become prostitutes as a way of showing their filial duty. Others responded more actively and were aware that there are levels of inequality within their own circles which they could exploit and use to form power bases (Hanks 1962). The older children formed entourages of younger children that they could control and grant favors to in the knowledge that these younger children were then indebted to them. In this way, prestige, status and power were built up as certain children could command the time and attention of others. It may not seem a very great power to outsiders but it indicated the skillful way in which the children sought to optimize their status and make use of the limited options.

Such discussions show up the difficulty of talking about choice and force in relation to child prostitutes. On a macro level it is hard to see them as having any choices. Their poverty and poor social status consigned them to the margins of society from where they had no structural power. With no welfare state or social safety net, there were few options which enabled them to exist even at subsistence level. Their right to live on their land was tenuous and they could be evicted at any time; their rights over their children were also under threat and the income generated by their children fluctuated. Yet on a smaller scale, they did not passively accept their low status and lack of choice, and their own sense of worth and identity were bound up in being in control of their lives. The money that prostitution brought in did enable the community to function and to stay together and this was a real achievement by the children. It was their money that supported their parents and kept the families together. Even though they were socially and economically very marginal, by most definitions they were dutiful children whose respect and difference towards their parents was honorable and admirable. For people who are poor and powerless, prostitution does not seem a unique and ultimate horror (as many outsiders view it) or something they have to be forced into but one difficult choice among many. They can be forced into many forms of work that they dislike such as scavenging or collecting garbage, neither of which pay nearly as well as prostitution.[6] It is unlikely that given a full range of choices and options, many of the children would choose prostitution, but these options have never been open to them. Their choices are limited but they do attempt to exercise these, despite the limitations. They choose not to represent themselves as victims and not to align themselves with negative connotations that others have placed on prostitution. Their power and ability to change their situation are extremely constrained but their constructions of their own identities and ways of viewing the world show a clear difference between them and the passive victims that child prostitutes are constantly assumed to be.

Conclusion

The children that I worked with were undoubtedly exploited and forced into lifestyles that exposed them to many forms of abuse and oppression. Whatever the children said about prostitution, it is difficult to examine other ways of seeing their situation without encountering suggestions that understanding is the same as condoning that which is indefensible. It is hard not to sound like a moral relativist and argue that if the children do not see abuses, then no abuse has occurs. Personally I felt that these children were exploited but that this exploitation came not through prostitution but through their general poverty and social exclusion. There has been no intention or attempt to justify that in writing this chapter but I do not wish to position it as the ultimate evil. The children did not have a choice as to whether they were exploited or not or between prostitution and work-free childhood. If they were not prostitutes, they still would have been impoverished and probably forced into the illegal labor market in a sweat shop or as a scavenger. These children were neglected by the state and given few viable options by their society. In this situation examining prostitution in isolation from other economic and social choices is pointless and leads only to narrow moralistic arguments about whether prostitution is "right" or whether any prostitute, either adult or child "really" chooses prostitution. Child prostitution has been a major cause of concern in recent years but there has been no widening of the debate and instead, campaigning groups have simply become increasingly shrill in denouncing it. Yet, despite the passion that child prostitution arouses, the children themselves have been largely silent. Many people are speaking in their name but very few people have listened to them and know who they are or how they perceive what they do. In this chapter, I have not given any definitive ways of viewing child prostitution or made claims that all child prostitutes think of themselves in these ways. Rather, by giving a context to the children's lives, it is possible to understand better what motivates and sustains them and their families. Through this contextualization, I have suggested other ways of understanding children who work as prostitutes and added complexities to what is becoming an increasingly simplistic debate.

Notes

1. Australia has passed a law which would imprison its citizens for up to seventeen years if they are found guilty of sexual offenses against children abroad. Norway, Germany, France, Belgium, New Zealand, Britain and Sweden have passed similar laws allowing for the prosecution of their own nationals at home if they cannot be convicted abroad.
2. Head of ECPAT France. Personal communication September 1994.
3. In the most notorious incident, a brothel in the seaside town of Phuket caught fire in 1995, killing five young prostitutes who were chained to their beds and unable to escape. In a similar fire in 1994, two women died.
4. However, I have used the word prostitute and prostitution throughout this chapter simply because it is the easiest understandable way to describe what the children that I am writing about do. It does not imply any moral judgment on them or attribute any characteristics. It is used simply to describe an economic activity. I have also used the word prostitute interchangeably with sex worker when discussing adult prostitution, which is many Western prostitutes preferred term (Bell 1987) because the concept of work is so problematic for the children and I did not find this term very useful when referring to children. Also, there is also no Thai equivalent of the term sex worker whereas *sopheni* (prostitute) is readily understood, if not always liked.
5. In other societies also, prostitutes dislike the labels forced upon them. In Jakarta, young prostitutes use the word "experimental girls" about themselves rather than the word prostitute which they use about other people (Murray 1991: 119).
6. The children could earn between 750 and 3000 baht ($30–$120) a month from prostitution compared with about 500 baht ($20) a month if they sorted garbage every day for around ten hours a day per month.

11 Hustling for Dollars *Jineterismo* in Cuba

Coco Fusco

In January 1996, I travelled to Cuba to conduct interviews with *jineteras*, women who exchange a range of favors, including sexual ones, for money from foreigners. Having visited Cuba regularly over the past twelve years as a journalist and artist, I was already familiar with *jineterismo* as a social phenomenon on the island. My interest in the special role that women of color were playing in the burgeoning sex tourism industry there, coupled with my awareness that since 1993, there had been a marked increase in prostitution in Cuba, prompted me to write an article about the women involved. I was also particularly interested in the issues that prostitution raises for a Third World socialist country that is in the process of making a difficult transition to capitalism.

An earlier version of this chapter appeared in the September/October 1996 issue of *Ms.* magazine. The research also served as the sociological basis for a new performance created with Chicana artist Nao Bustamante. The piece, entitled STUFF, deals with the role of Latinas in the peddling of spirituality and sex for first world consumers.

First Impressions

I am sitting one night in Havana's Cafe Cantante, a bohemian chic watering hole for the country's cultural elite. On the dance floor, a young woman with the tawny complexion, oval face and aquiline nose of a young Josephine Baker twists her hips and rib cage in opposite directions, her creamy yellow baby doll dress swinging from side to side. The way she gyrates her torso is called a *mono*, or knot. It's nothing short of a simulated sex act, and brings on erotically charged smiles as couples mime lovemaking to the music. But this girl, who can't be more than seventeen, is dancing alone. Her look, her age, her hip clothes and her foreign date are tell-tale signs that she's a *jinetera*, the popular term for Cubans who exchange a range of services, including sex, for money from foreigners.

A well-groomed YUMMY (Young Urban Marxist Manager) in Benneton sportswear struts over to the table where I'm sitting with a friend of his and kneels for a moment to light a cigarette. "I've read every manual about cross-cultural exchange that exists," he says to me, not yet realizing that I am not a resident Cuban but a visiting Cuban-American, "and I'll tell you one thing. No one comes to Cuba for ecotourism. What sells this place is right on the dance floor—rum, cigars and *la mulata*." My table mate Anita, a Cuban who now resides in Spain, gives me a weary look. "It's the foreigners who are out of control, not the *jineteras*," she says "Everyone in Madrid thinks every Cuban woman is a *puta*. I keep asking them why they don't worry about prostitutes in their own country and leave us alone."

I don't tell her that I, too, have come to Cuba to engage in some *jinetera* watching. Magazines all over Europe have been running stories about Cuba as a sex tourist's paradise since 1993. The press in Miami has been accusing the Cuban government of being the country's number one pimp. A marathon meeting on women's rights was called by the United Nations Committee on the Elimination of Discrimination against Women in January of 1996, in which a Federation of Cuban Women spokesperson fielded questions for two hours about this "new wave" of *jineteras*. This renewed international scrutiny is due as much to the real explosion of sex work in Cuba as it reveals the particular irony that such a resurgence of prostitution represents for a Third World socialist nation.

The Background

Prostitution is hardly new to Cuba. As early as the eighteenth century, a Spanish captain was dispatched to the island to suppress a scandal by closing down a string of brothels run by the local clergy. In a society that once adhered to a strong Latin Catholic tradition of separating men and women in the public sphere, brothels were among the few spaces available for casual exchanges, and particularly for encounters between white men and women of color, which accounts for the island's extensive mythology enshrouding the sexuality of mulatas. While there were always plenty of opportunities for exploitation of disenfranchised women, it is also true that the world of the brothel served as the wellspring for much of Cuba's popular culture.

By the 1920s, an extended network of brothels managed by Cuban pimps was operative primarily in Havana and Santiago, as well as around the U.S. military base in Guantanamo. Those pimps employed poor Cuban women (black and white), as well as many dancers and actresses. At the other end of the social spectrum were the many high class Havana salons featuring French and Spanish hookers which were run by Europeans. With tourism emerging as the island's second largest industry in the 1940s, and the Mafia's takeover of major hotels and casinos in the capitol by the mid-1950s, prostitution connected with Havana's infamous night life was firmly entrenched. It was that demi-monde that gave Cuba an international reputation as a whorehouse for visiting Americans and former Cuban dictator Fulgencio Batista's cronies.

Fidel Castro had promised to change that—one of the first moves by the revolutionary government nearly forty years ago was to reeducate the hundreds of Cuban prostitutes who had serviced the island's foreign and home-grown elite. The government then provided them with jobs as clerks, bus drivers, and waitresses. Their "liberation" from sex work was touted as evidence that the Revolution had eradicated the corruption and immorality associated with capitalism. Indeed Fidel Castro's public image as a benevolent savior was substantially enhanced by the sympathy he expressed toward these supposedly "fallen" women. By the standards of today's pro-regulation sex work activists, such a position would be interpreted as extremely paternalistic. Nonetheless, for many supporters of the Revolution, as well as for the exiled opposition, the reemergence of prostitution is the ultimate sign of the system having failed Cuban women.

The truth, however, is that *jineteras* emerged in Cuba long before most of the Revolution's supporters suspect. When I started visiting the island over a decade ago, it wasn't unusual to find a few well-dressed young women circulating in hotel cabarets, at festivals and embassy functions. All my Cuban friends would warn me to be careful around them, they were sex workers operating with the approval of the Ministry of the Interior, who would report on exchanges with foreigners in exchange for immunity. The two men I was filming a documentary with in Havana in 1986, for example, were offered a package deal of two women and a gram of cocaine by a pimp hovering around our hotel bar. We took it as an indication that we were being followed by the state security. And before the current wave of prostitution that has made foreign men the main objects of desire, Cuba went through a phase called *titimania*—in which older men, usually high-ranking members of the military or the political machine, would play the role of sugar daddy to younger women who served as trophy mistresses.

Since the bottom fell out of the Cuban economy in the early nineties, however, the tourist industry has become the country's main source of hard currency. The Cuban Ministry of Tourism claims that 750,000 people visited the island in 1995, up from 640,000 the year before, and it projects 1,000,000 tourists for the year 2000. Among these visitors are planeloads of men from Spain, Italy, Germany, Canada and the United States, whose buying power and social status is multiplied tenfold upon arrival in a cash-starved country. "Pussy Paradise" as Cuba is now called over the Internet is a place where these men can act on their fantasies without any threat of police intervention—not unlike multinationals looking for cheap unregulated labor across the border. Once there, they meet up with Cuban women who are looking for dollars, a good time, and very often, a ticket out of the country. It's no secret that many Cubans see the *pepes* (foreign johns) as replacements for a paternalist government that can no longer provide for them. One of the top salsa hits on the island, when I arrived in 1996, called on Cuban women to find a "papiriqui con mucho juaniquiqui"—a sugar daddy.

Jineterismo **Today**

As the Cuban economy totters on the brink of ruin brought about by the withdrawal of Soviet subsidy and the U.S. trade embargo, the number of women offering themselves as temporary partners or potential wives to foreigners escalates. When this last wave began in 1993, a substantial number of the women were white, but as client demand has grown for Cubans whose appearance corresponds to the tropicalist cliche, women of color have become the majority, which is also attributable to their generally being poorer than the mostly *criollo* elite. A sizable number of the *jineteras* are minors, and the majority of them these days have no direct connection to any state enterprise. Some women work on the their own while others, particularly the young ones from the provinces, are managed by *chulos*, or pimps. From the salsa singers, the cab drivers' quips and the bawdy folk art renderings of *jineteras* I encountered around Havana, I got the sense that on the street these women are perceived as heroic providers whose mythical sexual power is showing up the failures of an ailing macho regime. As Paco, a young hustler I met in La Habana Vieja, explained, "Everything is upside down now. The men are at home with aprons cooking and taking care of the kids, while their wives are on the street working."

The more affluent Cubans tend to be outraged about the rising tide of *jineteras* for politically motivated reasons. In January 1996, after being pressured by Brothers to the Rescue leader Jorge Basulto, Miami pop star Willie Chirino pulled off the air a music video produced for his hit song, *Eva la Jinetera*. Chirino removed scenes in which he appears to be touching *jineteras* while dancing with them. The official explanation given by Chirino and his producers Sony was that flirtatious physical contact with *jineteras* might imply that the singer condoned the women's lifestyle, an attitude which the Miami right interpreted as too soft on Castro. Some other Cubans, however, tend to be more concerned with the potential for exploitation, likening the *jineteras'* situation with that of prostitutes in other sex tourism hot spots such as Bangkok and Manila. Cuban friends exiled in Barcelona were indignant when they explained to me last spring that the latest Christmas bonus for Spanish executives was a trip to Varadero Beach with an "escort" waiting at the airport, a story made more credible by a *Miami Herald* report last year claiming that a Spanish businessman had set up an agency specializing in such matchmaking. Upon coming back from visits to the island, other Cuban friends had told me that some families were practically selling their daughters to prospective foreign husbands as a way either to ensure a constant source of hard currency or to eventually get themselves out of the country.

To get to any sort of truth though about Cuban *jineteras*, you have to plow through the myths that make any discussion of mulatas, tourism and prostitution in Cuba so incredibly complicated. Throughout Cuba's history the *mulata* has stood for illicit sex—stemming from the reality that from colonial times onward, many mixed race women were the "love children" and mistresses of white men. According to the old adage of the Caribbean plantation, white women were for marrying, black women were for work and *mulatas* were for sex. That legacy, told and retold through scores of songs, poems and novels made the mulata a national symbol that the country's tourism campaigns simply take advantage of. Even though not all of today's *jineteras* are actually mulata (although demographics indicate that Cuba's youth are majority mixed race due to greater population growth among people of color and higher immigration rate among whites), the stereotype still carries enormous power, so much so that to engage in sex work practically means to assume a mulata identity by association.

The current wave of attention to *jineteras* also obscures the fact that Cubans aren't the only ones who have turned to sex work when their country's economy faltered—or when, as in certain Asian countries, as capitalism develops in some sectors, the need for dollars grows faster than there are legal jobs available to provide them. Sex tourism thrives in other parts of the Caribbean, but on other islands such as Jamaica, the sex workers are predominantly male. In Eastern Europe, similar economic crises to Cuba's have prompted many women to make drastic career changes, moving into exotic dancing and prostitution at home and abroad.

Sexual Freedoms

Images of Cuba's past flickered through my mind as I watched the current *jineteras* in action. Having something of an insider's perspective kept me from jumping to easy conclusions. My mother is a tough-as-nails doctor, who is also, like many of the *jineteras* of the 1990s, a mulata from the Southwestern province of Oriente. She set out for the capital in the 1940s, worked her way through school, then left the island in the 1950s. Eventually she married a foreigner to stay out for good, sensing she could never have the life she wanted in her homeland. She also instilled in me a healthy degree of skepticism about what Cubans with power say about their country, wherever they might be. I thus acquired a special distaste for the hypocrisy of the Miami extremists who throughout my adolescence ranted about freedom from tyranny while thrusting repressive Catholic morality, complete with chaperons, virginity cults, and unquestioning acceptance of male dominance, on their daughters.

Because I was used to seeing such an extreme form of patriarchal control in Cuban exile households, I was duly impressed by the much more relaxed attitudes towards sexual assertiveness among women that I encountered when I first visited post-revolutionary Cuba. The stigmas attached to women having an active sex life before or outside marriage had diminished considerably among people of my generation. More than thirty years of free birth control, sex education, co-ed boarding schools and a social system that reduced parental control laid the groundwork for this increased permissiveness, and set the island apart from most other Latin American countries, not to mention most Cuban exile communities. Not only that, but attitudes toward sex became somewhat more liberal. In a country where consumer pleasures were few and far between, casual sex had become the most desirable leisure activity for the younger generations on the island. In addition, Cuban intellectuals I have spoken to who are attempting to evaluate the meaning of the increasing openness about extra-marital sex—including gay, lesbian and bisexual activity—have interpreted it as an unspoken revolt against both the socialist emphasis on productive labor and the revolution's puritanical morality.

What Cuba's current situation brings into relief is the connection between sexual freedom and affluence. That a tropical socialist utopia that became famous as a site of sexual liberation in the 1980s would be transformed into a impoverished island ripe for sexual exploitation in the 1990s is just one of the more painful indicators of what is means for Cuba to be reentering a global post-industrial economy. At the heart of Cuba's current transition from state social-ism to a mixed economy lie thorny questions about the state's authority to intervene in the private choices of adult women .

Into the Nightlife

I decided to hit the streets in La Habana Vieja to get the perspective of prostitutes who were in the business long before the recent explosion. Nestled around the Havana port area, La Habana Vieja is the most heavily touristed neighborhood of the city. It happens to be one of its poorest neighborhoods, and is famous for illegal activity. By the time I reached the Plaza de la Catedral, with its bustling craft market, a mischievous looking street hustler had latched on to me. Paco was a thin, small framed twenty-four-year-old mulato with short hair, crisply ironed jeans and imitation Ray Bans. We strolled past the cathedral towards the Malecon, Havana's waterfront boulevard that wraps around half the city. Even-tually, he agreed to introduce me to two women, Helen and Margarita, both in their late twenties, and both of whom had been working the streets of La Habana Vieja for over ten years. Margarita had a young son whom she sup-ported, while Helen lived alone.

When they first started, Margarita explained, their main clients were mer-chant marines and foreign technicians. At that time, dollar possession was ille-gal, so they would hide their money in their vaginas and get visiting African stu-dents to buy consumer goods for them in the dollar shops. They were careful not to be too ostentatious so as not encourage envy that might lead someone to inform on them. They were lucky and had never been arrested, but they had friends in jail. They said at least two thirds of the young women in the barrio were *jineteras*. When I asked what the men in the neighborhood think about it, they both laughed. "They see the *gallego* (Spaniard) coming in with a girl, and they don't see him," says Helen. "They see a chicken, beans, rice—a full fridge."

What did come across clearly in our conversation was these women's sense of what constitutes fairness in dealings with clients, and their willingness to defend their sense of their own rights as women providing a service. "The guys some-times show up with bags of bras and underwear, thinking that's enough to get us into bed," said Helen with a smirk. "There are a lot more younger guys com-ing now, and they try to tell you it's for *amore, amore.*"

Sensing that I was dealing with sophisticated traffickers in fantasy as much as sex, I asked them to classify their clientele according to tastes. Helen and Margarita leaned towards me, as if we are high schoolers engaging in juicy gossip. "Look, the Italians are the ones coming here most now, and they like *tortilleria* (lesbian sex)," they began. "The Mexicans used to come a lot, but since the peso devaluation they don't show up that much anymore. They used to ask for marathon sessions of oral sex. It was awful!" exclaimed Margarita. "The Spaniards tend to be older," Helen added. "Some of them just want to talk. Others want to come and live with us for a while. I used to bring guys home with me for a week at a time. They loved it, and didn't mind the blackouts and water shortages. They'd show me pictures of their wives. Now though, most guys want a different girl every night."

I told them about the image of *jineteras* outside the island, that they are often described as brash tarts with bleached blond hair and stretch pants. Helen was wearing a white sweater, loose fitting white pants and a tan jacket, with a little white cap. Margarita had on jeans, a light blue pullover and plastic earrings. Neither of them had colored their hair. If anything, explained Margarita, "the natural look is back. Even the white girls are perming their hair so they look more like mulatas." Both acknowledged that styles cater to client tastes. "The Spaniards really like black girls with braids, so all the *negritas* are wearing their hair like that now. The Italians like mulatas with wild hair."

What about the possible dangers? The only case of violence they could think of was the 1993 case of a *jinetera* who was impaled on a mop by a European tourist who then threw her body from the balcony of one of the hotels in the Vedado. Of course, the murderer was out of the country before the *jinetera*'s body was found. Health risks? Helen and Margarita immediately answered that they insisted on condoms, and that health was the one thing that the government still had under control. Knowing about the declining conditions in Cuba's hospitals, and chronic shortages of medicine, I wondered if they were not just convincing themselves that the old revolutionary promises still worked just to ward off fears. No one I spoke to throughout my entire trip wanted to accept the idea that an STD epidemic, including but not limited to AIDS was in the making, which seemed to me an almost criminal oversight.

When I asked them if they ever thought about getting out of the business, Helen told me a story that perfectly illustrated the dilemmas facing Cuban women who've been socialized to believe in their equality but who now face an extremely polarized world that leaves them little room to maneuver in. "I got married once," she confessed with a wry smile. "But it didn't work. I thought I'd go to Spain and start a new life. I thought I would work, and that we would live together. But he was nuts, crazy," she continued. "He wanted to keep me at home all day. He wouldn't let me work or go out. I lasted two months, and then

I realized that I had to get out. I sat him down with his mother and explained. I had no money, and no place to go, so I had to come back here. He's so mad that he won't even give me a divorce now because he says it's too expensive." Both Margarita and Helen knew that some *jineteras* triumphed in Europe, but that others were stuck in awful situations, and forced by pimps to work long hours seven days a week. At least in Cuba, they could survive working a few times a month.

Race, Class and Gender Biases

In search of more upscale *jinetera* action, I grabbed a cab one night with a Cuban journalist friend named Magaly and headed out for the disco at El Comodoro, a hotel wedged between the embassies and Party officials' homes of the swanky Miramar district. The Havana Club disco at the Hotel Comodoro is the capital's most famous den of iniquity. Being there is like taking a trip out of Cuba to a teeny bopper club in Rome or Madrid. It's a labyrinth of chrome and vinyl, with Europop dance music blaring so loud I got hoarse from trying to have a conversation. We stood at the railing of the sunken round dance floor, while Magaly showed me how the girls positioned themselves in full view while they danced so they could attract a *pepe*. These were the five star *jineteras*, Magaly explained, they could afford to pay their own way into the club. The men tended to look a little older than those on the street, which I attributed to the high cost of entry and drinks, and the steeper prices charged by many of the *jineteras*. Magaly and I walked over to one of the bars where a dozen overweight, middle-aged men were having have their heads massaged by teenagers.

I was wrestling with what I saw, asking myself what, if any, difference there was between this scene and the action inside any downtown chic club in New York, where dark-skinned girls are also all the rage. The fact that sex work was the best way for many young women to make a living in Cuba, I silently acknowledged, made the stakes quite different than in a place where other viable job options abound. On the other hand, the negative factors associated with working class prostitution in places like New York—its association with drugs and drug addiction, for example, or the stigmatization of the women involved—seemed to be less of a problem in the Cuban context.

What irks me as I discuss *jineteras* with many privileged Cubans, however, is the snobbery that too many Cubans indulge in over this issue. No one I talk to takes into account that most Cubans, *jineteras* or not, always expect foreigners to pay the bills when they are in dollars, a habit that comes from years of not having had legal access to them. And few Cubans seem willing to see a parallel between the *jineteras* and the many artists, musicians, and professionals with exportable skills who are also looking for opportunities to socialize with—and occasionally have sex with—foreigners to secure invitations abroad and even foreign jobs, not to mention to enjoy the best of Havana's nightlife. When Cuban men do it, or when women involved are part of the elite, everyone looks the other way. It's the poorer, non-white women who always take the heat. I'm convinced that much of the fuss over the *jineteras* reveals certain biases regarding race, class and gender that Cubans have not shed. One of the most glaring aspects of Cuban's re-insertion into the capitalist orbit is the way in which racial divisions have become more apparent. Cuban blacks are far less likely than whites to have wealthy relatives sending dollars from abroad, a factor that has played heavily in their disproportionate involvement in illegal activity. Now that tourism is the main source of hard currency, the state is less invested in an image of itself as a modern industrial nation, and instead showcases "traditional" Afro-Cuban religious rituals and art, "traditional" Afro-Cuban music and of course, Afro-Cuban women. Those are the sorts of tropicalist clichés that used to drive many upwardly mobile Cubans up the wall. The prospect of developing a modern society with a diversified economy was linked in the minds of many with no longer having to service first world desires for exotica. Ironically, Cuban economic decline has led to a situation in which those who represent marginality within the Cuban system are quickly becoming the island's nouveau riche.

The current obsession with controlling the *jineteras*, I believe, is linked to deeply rooted cultural attitudes about sex between black women and white men. Most of the black Cuban women I know who are involved with white men are with foreigners, whether they are *jineteras* or not. This not unrelated to the fact that white Cuban men would rarely even consider marrying black Cuban women, due in part to a colonial history that marked them "for sex only." It's also due to folk wisdom that has circulated for ages among black Cuban women that European men's fascination with us as exotic objects was a better, safer basis for a marriage than the options offered by black Cuban men. Liaisons with Europeans, whether they culminated in marriage or not, implied more economic security and social status than did relations with other Cubans. The fact that black and *mulata jineteras* are succeeding in marrying Europeans at an unusually high rate also makes these women the objects of envy in a country where many people are using every means possible to emigrate. The more affluent, and mostly white sectors of the female population are not accustomed to such steep competition over foreigners, and often resort to moralizing rhetoric as a mask for their resentment. A black Cuban artist who married a white American years ago endured endless harassment from her compatriots, who simply wouldn't believe she wasn't a *jinetera*. The only Cuban *mulata* I know who is married to a white Cuban is an actress who was mistaken for a *jinetera* when they tried to rent a hotel room in Varadero last year. "The guards kept saying that they had seen me before," she told me. "I had to explain to them that they recognized me from TV, not police records."

Other Latinos reject the *jineteras* strictly out of Catholic-inflected prudery. In the summer of 1995, for example, *The Miami Herald* ran a hilarious report on touring troupes of Cuban nightclub dancers. According to journalist Andres Oppenheimer, the dancers' brazen sexual behavior was luring many of the wealthiest men in Merida, the capital of Yucatan, away from their wives. The ladies of Merida took to the streets to protest the disintegration of the Mexican family at the hands of the Cuban *mulatas*, who, they claimed, were turning tricks after every show.

Changing Climates

In the months before I left for Cuba, I periodically picked up stories in the news about a Cuban "crusade" against *jineteras*. This signaled a drastic change in attitude. In 1992, Fidel had commented somewhat cynically that Cuban women were *jineteras* not out of need, but because they liked sex, and that they were among the healthiest and best educated hookers in the business. This famous speech was interpreted by many Cuba-watchers as a cynical invitation to male tourists to take advantage of the sexual prowess of the Revolution's children. Three years later I found Federation of Cuban Women leader Vilma Espin denouncing *jineteras* as decadent trash whose parents had lost control of them.

Seconding her position during a press conference last December, Deputy Tourism Minister Miguel Bruguera announced that Cuba "rejected" prostitution, and sought instead to promote "healthy, family tourism." These recent pronouncements spearheaded an offensive that included police sweeps of key areas, stiffer penalties for prostitutes, and a crackdown on hotel guards who had been accepting bribes from tourists. In Varadero, I heard rumors of work camps nearby where many jailed prostitutes were supposedly being sent, which reminded me somewhat chillingly of the camps that held homosexuals, hippies and other social outcasts in the mid-1960s. While these moves might suggest that the Cuban government was acting on the same revolutionary principles that informed its 1959 campaign to save prostitutes' souls, they seemed to be more directly the result of accusations from exiled opposition leaders that the Cuban government had been encouraging prostitution for years to lure tourists. At the Havana Club nightclub, when I checked my bag, a guard took it, saying that picture-taking had been banned due to "negative publicity outside the country." I added that comment to my mental list of Cuban government moves that show how saving face means more than protecting the women involved.

Such inconsistencies in the Cuba's position on prostitution were also noted by international women's rights experts who gathered at the United Nations last January to discuss the situation of Cuban women with Yolanda Ferrer Gomez, Secretary General of the Federation of Cuban Women and a member of the Cuban Communist Party's Central Committee. Ferrer Gomez referred back to the official line at the meeting, stating that prostitution had resurfaced due to a growth in tourism, that it involved a minority of young women who were healthy and highly educated, that the women involved were not doing it to survive but simply to buy luxury goods, but that their activity represented a health risk and that it was linked with crime and drugs.

Were I convinced that the Cuban government was seriously concerned about the well-being of teenagers engaging in sex work, I would actually be impressed. The government's exaggeratedly moralistic rhetoric masks more significant economic concerns as much in the case of the *jineteras* as it has for other freelancers in Cuba in the past. In the early 1980s, for example, Fidel Castro denounced peasant farmers when they started to prosper in private markets, and then a few years later lambasted artists who did well selling their work without state intermediaries. Whenever an authorized private practice gets big enough to threaten the state's control over the economy, the government launches a clean-up campaign, and many people land in jail, often stuck there even after laws change.

These days Cuba's emerging class of self-employed vendors, beauticians, cab drivers and private restauranteurs are having their profits taxed heavily by the Cuban government. Most of those new fangled petty capitalists, incidentally, used to be engineers, architects, and economists, but can no longer make a living in their professions; *jineteras* aren't the only Cubans who've switched careers. However, freelance *jineteras* don't pay dues to the state—they are part of an illegal economy that also includes chulos and the homeowners renting rooms to them. Thousands of dollars of bribes pass among chulos, *jineteras* and cops and hotel guards each day. That underground economy is hedging in on a tourist industry run primarily by the Cuban Armed Forces and the Ministry of the Interior.

"What bothers the government now isn't that women are selling themselves," explained political scientist Maria de los Angeles Torres, an expert on Cuban affairs at DePaul University, "It's that the business is now out of their hands. The state has been directly involved in promoting sex tourism for years." Torres recalled that in 1991, when Cubans were supposedly not allowed past hotel lobbies, the Comodoro Hotel offered male guests—for a price—special certificates authorizing those "with intent to marry" to take Cuban women to their rooms. "They are just repressing *jineteras* now while they try to figure out new ways to regulate prostitution and extract profit from it," she asserted.

Indeed, who can and who does profit is the key issue. What one's position is on adult's women's resorting to prostitution in Cuba hinges on the degree to which one can entertain the idea that sex work, even for a woman in a poor Third World country, involves an exchange of benefits, and that it could be a viable option by comparison to other choices available for survival. That the range of profitable activities has dwindled since 1989 is obvious. When Cuba entered its Special Period in 1993 and the country faced the worst food shortages and highest black market rates it had experienced in decades, the choices for those who didn't have relatives abroad who could bail them out narrowed down to two: work in or around tourism and make dollars or make a pittance in pesos and watch your family suffer. Legitimate jobs in hotel construction, maintenance, tourist entertainment and sales were not plentiful enough to satisfy the population's demand for dollars. I remember a conversation I had in 1993 with the granddaughter of a respected but humble *santero* (priest of an Afro-Cuban religion in Regla). Walking me to a nearby bustop, she burst into tears when she told me that all the female coworkers at her office were turning tricks after hours. "You see my daughter and my grandparents, how thin they are, Coco," she cried. "But I just can't do it. I think about it, but I can't."

While the hardship that led many women to take up sex work is real, the frequently invoked image of the *jinetera* who's selling herself for a pound of meat doesn't explain the range of motivations for the women and men involved. The desire among the populace for the kind of nonproductive leisure and pleasurable consumerism that the Revolutionary government had once linked with capitalist corruption is another extremely important and explosive factor. When the Cuban government began to stimulate tourism in the early 1980s, it created a world of consumer pleasures inside Cuba that was off-limits to most of the citizenry. Area Dolares, as it was called, reminded more than a few Cubans of de facto race and class segregation that restricted their use of clubs and beaches prior to 1959. It generated enormous resentment in a mostly working class populace who watched the same government that would pontificate to them about nationalism and the Socialist work ethic offer pleasure, leisure and the finest resources of the country to visiting capitalists with bucks and the Party elite.

The Union of Communist Youth tried to stem the growing tide of disenchantment among Cuba's under twenty-five majority during the early 1990s with street parties and rock concerts. But those sporadic activities can't compare with the mobility and lifestyle many adolescent *jineteros* and *jineteras* can buy with the dollars they make. The legalization of dollars possession in 1994 further facilitated these youths' access to "el hi-life", offering them respite from power shortages, overcrowded housing, interminable lines, and lousy TV fare. "What would I do with a Cuban boyfriend on a Saturday night?" a *jinetera* asked me rhetorically while we shared a drink one afternoon. "Wait for a bus for two hours, and then go home to an apartment with no privacy. These guys might be old and gross, but at least when I'm with them, I sit in a nice place with air-conditioning, listen to good music, and have a real drink. That helps me forget about bad breath and a big belly."

The Younger Generation

All the adult pimps and *jineteras* I interviewed noted the marked rise in tourist demand for adolescents and even children, and most sex workers I spoke to agreed that this was alarming. When I first met Paco, I asked him about the rise in demand for child prostitutes. A recent client from the Dominican Republic, he said, offered $2,000 for a girl under fourteen, "without a scratch" to work in a brothel there. He also mentioned that some arriving Europeans were using lollipops to bribe kids into performing oral sex.

On a windy Sunday night, I went out on my own looking for teenage *jineteras* and decided to pay a visit to the new and very pricey Melia Cohiba Hotel. It's a monstrously oversized high rise building dwarfing the old Hotel Riviera just next to it, full of marble and glass, too many indoor fountains and $400/night rooms. As I approached the door, a guard with a mysterious earphone in one ear gestured for me to stop. I knew what he was thinking, so I told him in my best imitation of gringo Spanglish that I was visiting from America, and he immediately looked embarrassed, whispered an apology and let me through. At the bar in the lobby, I ran into a Chicano academic I had met on the plane the week before. "See those guys," he said to me, pointing at two middle-aged men at the other side of the bar. "They're from Canada. I asked them what kind of work they had come to do here. They laughed. 'Work?' they said. 'We're here for the women. The only thing that bugs us is that they have to go to school in the morning.'" He was visibly disgusted. "This is awful," he said. "I keep thinking about my own daughter."

I stepped outside and spotted two teenagers chatting up a short, fiftyish man in a gray suit. One girl had over-the-knee, spike-heeled leather boots and a peroxide blond Afro. The other was wearing a smoky blue long dress, had long dark unstyled hair and a lot of acne. At one point in their exchange, the man stepped inside. In a flash, three cops descended on the girls, and pulled them over to the other side of the entrance. The ensuing exchange looked calm, and within minutes the cops had let the girls go. I approached them and invited them out to eat. As we made our way through the parking lot, a wild-eyed blond Italian in a Hawaiian shirt and jeans hopped out of a Havanauto rental car. The faux blond, clearly the more assertive one, made plans to meet him—in flawless Italian. I asked her how she learned Italian. "Italian? I speak Italian, French, German, even some English—whatever you want," she exclaimed with pride. Katy and Sussy told me they were eighteen, but they looked about fifteen. They said they had been in the business for four years. They claimed that the clampdown was so tight that most hotel guards wouldn't take the $25 bribes to let a girl upstairs anymore, since the penalty for doing so had been raised to two year's imprisonment. An old vagrancy law has been resurrected and was being used against the *jineteras*, who got three warnings before they faced up to eight years imprisonment, up from four years. Their being underage didn't protect them from such punishment. Katy, the faux blond *mulata*, did most of the talking. I asked her if she was supporting anyone. "We're helping the country!" she told me, reiterating the most common line of those defending the *jineteras'* right to engage in sex work. "I'm too used to this life to give it up," she said. "I'm used to the having money, and I love to go to the clubs."

How much does she charge, I asked. "I won't work for less than $50," she claimed adamantly. "Some girls are ruining things by taking $20 or $30." Katy said she had seen as many as three clients a day. And they both insisted that they went to school, though they didn't see any point to it. I asked Katy if she'd like to leave the country. She explained that regulations didn't permit someone her age to marry and leave. She had visited Italy, where her older sister lived with her Italian husband, and liked it, but decided not to overstay the three-month period her visa permitted. That sister got her started as a *jinetera*. "She told me that she didn't want me to 'become a woman' with a Cuban man who would mistreat me. She found me a nice Italian guy. He spent a month here with me, and then left me $500. He's waiting for me to be old enough for us to get married," she claimed. Between the lines of her story I heard old and new Cuban moralities converging: on the one hand, there was the post-revolutionary pragmatism of strategically planning how to lose one's virginity before marriage, and how to get around Cuban immigration restrictions; on the other, there were the older beliefs that white male foreigners protect women of color from the archetypally controlling, even abusive Caribbean male. I asked the girls what they do with the really old men. Sussy blurted out, "We just have to suck 'em a long time," and then went back to munching on her French fries.

Listening to them, I felt I was watching the saddest part of the Cuban socialism's last chapter—living proof of the island's own nihilistic version of a Generation X without any dreams of a future beyond the next purchase. But my conversation with Katy and Sussy came to abrupt end as a Cuban who was clearly an illegal cab driver pulled up nearby and waved to them to get in the car. That the girls interacted with everyone in the environs of the hotel with an easy familiarity—the guards, the cops, the drivers, and waiters—was yet another indication of the popular sympathy for the *jineteras*, and of a bond among struggling Cubans in many sectors of that society that comes from their shared weariness of excessive state intervention in their lives, as well as of spartan living. I'm not trying to suggest that there isn't something fundamentally wrong with a society in which sex work is the best paying job for women, but the current moves to repress *jineteras* are misguided, wrongheaded, and nothing if not hypocritical. That doesn't mean I want to forget about the abuses and inequities that are built into sex tourism. It just means that Cuban women deserve more culturally acceptable ways to express their sexuality than a still harshly patriarchal society permits, and that the moralizing of the power brokers—be they prudish liberals, fanatic Catholics or Communist bureaucrats—would concede.

Part Three Sex Workers' Organizations

Introduction

Sex workers' organizations are the heart of the global movement for sex worker's rights as it is through such collectivities that common problems are identified, identities claimed, redefinitions formulated, and strategies for change developed. This section represents just a small part of the organizations that exist worldwide, yet describes some the diversity and specificities in the global sex workers' movement, as well as commonalities between sex workers' positions and resistances across the globe. The majority of these organizations were formed in the 1990s, representing a new wave of global sex workers' rights activity and movements. Writings in this section capture the initial aims, struggles, accomplishments and visions of organizations, in the words of the principle activists.

The Association of Autonomous Female Workers in Ecuador was founded in 1982, and is one of the oldest sex workers' organizations in South America. Ecuador is also one of the few countries in the world where prostitution is state regulated and legal. Run by a group of feminists, health workers and sex workers, the activities of the Association are aimed at improving education, providing health care and vocational training and obtaining credit facilities for sex workers. The group also continually exposes police mistreatment, brutality and corruption, as well as exploitation in the sex industry. As part of this work, the organization called a general sex workers' strike in 1988 to protest conditions in the sex industry. In the 1990s the Association held two national meetings or "Encuentros," for Ecuadorian sex workers. This chapter reflects on the development of the organization, describes the national meetings and takes a critical look at some of the problems it faces. The chapter is a revised version of a letter from the Association published in *Black Light,* the magazine of Red Thread (the sex workers' organization in the Netherlands), in 1993. It has been updated with a report on the national meetings and an interview I did with Tatiana Cordero in July 1996.

SWEETLY (Sex Workers: Encourage, Empower, Trust and Love Yourselves!) is a newly formed sex workers organization in Japan for *fuzuko girls* (female sex workers), *fuzuko boys* (male sex workers) and *fuzuko new half* (transgendered sex workers). Its aims are to empower sex workers, research conditions in the Japanese sex industry and to challenge exploitation and slavery in the industry. The most prominent activities of the group focus on education and AIDS prevention. SWEETLY publishes and circulates "Pro Sex," a small guide booklet for safer sex, and a newsletter, which provide information about sexual harassment, sex workers' rights and physical and mental health. The organization broadly includes prostitutes, dancers and models in the sex industry as well as non-sex worker activists. In this chapter Momocca Momocco, founder of SWEETLY, describes conditions in the sex industry in Japan and outlines her personal history that led to the formation of the organization.

The South African organization, SWEAT (Sex Workers Advocacy and Education Taskforce) is one of the few sex workers' organizations in Africa. Founded in 1994, it is a health and human rights service organization assisting sex workers in health education, psycho-social care, legal and advocacy support and HIV/AIDS and STD education. It seeks to ensure that sex workers' human rights and freedoms are enshrined in the Constitution. This chapter by one of the founders of SWEAT, Shane Petzer, and Gordon. M. Isaacs, describes the emergence of the organization, its activities and its democratic vision for the future of sex workers in South Africa. The chapter highlights the importance of alliances and cooperation between sex workers' organizations and a variety of others concerned with HIV/AIDS, child labor, and gay and lesbian equality.

Started in 1992, the Exotic Dancers' Alliance is one of several organizations for self-identified female exotic dancers that exist in the United States. Based in San Francisco, the collective works towards obtaining adequate working conditions and civil rights within the sex industry. Their primary objective is to support exotic dancers by providing information, referrals and services while advocating sufficient working conditions for the extremely diverse population. For years, exotic dancers have been regarded as second-class citizens and have been subjected to unfair treatment by management. Individual dancers have often complained about intolerable working conditions but have either been suspended or blacklisted as a result of speaking up against management. The Alliance represents a strong unified voice in the struggle to gain civil rights and protection in accordance with the law. It works closely with prostitutes' organizations in California, such as COYOTE and the Sex Workers' Caucus of the Harvey Milk Democratic Club in San Francisco, is linked to the PENet (Prostitution Education Network) web site and collaborates with the Asian Aids Project in San Francisco for outreach and prevention work among Thai, Korean and Vietnamese sex workers in the city. The Alliance also regularly distributes a newsletter among its members and allies. Dawn Passar and Johanna Breyer talked to me about the organization and some of their struggles during an interview in California, January 1996.

Claudia Colimoro is president of a sex industry advocacy association in Mexico City, La Únion Unica, which she founded in 1993 and which has a membership of around 20,000 night-workers. Calling herself "La Mega-Puta de Mexico," Mexico's Mega-Whore, she appears regularly on radio, television, newspapers, university campuses and academic conferences to advocate for the human rights and dignity of those working within the sex industry. She has also worked in the sex industry as a sex worker and manager for over twenty years and is a founder and director of the AIDS organization, Mujeres Por La Salud En Acción. Colimoro has participated in major international sex workers' rights meetings and is a leading voice in the Latin American sex workers' movement. The essay here is excerpted from an interview that she did with Amalia Cabezas in August 1996 in Mexico City. At the time, Colimoro was planning to run for a seat in the Mexican Parliament.

The Mahila Samanwaya Committee is India's first sex workers' organization and is one of the world's largest. Founded in Calcutta in 1994, it quickly grew in strength, size and prominence. By 1997 the number of sex workers in West Bengal associated with the Committee was around 30,000. The Committee's activities have included public rallies against an eviction campaign launched at prostitutes in Tollyganj and against police raids in Sonagachi, as well as protests around the torture of sex workers by local impresarios in Khidderpur. The group has demonstrated against the harassment of sex workers for large contributions demanded from them around Puja time, and has called attention to an unauthorized experiment by a NGO in West Calcutta with an untested AIDS vaccine. It has shown solidarity with others through collecting money and goods for flood victims in West Bengal and celebrating International Women's Day with other women's organizations. Various activities for children of sex workers have also been organized. The committee participates in the Steering Committee meetings for the West Bengal Sexual Health Project and STD/HIV Intervention Program, and is a member of the NGO AIDS Coalition. In April 1996, the Mahila Samanwaya Committee organized its first conference at the University Institute in Calcutta. The aim of the conference was to present the organization to the general public, to highlight legal rights of sex workers, and to protest all forms of oppression against women in the trade. In November 1997, a second conference took place. The essay in this section was one of the first written public statements made by the organizers in 1995, describing their aims and goals.

Cheryl Overs is coordinator of the NWSP (Network for Sex Work Projects), an information exchange and advocacy organization that is based in London, United Kingdom and in Rio de Janeiro, Brazil. The organization was founded in 1991 and today has links and provides services to around forty organizations and projects worldwide. It provides practical information and seeks to raise awareness of the health and welfare needs of sex workers. At regional and global levels, the NWSP advocates for policies and actions which further the human rights of sex workers, develops links between service providers, sex worker organizations and international institutions, and facilitates opportunities for the voices of sex workers to be heard in international forums. It operates a web site and in 1997 published "Making Sex Work Safe,"a practical guide on safe sex work for program managers, policy makers and field workers. This chapter is an interview with Cheryl Overs, founder of the NWSP, who began campaigning for prostitutes' rights in the mid seventies. She established VIC, the Australian Prostitutes Collective, in 1981 which went on to become one of the most active and influential sex workers' organizations in the world, and is now known as the Prostitutes Collective of Victoria (PCV). Since then she has lived in London and Paris working in local services and organizing internationally. This interview was conducted in London in 1995, and reflects on Overs' many years of advocacy work for sex workers' rights.

Khartini Slamah is the national organizer and international spokesperson for transgender sex workers in Malaysia. She is project manager of the sex workers program at the Ikhlas Drop-In Center for transgenders, sex workers and drug-users that was established in 1992 in Kuala Lumper, and is the former secretary of the National Transgender Association. She is both a transgender and an ex-sex worker. This chapter draws from talks she gave at the 1996 International AIDS Conference in Vancouver, and the 1997 International Prostitution Conference in California. In it, she describes the history of the development of transgender

organizations in Malaysia, the problems and discriminations facing transgenders, and some of the reasons for transgenders entering the sex industry.
Clearly, in the Malaysian context, "transgenders" is used to refer exclusively to
male-to-female persons.

The Maxi Linder Association is an independent NGO for sex workers in Suriname. It began in May 1992, with the aim of improving the socioeconomic and
health conditions of female sex workers in Suriname through education,
research, counselling, building solidarity among prostitutes and with other
women's groups, and securing legal rights. The Association was formally
founded in 1994 due to a demand from sex workers for an organization with
which they could identify and from which they could receive support, protection and advice. The Maxi Linder Center, a spacious, bright, two-story house in
downtown Paramaribo, operates as a meeting place, daytime shelter and training center, and opened in January 1995. The Association has also secured a plot
of land from the government for agricultural purposes, enabling the women
to grow food for their own consumption and to sell on the market. Among
its activities, it provides counselling and runs a support group for HIV-positive
sex workers, holds weekly workshops, sewing and cooking classes, has a job
referral system, and provides day-care for children of sex workers. Over 200
street-based sex workers are registered with the Association. In 1996 it became
closely allied with the newly formed national network of women's organizations, Konmakandra (United). The program manager of the organization,
Juanita Altenberg, and former sex worker and senior health educator with the
Association, Dussilly Cannings, talked to board member Judi Reichart and
myself about the Maxi Linder Association and prostitution in Paramaribo in
January 1995.

Kamala Kempadoo

12 The Association of Autonomous Women Workers, Ecuador: "22nd June"

Angelita Abad, Marena Briones, Tatiana Cordero, Rosa Manzo and Marta Marchán

Our organization was set up in 1982, as the first of its kind in Ecuador. In 1987, we acquired official status as an organization, but we have kept our pioneer spirit. Our offices are in Machala, the capital of the El Oro Province in the south of Ecuador. It is an area with approximately 480,000 inhabitants, rich with agricultural and animal produce (bananas, coffee as well as shrimp, etc). The wealth is, however, in the hands of a few, while the majority of the population struggle against poverty and distress. Terrible conditions, such as unemployment, malnutrition, illiteracy, and social violence, are a visible part of our daily reality. In addition, discrimination of women is a daily occurrence, legitimized by habits, traditions, ideologies and laws. We carry the full weight of this crisis on our shoulders. In this disadvantaged and marginalized social position we have to accept that we are the head of the household and therefore that we are responsible for our own survival and that of our children and other family members.

We, sex workers of El Oro, organized ourselves in fourteen districts, in search of mutual support, for self-defense and with the desire to fight for our rights as women and human beings. To date we have held solidarity actions with colleagues. These activities had a cooperative character and were aimed at improving education, credit facilities and vocational training. All of these activities were realized through our own strengths, and we were successful in obtaining some assistance from government departments dealing with health, education and social welfare.

Our most important struggle focussed on the extensive malpractice within the police force and on the exploitation by brothel and club owners. In 1984 we called a strike that gained national attention. We closed down the brothels, cut the telephone lines, padlocked the rooms and made sure that those who profited from our work were unable to do anything during those days, from the boys who fetched water, to the cleaning staff, to the taxi drivers. There was full radio coverage during the strike. Authorities were held hostage in the place where the association operates until the demands were met. Marianna Guevara, then president of the Association, directed the strike. It was a successful struggle that brought us public visibility and a means to end the institutionalized exploitation and violence. But more than that, the fight was an extremely encouraging experience because it made it possible for other sex workers to join us and to decide to follow our example of organization. Various other sex workers' organizations were established after that in all the main provinces in the country. However, it would be wrong to suggest that because of the strike our problems were solved. They continue to exist in a society that is completely against recognizing the prostitute as a woman or as a worker.

In order to continue activities that would strengthen, not only the Association in Machala, but the organization of sex workers in the country, a first national encounter was planned. It was held June 28–29th 1993, as the first meeting of sex workers in the country. It grew out of an awareness within the Association and among its supporters, locally and internationally, and from a need to consolidate efforts in the face of increasing violence in the sex trade. The Encounter was an initiative taken at national level, and was the result of ten years of organizing by Ecuadorian sex workers.

The general aims of the First National Encounter of Ecuadorian Women Sex Workers were varied. In the first instance, it was to facilitate the sharing of experiences, doubts and problems related to the practice of sex work. Secondly, it was a time for reflection upon social, juridical and health conditions under which sex work is done in Ecuador and on the living conditions of female sex workers. Third, it aimed to design strategies to cope with difficulties commonly faced by sex workers, and to urge the rest of society including brothel owners and the government, to recognize the rights of female sex workers. Finally, the Encounter was to set up a national organization in order to have the voice of female sex workers represented in the political arena. The organizing group decided to use the workshop method because of its participatory character and because it was important to create a space in which women could speak and voice their concerns. This would be the first time they would be subjects of their own history and life stories.

Women of the Association went out of their homes, working spaces and cities during the weeks prior to the Encounter to invite other sex workers to the event. Posters and invitations were also distributed to other organizations, women's groups and local authorities. Eight leaders of the Association covered twenty-eight cities of the country and decided to have each province represented by three women, totalling forty-five to represent the whole country. We made this decision to take into account the situation of each province and the finances available.

Women from all over the country arrived in Machala (a southern city) on June 28th. From there we moved to Pasaje, a small town ten minutes away from the conference site. Thirty-four representatives of female sex workers from thirteen different provinces, eight observers, three staff persons and the support committee participated in the Encounter. With the exception of the organization in the Province of Manabi and representatives of Cuenca, all sex workers organizations were present. We learned that the representative from the city of Cuenca could not attend because the women were threatened with death by brothel owners if they participated in the meeting.

Three parallel workshops were held: on health, working conditions and organization. Discussions were held in the workshops of the first day and the morning of the second. These were followed by a plenary session to synthesize the conclusions and to formulate resolutions. Part of the agenda of the meeting was to have social events. On the first evening the founders of the Association and a representative from each province were awarded by their colleagues as symbols of strength and courage. A special party was organized which was designed to respond to the Latin spirit of dance and music as well as to the spirit of the women and to their particular life histories and their struggles. Finally a theatrical performance of "Nosotras, las Señoras Alegres" (We, the Happy Ladies) was given by the actress, Marina Salvatierra of the literary group "The Women of the Attic." "Nosotras, las Senoras Alegres," was the first visible product of the work between the support group and the Association. It reclaimed life histories of the women, their struggles, the struggles of the organization and the, so often disregarded, humanity of the women. The performance was a theater production of the book with the same title, written by Marena Briones, Rosa Manzo, and Tatiana Cordero. The book made no distinction between the people who recuperated the stories and those who it was about. There was no "them/us" distinction, but written in the third-person "nosotras" (we women). It was a way of giving back to the women their own stories, in their own voices. It was a literary expression of the life experiences of women, their feelings, worries, relationships with clients and with loved ones and families, and drew from other writings about prostitutes, such as Jorge Armado's *Therese Batista Cansada de Guerra* (Theresa Batista Home From the Wars) and Alicia Yanez Cossios' *La Casa del Sano Placer*. It recovered the women's oral histories. The Encounter concluded with a number of resolutions and the identification of many issues and needs of sex workers which required attention.

The outcome of the event was beyond our expectations. Not only were the objectives achieved, but most importantly there was an exchange of experiences, a possibility to speak and to share the recognition that one was not alone, that a problem was not one woman's, but ours, and that these problems did not have to do with us as women prostitutes but with the way in which society treats women and hypocritically treats the issue of prostitution. This knowledge brought great courage to the women and strengthened our solidarity. We believe that the evidence that female sex workers continue to be in touch with each other, that the organization became stronger at the national level, and that other sex workers' organizations acquired their legal status, is clear proof of the power and effectiveness of the Encounter.

Quite incredibly, for the first time in the history of treatment of prostitution in the media, all the main television channels and newspapers covered the meeting with respect. They even went to the extent of calling us by the name we have chosen for ourselves "autonomous women workers" instead of "prostitutes." It was our voices that were heard. We spoke for ourselves, and were widely listened to. We spoke about our problems, talked about the Encounter and demanded recognition of our rights.

In short, beyond the objectives of the meeting, women sex workers started to construct themselves as subjects, as actors in their own right, to affirm their existence, and their ideas. On the other hand society was forced to look at sex work and sex workers through a different lens which, without doubt, is beneficial for the raising of consciousness about the issue. The commitment to this process which started at the first Encounter, was to enrich ourselves as women and human beings.

In 1994 a second meeting was held which aimed, on the one hand, to analyze the root causes for women entering into prostitution. On the other hand, it was to try to increase political negotiations and to develop alliances. This time it was held in Cumbaya, a town in a valley on the outskirts of Quito. Once again, women from Manabi and Cuenca could not attend, but the number of organizations had grown, with around seventy participants. The issues were similar to those of the first Encounter—health, commonalities and differences among women and women's work, a view on health from a gender perspective, political platforms, strategies and organization, and the revision of law with regards to the treatment of prostitutes.

Of central importance to this second conference was the creation of a national federation and to address the issues from a gender perspective. Furthermore, the conference outcome and demands were to be presented to health, police and local government authorities and to representatives of the UN system. This was done through a theatrical presentation by the women, which highlighted the violence sex workers faced from public health authorities when they are harassed for their health ID cards, the harassment by owners of sex businesses through certain imposed conditions of work such as alcohol consumption, and harassment by the public health authorities through such things as the genitalization of medical service, delay in provision of care, and the stigmatization that goes together with the provision of health services. The performance also described the violence exercised by school teachers and members of community towards sex workers' families, as well as the kinds of violence experienced in their closest relationships, such as the pressure from a pimp/lover to continue working, to have more clients, or to make their money. An idea that also came out of the meeting was to request land and credit from local authorities to build new brothels which could be controlled and managed by women sex workers.

Despite the enthusiasm and energy that went into the second Encounter, the national federation did not get off the ground. Also a set of problems internal to the organization of sex workers arose, which were not adequately addressed during or after the conference. The main ones were that health providers in Quito, as opposed to sex workers themselves, directed the meetings, that funds within the organizations were not managed well, and that there was a steady reliance on male advisors and consequently a continuous dependency on men. By 1996, a number of stumbling blocks hindered the national strength and organization of sex workers in the country. Firstly, little or no in-depth evaluation of the process had taken place, therefore leaving aside any analysis of the momentum to create a national organization, or how to sustain a long-term project beyond denouncing the existing situation and exploitation in the sex trade. There was no discussion of how to move from a response to conjunctural events to the development of an empowering political agenda and program, or how to combine denunciation with an vision of alternatives and future and to construct a simultaneously re-active and pro-active organization.

Furthermore, the idea to run the brothels ignored very important and critical issues: it was based on an assumption that if women control their own brothels, exploitation would cease to exist and all problems would be solved. Consequently neither financial management nor relationships of power between prostitutes within the new working relationships of mangers/owners of sex businesses and workers were explicitly addressed or discussed, leaving any initiative open to possibilities of mismanagement and continued exploitation of some women in the sex trade.

Nevertheless, even with the failure of the national federation, the lack of success in obtaining land and credit for new brothels, and the absence of critical self-evaluation, the grass-roots and local organizations for and by sex workers remain important and necessary, drawing new members and addressing immediate local problems and concerns. The Association in Machala continues to be strong, and the organization in Guyaquil has grown in size considerably. The struggle against the oppression of women sex workers in Ecuador continues.

13 Japanese Sex Workers

Encourage, Empower, Trust and Love Yourselves!

Momocca Momocco

I was married for six years and taught art for seven years in school. I chose sex work as a way to consider the meaning of being a woman in Japanese society. It is difficult to build relations between men and women because of the influence of gender dynamics. I wanted to know how I felt when I sold sex, and what and how men as customers feel. Of course, there are instances of men selling sex to women and men as well. I can only speak about women selling sex to men in Japan because that is my own experience.

The Structure of the Sex Industry in Japan

The Prostitution Prevention Law in Japan prohibits direct sexual intercourse for money, so other forms of sexual services have developed. For example, in the sex bar "Pink Salon" sexual service consists of a blow job and a hand job, in the "Fashion Massage" the service consists of giving fellatio and receiving cunnilingus. "Soap land" is equipped with a bath tub next to a bed, and sexual intercourse is part of the service even though it is illegal. Other types of sex work include S&M services, telephone sex and fantasy costume play services. There are also escort services, in which a woman travels to the customer's hotel or home to give a "sexual massage."

I worked in the "Pink Salon" for three months. The working hours were from eleven in the morning to five in the afternoon or from five until midnight. I had from three to eight customers a day. The bar charged 7,000 Yen (approximately $60) for a half hour with hand job, 12,000 Yen for forty-five minutes with a hand job and oral sex, and 15,000 Yen for sixty minutes with the same service plus a bottle of cheap brandy. In the "Date Club" I had two to five customers a night, and 25,000 Yen was paid for every seventy minutes. At my current workplace I work eight hours a day, from four in the afternoon until midnight. For thirty minutes the charge is 12,000 Yen and for one hour it is 20,000 Yen.

There are a lot of workplaces with tougher conditions and where women have more than ten customers a day. It depends on the workplace, but in general sex workers receive forty to sixty percent of the fees. Our income seems high, but it's not, because we are obliged to stay inside the workplace even if there isn't a customer. If we work hard, we earn more, like in any other job.

In all the salons, the girl with the most sales is called No. 1, the one with the second highest, No. 2, and so on. While working at the "Pink Salon" I gradually learned that No. 1 was also the mistress of the boss, and No. 2 was the manager's mistress. My sales increased and I became No. 3. At the same time, I found myself in the position of mistress of the submanager. It was surprisingly well-planned. The "Pink Salon" had an atmosphere where anyone would feel mentally damaged. In such a place a woman depends on a man who personally supports her in her private life. It is an extremely regulated workplace with money and power as the dominant principles. I also think the sex that is dealt there is distorted. So I quit.

In my present workplace, which derives from traditional Japanese brothels of the nineteenth century, the manager is a woman and the employees are all women as well. Women working under male managers are subject to the principle of "divide and rule" by management for the sake of profit. In contrast, in my present workplace, despite occasional conflicts, the women have a sense of community. We don't disturb each other's privacy, but privacy is maintained because we respect each other. At the "Pink Salon," women guard their privacy to protect their own profit and position.

While working at the "Pink Salon," I became aware that it was wrong to identify sex workers as disease carriers and as a "high risk group" for HIV. Sex workers know the importance of their sexual organs. They are business tools, just as appearance and communication, and sex workers take good care of all three. My vagina is healthier now than it was before I started sex work. We have to protect our bodies ourselves. This refers to all people. The reaction of customers to condom-use varies. Some think it's a must and have no problem wearing them, others plead not to use them but will eventually accept, and some refuse. With a customer who initially doesn't want to use condoms, I tell him in words and I demonstrate with my behavior that he can be sexually satisfied while using a condom.

Sex Work and Society

Sex work should be regarded as an established form of labor like any other. Any pleasure is now a commodity in society, and sexual pleasure can also be seen as a commodity. By regarding sex work as labor, we'll be able to revitalize non-business sex, to create sex without power imbalances. Forced labor is however, slavery. We should change the social structure that allows forced labor before commenting on forced prostitution. Also, in Japan the border is blurring between professional women and amateurs. Housewives and students can easily get involved in the sex industry as a form of part-time job. It is true that a lot of men in Japan like a sex worker with a "non-professional" image.

Many customers need mental liberation just as much as they need physical liberation through an ejaculation. With a sex worker, they talk about things which nobody in the family or workplace will listen to. Or they can talk about personal things because they are more able to relax with a sex worker than in the front of their colleagues or their wives.

I appreciate my work. Within the restrictions of time and atmosphere, I try my best to offer a desirable and luxurious service. I'm truly happy when a customer says "thank you" when he leaves a room. But I still need courage to speak out like this. I always try to tell my friends about my work, but don't want my parents to find out. I do wonder what my friends will think of me: I wonder if he or she will be upset and I hesitate.

SWEETLY

I became acquainted with some members of the Network of Sex Work Projects (NWSP) when I first spoke out as a Japanese sex worker at the 10th International Conference on AIDS/STD at Yokohama in 1994. Before that, there had been no group organized by sex workers themselves in Japan. Of course there have been some groups of Christians, moralists and reformers who regarded prostitutes as victims and were concerned with "rehabilitation," "remedies" or "salvation." But there was no group or network for sex workers to empower themselves and to help themselves work safely.

In the beginning I did not know how to go about protecting our health—both of mind and body—bettering our legal position, and promoting economic independence and sexual rights. But I was helped by discussing things with Cheryl (in London), Maryann (in Sydney), Jo (in Amsterdam), Noi (in Bangkok) Irene (in Manila) and Priscilla (in New York). I gradually began to formulate some clear ideas and I found collaborators in Japan as well. Finally we started a group. It's called SWEETLY: Sex Workers! Encourage, Empower, Trust and Love Yourselves!. The members of the group include sex workers, dancers, nude models, a lesbian counselor, an acupuncturist, lesbian activists and AIDS activists. Our aims are:

—to make it possible for sex workers to find our own values, dissolve stigmatization within ourselves, and empower ourselves to create out own lives and work;
—to research situations of sex industries in Japan and recognize the difference between sex industries in Japan, other Asian countries and Western countries;
—to find out what we can do against structures of sexual exploitation and sexual slavery.

We are very careful about media coverage of our group because we've just started. We're afraid that inaccurate information about SWEETLY may be circulated by the mass media before we ourselves can hook up with other sex workers. Our main job now is to distribute brochures about HIV/AIDS, STD's, physical and mental health, sexual harassment, sexual rights, private sex etc., and to publish a newsletter. This is information for sex workers in Japan, regardless of nationality, gender or sexuality.

14 The Exotic Dancers Alliance An Interview with Dawn Passar and Johanna Breyer

Kamala Kempadoo

The Spark

Johanna: The main reason for trying to organize women together in 1992 was to look at the working conditions and the situation at hand with regards to the stage fee. The management at the Market Street Cinema had just decided to raise the stage fee from $10 to $20, and there wasn't really any justification for this. Conditions were still the same, the dressing rooms were still substandard, and the customers weren't necessarily being charged any more money. A stage fee, in translation, is just a fee you pay in order to work in the clubs. As an independent contractor the management requires that you pay them a certain percentage of what you make. Usually it ranges from $10–$25. In other states it has gone up to $75 or sometimes $100 per shift. If you work two shifts in one day you pay the stage fee twice. If you don't pay your stage fee, you don't work. So that was really why we started to get people together—to look at why we were paying management this high fee when they were not doing anything in turn for us.

Dawn: I had worked in this industry for around ten years by that time, and I found that there was a lack of a lot of things, such as social support, and other information. In 1982 when I started working at the Mitchell brothers' O'Farrell Theater, we were paid a salary—a minimum wage an hour—and we would report our own tips at the end of the year. It didn't matter how much we made, we would take care of our tax paying at the end of the year. That stopped in 1987. In the city of San Francisco, the Mitchell brothers were the first to implement stage fees, although they didn't call it that at the time. But anyway, they took away the salary, and made the dancers pay.

Johanna: They changed the status of employment so that dancers were no longer employees, but were "independent contractors." I think its very important to tell it from a San Francisco perspective, because that's also how most of the clubs, nationally, are now working.

Dawn: One of the ways the management justified the change in the system was by saying that the business was a "joint venture."

Johanna: Yes, almost like a co-op or joint partnership between the dancers and the management. But we're not receiving any percentage of the customers entrance fee, or anything that the club is generating, so that justification is totally absurd.

Dawn: So we wanted to have a voice of our own. I had been in the business for quite a long time and had heard a lot of things from other dancers and friends. I was frustrated too, at the time. When the stage fee went up from $10 to $20 that just drove us to organize a group and to call for dancer meetings. A hundred percent increase in one year, without improving any working conditions!

The place was in even worse condition than before, but they increased our stage fees. From that increase of $10, they provided us only with filtered water.

Johanna: They gave us water. They said they were going to make changes in the club, improve all the conditions for the dancers, to legitimize what we were paying. But the only thing that really happened was a water filter. We got water!

Dawn: Johanna and I were the main organizers, and we had a lot of support from other dancers who are still working in there. But it was not easy. The nature of the work is that if anyone makes trouble, you get fired. Neither of us were prepared to be fired at the time. Johanna had just finished school and I had just finished an education in Fine Arts. I decided that I was the one who could afford to get fired. So I filed against the club managers.

At first it was Kaya and I as spokespersons—we were out in the press. We can't go back there now. A lot of dancers who organized in the beginning can't dance there anymore. We weren't really "fired." How it operates is that you work from day to day. You call in, for example, at eleven o'clock for the day shift, and you come in at the time you have to dance. After I filed, I kept calling in to get on a shift, and I was told that the shift was full. They kept doing that, so there was nothing that I could contest.

Johanna: They can't really say "you're fired" because that would be indicative of an employer-employee relationship rather than that of an independent contractor. So they came up with these round about ways, saying "the schedule is full" "you called in too late," or "there's a lot of people ahead of you"—all of the excuses they could possibly make.

Dawn: However, once we started filing, we began to do everything at once. We filed with the Equal Employment Opportunity Commission for sexual discrimination and sexual harassment. The case is still pending but they did conduct an investigation and found a lot of suspicious things at the Market Street Cinema.

Johanna: There were incidences of physical and verbal harassment by managers, with myself and Dawn as well as other witnesses that they spoke to. The discrimination factor came into play with the other theater that had opened, which is called Campus Theater—a male club. The male dancers are paid wages or supplemented in some way—they get a salary—whereas women working at the other clubs are not given hourly wages. Yet the clubs are under the same management

Dawn: The Bijou Group, Inc. own a lot of different businesses, several theaters where women dance, a few theaters where men perform, and then other outside businesses, like adult bookstores. It's a big corporation, not just a small operation.

Johanna: They have a monopoly of many of the clubs in San Francisco, so that if the working conditions are such a way in one club, it's indicative of how the other clubs are run.

Dawn: In conjunction with that action, we called the California Occupational Safety and Health Administration, telling them to investigate for occupational safety. Our first victory was to have a door fitted to the dressing room toilet, because the door had been taken out.

Johanna: There was no privacy. There were only these two bathroom stalls where all of these women on two daily shifts come in.

Dawn: Eighty or more dancers per day.

Johanna: So that's why we also called the fire department, to see what the maximum occupancy was. The management wasn't really upholding a lot of the conditions that they were supposed to, so it was almost like a snowball effect once we put out the initial complaints. It was like "wow—they're doing all of these other things wrong," and we started networking with the various government agencies in San Francisco. We really had to knock down some doors because they didn't take it seriously at all, especially because we weren't really legitimate employees.

You know, we were going into offices saying, "we're strippers and we work in this club, the managers are really horrible, and they're not upholding the conditions". Even when we tried to make the complaint with the Labor Commission, we were told that since we weren't employees, we could not even use the agency. Our argument was, "well, that's the problem: we think we are employees and we're not being treated as such, so that's why we're coming to you." All the businesses are licensed, they're set up like that. But there's no protection for the actual workers.

Dawn: Sometimes you are forced to do a love act with a girl. You can't just do a show, you really have to go down and do the real thing, and if you don't you're not scheduled to work next time. It's that kind of thing.

Johanna: Yes, there is coercion on various levels. Generally you are going to be coerced to do something. There are always these conditions that are predetermined for you. So if the level of coercion isn't at the performance level, then its within having to pay a stage fee to work, or having to give up a percentage of the money you make to the manager so that he'll put you on the schedule the next day, or in some cases having to perform sexual acts with the managers to keep your job. The managers are at the top of the pyramid and they hold the key to the business, even though the women are the bread and the butter in the industry. And when you have people who don't have self-advocacy skills, who don't have adequate information about their rights, they are more susceptible to that type of coercion. And it happens all of the time: managers can really see who is a "victim."

Its not like you can bargain with these people. Its not a democracy but very much a dictatorship. And certainly the same type of mentality is running the other clubs too.

Dawn: And the largest population who suffer are young women.

The Dancers

Dawn: They are mostly young women. Some are students, others are single parents, most are Whites and African Americans, some Asians and Latinas. But it's a mixed group—a lot of diversity. A small percentage are retail or restaurant workers. A small number are undocumented. There are a large numbers of young women working. Maybe they're new in town, or trying to work their way through school, or just planning to make a living and they don't know what the situation is or what they are getting themselves into. To be in this kind of work, without any status or support, can really drive you into isolation, until you don't know a way to get out.

Johanna: It is definitely connected to a lack of jobs for young women elsewhere. If you have to go home and put food on the table for your children, in addition maybe to having an unemployed partner, there aren't really a lot of jobs that will give the kind of money that you need, especially living in this city. There's a lack of affordable housing on top of that, and I mean welfare in San Francisco is $345 a month, so if you're not working, if you don't have some type of salaried position, then there really is not a lot you can find for yourself. Where else can you make instant money? Generally people are making at least $100 a shift with dancing.

Dawn: For most, it's their main job—their main source of income. Some may work a shift five days a week, six days a week. Some people work double shifts. The old time for a shift was eight hours, but under the new system it's four to five hours.

Johanna: We're shown these stereotypical images of people working in performance venues, strippers and exotic performers, in the media, television, movies, and they're living this high style life, glamor in Las Vegas or whatever, but its not like that for the majority of the population. It's only a very small percentage of women who actually work at this full time and are able to buy houses, or secure investments for themselves. Its a very, very small proportion.

Dawn: Most likely they live in a hotel, and from day-to-day.

Johanna: Or they're trying to work their way through school, or maybe have a part-time job outside of that. But the stereotype is reflected in the public response. There are ideas such as, "what do you mean that you want to organize? You're making all this money." But that's not necessarily true. Its a fluke if you do. You don't have any stability whatsoever. You don't know what you are going to make from day to day.

Dawn: There are only two clubs in the city that have male dancers, and usually its gay centered. So its men performing for men. These men are a small percentage of the dancers population, but I can guarantee you that their working conditions are very depressing. They have it worse than us. I've heard reports of dirty dressing rooms, needles all over the place—there seems to be a high level of drug use. A couple of years ago, one of the male dancers killed another. Talk about isolation, violence, and drugs.

Building Power and Self-Advocacy Skills

Dawn: Management really plays on the weak, especially the ones who have substance abuse problems, and other economic problems. If they have no other vocational training or skills they are usually unable to leave that work. So management is really mean to those people. The group that has self-advocacy skills and can bargain, can say "hey, you can't treat them like this," and the management will lay off a little bit.

We're here to give people information and referrals to different services, but not to necessarily hold anyone's hand through the process. We want to give exotic dancers the support necessary so that they can stand up for themselves, to say "I think what you're doing is wrong, and I'm not going to stand for it, and this is what I am going to do about it." Johanna and I constantly meet to strategize on different ways to reach out to women and to build a network with other city and government agencies to advocate on our behalf, and take us seriously as workers.

Johanna: We also hold general monthly meetings where there is an exchange of information, so we're keeping other dancers up-to-date about the progress with the different cases, with their legal rights, about access to different services, and giving them the facts about what already is in existence: different labor unions that are around that would possibly support us, about the Labor Commission and what its regulations are as far as the clubs go. And so on.

Dawn: One of the big agencies in the city that does drugs detoxification, family and mental health counselling, just signed a memorandum of understanding with us. If we need their services, dancers can now directly access them, using our name as a referral source.

Johanna: And that's what we're trying to do: to embellish upon those resources that are out there, to formalize agreements and to let the services know who we are. Hopefully there won't be the level of stigmatization that there would have been had the dancers called themselves. We do legitimate social service referrals.

Dawn: Also for vocational training, career changes, transitions, schooling perhaps, information about how to work part time and still dance—things like that.

Johanna: It's a lot of exchange of information. Our meetings almost take the form of a support group. And because the workers are so independent, there's a fountain of different ideas, and views. Sometimes its hard to contain those meetings. We have a lot of stuff coming up, it's not like everyone's focussed on one certain way to work or one particular issue.

Dawn: We do a lot by phone—people call for advice. Having a phone line open so that everyone can call—that's the main thing. People can call and ask when the next meeting is, or talk about something that is happening to them. You know when you do this type of work, you can be very isolated from the rest of the world. If you're focussed on making a living—and some people work double shifts—you can easily get lost. So we try to tell them that even if they can't come to every meeting, they know where to go to get help.

Links between Exotic Dancing, Sex Work and Prostitution

Johanna: The way that I perform, in theory, is sex work. I try to explain this to people. It's an exchange of money for a sexual act, whether you're doing lap dancing or stage performances, prostitution, peep shows, phone sex—it's all the same type of activity. The whole industry doesn't take on the term "sex worker." Sometimes we use the term sex industry, or refer to somebody who works in the sex trade, and many dancers are highly adamant about not being associated with prostitution. I think that's the reason why a lot of women don't necessarily organize together, and why we have these different sub groups within the sex industry. We try to network with many of those different organizations because we think it's important. When you look at it from a worker's perspective, it is all sex work. It doesn't matter if one is legal and one is illegal. Right now its a matter of human rights and making sure that the women who are working in the sex industry are getting the protection that they need. We're all working towards that one obtainable goal, of making sure that we are protected by law.

But still, you really have to be careful about what term you use, because a lot of people don't identify with it. Some identify as an exotic performer, and not a sex worker, even though the work is associated with sex. So, what I was saying before about there being many independent thinkers, that is definitely true in terms of the work they do and how they seem themselves. It's then hard to organize into one concise movement, or towards one concise goal.

Dawn: And for me: if you keep sitting on the guy, and you keep rocking on his lap until he comes to ejaculation—you sort of cross the boundary. Is that prostitution or lap dancing? I mean, you're sitting on a guy's lap, and you use your butt to jerk him off, not your hands. That's still a part of your body. It's a fine line.

Johanna: This type of work has become legalized and the managers are commodifying the actual work that we are doing. They somehow manipulated labor codes or some law so that lap dancing is considered legal entertainment. Anything that falls under the codes of prostitution is illegal and its apparently against the law to do certain types of acts. That's also why a lot of people don't want to be associated with prostitution.

Laws vary from state to state, with regard to nudity and alcohol. Lap dancing doesn't always happen in every club, just topless dancing or nude dancing, where there's no customer contact, where you're hustling drinks.

Dawn: There are places where there's topless dancing, they can serve alcohol in a club and the customer is not allowed to touch you, or must be five feet from you. You know there are certain protocols. Or there's the strip club where the women go totally nude, and there's no alcohol.

Things change too. From my own personal history, I'll give you an example. At first, the Mitchell brother's place used to be just a porn X-rated movie theater. Then it moved to being a strip club. While I was working there, they adopted the "New York Live Stage" from a club in New York. It was where they would have nude dancing on stage and after, the women would go to the audience naked and sit with the customers, who could fondle them and finger them.

Johanna: But the clubs were constantly raided, because it was seen as prostitution.

Dawn: The Mitchell brothers adapted the show from New York because people were making tons of money. They started the trend here on the West Coast. I don't know how long they operated with naked dancers on the guy's laps, but they were busted. However, a San Francisco judge was in the audience when they were busted, so they got away without suffering recourse.

Johanna: So to get around the law, they threw some bikini's on the women. Now its legal.

Dawn: And all it is, is a G-string. You know, it's like dental floss. Just to call it legal!

Johanna: This is also one of the reasons why we really looked at formalizing a plan that encompasses outreach workers going into clubs as well as getting the information to women out on the streets too. Because prostitution and dancing—a lot of sex work—does overlap.

Dawn: The health department or the government social services agencies have not thought about the dancer population, even for issues such as AIDS. They will send an outreach team to the street hooker, but they overlook the clubs. They never investigate whether the women need any condoms or any health information. Its all focussed on the street workers, so dancers are left out.

Johanna: I know a lot of the women who are working in the clubs who may not engage in prostitution outside but are required to do female-to-female love acts. And the information about safe-sex is not there, not accessible for them either, unless they go and get it themselves. So its really about bringing the information to the population, which is the same for any type of outreach work, to any community.

Feminism and Exotic Dancing

Johanna: Some people remark, "How can you consider yourself a feminist if you are perpetuating all of these stigmatizations, and a situation where men are making money off of women?"

Well, I think this view doesn't necessarily take into account the root of the problem. I mean women are working in the industry, and we should be supportive of those women. If they make a choice to do that type of work, we have to respect that. When you chastise them, you're making the conditions even worse. Its not our fault that we live in this patriarchal society, but it is our responsibility to look at the needs of the women who are working. I just don't buy that feminist argument.

Dawn: It's not empowering women by thinking that way. Its just harming them and perpetuating the stereotype even further. Feminists say "you're a victim. I'm going to save you." What we want to do is help women who are currently working in the industry: to make sure that if you decide to be a prostitute or stripper or call-girl, there is help to make sure that you do it right, that you're safe from violence. But to say, "we want to rescue you," and then to send you to do weaving or arts-and-crafts is ridiculous. You know, some women may want to be a doctor, and are working to pay for their education.

Johanna: There is also this notion that the sex industry is the sole cause of acts of violence towards women. And I think when you look at it from that perspective, its a very narrow one. It does not take into consideration that we live in an environment where there is a lot of violence on an everyday basis. It's in the media, the movies, on TV, its everywhere. To isolate it to one particular field is not helping the women who are in that industry. In essence it just chastises and blames the victim. It doesn't get us anywhere. It doesn't solve the problems of violence, it doesn't solve the social problems or anything which contribute to violent acts.

Dawn: Other groups of women look at us as "victims." But prostitutes and dancers are as strong as any other woman, from the inside, and I think we have to encourage people to recognize that, and bring that out, not beat them down.

Johanna: As far as the philosophy of this organization goes, we look at sex work as a legitimate form of work. Women who work in this industry as well as the men, contribute to this society, as tax payers, as consumers, but it's important that people realize why the stigmatization occurs. It s the whole notion of how we consider sex in this society, why we are so conservative about it. All of that is completely reflected in the conditions within the sex industry. The reason why we have to form an organization like this is because people aren't taken seriously as workers yet dancing is the same as any other job that you do. The only difference is that sex is involved. It's not the women themselves, its a direct reflection of the ideologies of a particular country, whatever is happening politically, economically, historically.

So part of what we try to do is not only give this information to the women, but to educate the general public as well. To try to change those philosophies, or at least give people information so they can decide to change it for themselves. Exotic dancing is legitimate work, just like any other main-stream job, and simply because its associated with sex, doesn't mean that it is deviant or different from anything else that other working people do.

Dawn: I can't think of any other organization that has done this for dancers. I am sure many women have tried, but its very difficult to do. However, if we continue to work together as an organized group, we can achieve prosperity and protection as a unified community.

SWEAT The Development and Implementation of a Sex Worker Advocacy and Intervention Program in Post-Apartheid South Africa (with special reference to the western city of Cape Town)

Shane A. Petzer and Gordon M. Issacs

Introduction

South Africa is a heterogeneous, paradoxical and developing country. With a population of forty million people it is a diverse, multi-cultural, multi-racial society. Struggling to emerge from three hundred years of colonialism, racism and decades of apartheid it is nonetheless the economic powerhouse of southern Africa. Despite the miracle of a democratic process and reconstruction, the years of upheaval leave a legacy of political, social, economic, religious and civic inequalities and discrimination. Cape Town is the capital of the Western Cape Province. It consists of rapid urban sprawl, a growing population of three and a half million people, interfaced with existing pre-apartheid townships and squatter camps, middle-class suburbs, semi-rural and rural localities.

In the context of post-apartheid South Africa, SWEAT has emerged as an organization facing both the residues of colonialism and apartheid, and the challenges of a new democracy in a developmental context. This chapter highlights the macro, meso and micro components of a pro-totypical, dynamic sex worker education and advocacy organization located in Cape Town, South Africa. It also describes the development of an appropriate sex work development organization, dealing with a broad range of factors that influence an empowerment program.

The Development of an Education and Advocacy Program

In September 1994, Shane Petzer, a social worker and Ilse Pauw, a clinical psychology intern began consulting with various sectors of the city's diverse sex industry as to the viability of an education and advocacy program. Both were well known in the city sex industry and had a history of professional interventions with sex workers in preceding years, Petzer for his role in establishing a sex worker HIV initiative and Pauw for her research and fieldwork. In November 1994, SWEAT (The Sex Worker Education and Advocacy Taskforce) emerged responding to the need to address HIV/health issues and human rights abuses experienced by people working in the greater metropolitan sex industry.

SWEAT's focus and its vision is situated in the context of legal and civil discrimination and secondly the complicated hierarchy and diversity of the sex worker subculture. This has manifested itself in Cape Town as a microcosm of an equally diverse general population. With this premise the principles directing SWEAT have included accessing broader community issues so that sex work is acknowledged as a legitimate sector of, and alongside other, mainstream sectors of labor and the realities of broader society. SWEAT's aims are also that sex workers themselves will be empowered to access mainstream structures and delivery systems through a deliberate change in the social, legal and political status of sex work as a profession.

In order to understand SWEAT's educational and advocacy role it is important to have some insight into the macro, meso and micro components which have contributed towards SWEAT's intervention methodology. Macro components include inherent racism, a culture of discrimination and a socially negative bias towards prostitution in all its forms. SWEAT on the other hand seeks to situate prostitution within a human and civil rights platform. This has been met with interest in some sectors and opposition in others. However, advocacy in terms of the new Constitution facilitates access towards the debate of decriminalization. Legislation handed down through colonialism and apartheid reflects an anti-sex work position in terms of the South African Sexual Offenses Act 23, of 1957. To date, this criminalization of prostitution still exists in criminal law. Various other legislation in regard to loitering has been used to harass and mitigate against sex workers.

Regarding meso components, SWEAT has been linked to AIDS organizations, medical services, human rights organizations and networks, and sexuality centers, both in the metropolitan area of Cape Town and nationally. So far

SWEAT has received some state and local municipal acknowledgement. In principal the State's perception of its legitimacy is articulated in its partial funding of SWEAT. It is also the only sex worker organization to have representation on the Government AIDS Advisory Committee and is recognized in its participation in other Civic Forums. The organization is also a member of the AIDS Consortium, the National AIDS Council, the Coalition for Lesbian and Gay Equality, the Coalition Against Child Labor and the Network for Sex Work Projects. These are mechanisms for advocacy, service provision and collaboration.

Recognizing that HIV/AIDS and health issues cannot be addressed solely in a developing country through vertical AIDS initiatives, SWEAT has undertaken to locate HIV education and health promotion in the context of development and advocacy. Inequalities in welfare and healthcare delivery systems have done little to change the means by which sex workers are able to access such services. Criminalization, societal stigmatization, police harassment, violence directed towards sex workers, substance abuse and poverty, means that intervention has to be integrated in a holistic program addressing the broad issues in a human rights framework.

There are several micro components. SWEAT, with its full-time coordinators and volunteer fieldwork personnel (sex workers and non-sex workers) have implemented a series of direct service-based interventions. Some of these services are supported by academic research, others are experimental and prototypical and are currently under evaluation. These include safer sex and HIV education integrated into a Life Skills curricula and skills building curricula, a Drop-In Center, a monthly newsletter, direct fieldwork, an extensive condom distribution network, legal advice, training, the establishment of direct sex worker and police liaison forums, and counselling.

Education is conducted in massage parlors, escort agencies and amongst street sex working people, at the SWEAT Drop In Center or in other suitable venues. Workshops using group work methods have proved a viable means of communicating health messages and information on other issues to sex workers. A vibrant Drop In Center was established in September 1995. Weekly Wednesday afternoon activities include meeting the social needs of sex workers (predominantly street women and transgendered workers) and an opportunity for the full-time coordinators to provide counselling services, give advice and provide information. Statements lodging complaints against clients and police are taken at the Drop In Center and handed over to authorities for investigation.

A skills training curriculum has been developed to attract sex workers to the Center for social activities and self development. Workshops have included massage skills training, hair care, manicuring, safer sex and primary health care.

A monthly newsletter, *SWEATnews*, has become a medium for sex workers to voice opinions and write articles. It is a vehicle for health promotion and communication within the sex industry. In addition an "Ugly Mugs" list, a secret list, is distributed by fieldworkers blacklisting dangerous and violent clients.

Regular fieldwork is conducted by volunteers. Volunteers are drawn from the sex working and non-sex working communities. Condoms and various media are distributed. Contacts are made and sustained with key people on the streets and in the agencies. Advice, information and some counselling is done by trained fieldworkers and sex workers are referred to appropriate resources for follow up, assistance and service. Training of mainstream medical healthcare workers, police, legal professionals and mental healthcare personnel forms part of SWEAT's ongoing mission of advocacy for integration and equity. SWEAT collaborates with various organizations in the city referring sex workers to amongst others, the Cape Town Drug Counselling Center, City Hospitals, the Legal Aid Board, sympathetic lawyers and Rape Crisis for assistance. It also facilitated the development of Direct Sex Worker Police Forums in four police precincts. These forums have arisen through fieldwork and the need for appropriate policing of sex workers. Significant success has been recorded with the forums addressing issues of importance to sex workers and in return, with sex workers assisting police in averting crime.

Democracy for Sex Workers

While the debate on sex work (prostitution) is both national and regional in respect of the parliamentary process, prostitutes are one of the most discriminated and marginalized sectors of the South African labor force. SWEAT's position on appropriate law reform in regard to sex work is rooted in a human rights perspective and governed by the World Charter for Prostitutes Rights (ICPR, Amsterdam 1985). In this instance the driving force behind SWEAT's mission is to ensure that the democratic principles enshrined in the new Constitution, namely the freedom of economic activity and freedom of association, are extended to include sex work. SWEAT's intervention thus far has included the formation of a national lobbying network (Decriminalization of Prostitution Network—DECPRO) in January 1996 with a primary emphasis on political lobbying, and has forged a formal link with a national association of progressive lawyers (Lawyers for Human Rights). Of fundamental concern is the ongoing violation of human and civil rights illustrated by violence towards sex workers, dismissive attitudes of police and health care workers and a unique hierarchy of sex work activity that exists in the country. Criminalization has ensured that sex work remains marginalized and without apparent legal redress perpetuates the ongoing struggle experienced by sex workers. SWEAT advocates that the fundamental definition and perceptions of sex work as criminal activity need to be changed.

16   **A World of People** Sex Workers in Mexico

Claudia Colimoro interviewed by Amalia Lucía Cabezas

On Sex Workers' Rights in Mexico

The business is good for us. We earn very well and have flexible hours, that's why we are here. In no other profession can we earn what we do here. I am going to run, I think, for the PRD (Party of the Democratic Revolution) or for the PRI (Institutional Revolutionary Party), it doesn't matter. But there has to be one of us women inside, so that the government will stop seeing us as part of society's negative social factors and so that, once and for all, they come out with a serious law that allows us to pay taxes and gives us rights. We need more than health projects; we need social security, low-income housing, medical assistance, tax rights as any other workers, education, as it says in the constitution. We generate a lot of indirect employment, we are a world of people.

What we need is legislation similar to labor laws. We already have our physical and mental health, but we need social health, to be integrated into society. We must have the opportunity for our trade to be seen by society like any other. We are all asking for respect. We need respect, each one of us.

On Organizations

La Únion Unica was founded in 1993, after there were closures of bars and discos. It is an association that does not distinguish between sex workers and business owners. The workers have to support the business owners, because if we don't, we have no place to work. We have to work closely with the bar owners, to start to sensitize them to our rights. Perhaps we will separate because we don't share the same interests, but, for the first time, we have an association in our country to help in the struggle and to end the closing of businesses. The businesses include hair and beauty salons, massage parlors as well as bars and brothels. We also try to get support for our struggle from men and women who work in the night-life at places like cafeterias, or as taxi drivers and parking attendants. They too, are indirectly part of the sex industry, and benefit from our work.

We have no guarantees in a place where we cannot sign a collective work contract. If you are a sex worker you cannot work on your own terms. There is always someone behind you, to whom you give one half of your earnings. The money that the businesses use for paying bribes to inspectors, or firefighters, could be ours if sex work were legal and we paid taxes.

We run literacy classes for children, and we develop courses on request about alternative kinds of work, such as typing, cosmetology, or sewing. In March 1996, we opened Casa de Mercedes, a shelter for young women who have been raped or sexually abused and become pregnant. The house gives the young women support and a better environment. We work hard to protect women and for basic human rights.

On Sex Work and AIDS

Nine years ago there was no talk of prostitution. We started talking after the HIV/AIDS epidemic. To be able to talk about AIDS, we have to talk about sexuality, and for that you have to talk about prostitution. An organized group is struggling to change the view that we are a high risk group, as we have been labeled since the beginning of AIDS. The risk is not the women who work in the sex trade; the practices are the high risk. We have gone to the press to say that we are sex workers, and that our group is not high risk. Our work is not to buy drugs; it's the same as other *work*. We have had to be very strong and courageous, to be accepted in different social circles. It is not easy for feminists to understand that we are not sexual objects. Instead, our work is like any other—only we do it with our genitals. It has been a very difficult struggle.

On International Sex Work and Organizing

I know that the organizing of sex workers is very attractive. Organizing did not happen until nine years ago, when we started coming out. The first to start organizing sex workers was Gabriela Leite, from Brazil. And in Uruguay, it was Raquel. Then it opened up, like a blossoming. If you go to international forums, we see in every country there is this restlessness. Sex workers want to be recognized, and their sexual work to be well thought of or at least accepted. There are many of us on a global level.

As advocates in the Third World, we have no financial support. There are sociologists, anthropologists and others interested in the different research and education projects. But the sex workers do not benefit. The academics are the ones on the board of directors, not the sexual workers. We need to have a group of academics around. But this does not permit us to advance. They are the ones who go to the congresses, the ones who take the organizations forward. It is a good business for the academics but not for the prostitutes.

17 The Wind of Change Is Whispering at Your Door The Mahila Samanwaya Committee

Minu Pal, Sadhana Mukherji, Madhabi Jaiswal and Bachhu Dutta

"Yet not deemed humans, merely prostitutes
Never men, they are women. . . ."

Times have hardly changed. What existed in ancient times, still persists. The character of the civilized man has not altered. Though born as humans, we are not regarded as such by the gentry. We stay in the midst of society, yet we are outcastes. We are recognized for the business we profess—a trade that has continued since times immemorial. This society and its respected citizens have sustained this trade for their own urges. Yet this profession is neither given its due in society, nor legal recognition. It is very simple to explain the state of affairs. Many tricks are manipulated to conceal the wicked propensities of men. These hapless women are marked as fallen. Our locality is earmarked as a forbidden area so that no questions are asked. There are a hundred and one ways of extortion, even in broad daylight. Local toughs as well as petty officials from police stations claim a share of the earnings of sex workers. They need not filch, a threatening eye is enough—as we are the fallen ones. Midnight looting is legitimate as these are brothels. When we are not even accepted as humans, can we expect to be honored as citizens of this country? The common rights and privileges accorded to every other citizen are not applicable to us.

Self-Deception

Since childhood we have been listening to moral teachings. These teachings do not satiate hunger. An empty stomach feels the pains and cries in agony. A mother cannot bear the cries of a child. No one enters the trade seeking fun and pleasure. We have seen the ugly face of the profession. But can one see the real picture from so high a pedestal? And the tragic glimmer on the face?

The compassionate often come with words of kindliness—to redeem the sex workers. They sprinkle words of morality which end in declaring us as the sinned, waiting to be delivered from the world of sin to remain forever their grateful slaves. This way or that, we are informed that we are fallen and sinful, deserving only their pity and charity. But there is no record of how many fallen women have thus been saved. Even the wise would not attempt to see through the reality of our profession, how deep and intricate are its hazards. Nobody dares to suggest ways and means to ameliorate the profession, for making the lives of the fallen a little bit more worthwhile or to transform the environment of the profession altogether. A hue and cry is raised if a demand is made to legalize the profession—the whole society unites against us. The truth is, no one in his heart of hearts can really endure the idea of a prostitute holding her head high.

Our Caste and Creed

Whether we like it or not, we have been identified and continue to be identified by the same name. We dare not leave this profession and this area, as the stigma of prostitution will accompany us with its innate hatred, contempt and humiliation. Even our children cannot elude the legacy—they are branded as bastards. Imagine the puny little baby in the mother's womb, dreaming about the exquisite world outside. Little does he know that the harsh society is waiting anxiously for his arrival to label him as illegitimate. In this milieu of despair, our profession is our life and death as also our caste and creed. We cannot aspire to differentiate.

Impassive Confines

Most of us cannot recall the hour when we abandoned our beloved homes. We have drifted to this city from the remotest villages—to a nook demarcated as a red-light area. Each of us was confined to a small cubbyhole. We are still there.

Yet we can hardly claim to know one another. In spite of living in the same room and sharing the same profession, we stand isolated. We are afraid to express our joys and sorrows. Hemmed in by high crumbling abodes and narrow alleys, the stagnant air has crippled us mentally. We are not only alienated from the society but also from ourselves. The sex industry is such that interaction among the sex workers is not encouraged. Besides, if we stand united the promoters will have hell to pay.

We Are In the Same Boat, Sister

As the sun sets everyday, we are out on the streets, standing in close proximity to each other, soliciting clients. We are close, but why are we not attempting to remove the barrier amongst ourselves? Can't we change the rules of the game? If we are unable to modify the rules and regulations of the trade, we will never succeed in reaching the outside world.

There is not much variation between the slave trade of yesteryears and the sex trade of today. There is one difference though—the slaves were not marked as sinners, but we are. As a result our struggle is much more complex. We need to consolidate ourselves if we would like emancipation from this inhuman and barbarous trade. Our endeavor is to institute our rights. For long we have lived in terror, it is time we overcame that fear and fought for our rights. We are so many. It is time to unite, and ignore all our trivial differences. It's time for a new chapter to begin.

We Shall Overcome, Certainly

Keeping these perspectives in view, a few of us got together from Calcutta and Howrah to form the "Mahila Samanwaya Committee" or Women's Coordination Committee. The primary aim of the committee is to achieve all round development for sex workers and their families. The attempt will be to participate in all sorts of endeavors at every level of society to attain social dignity, justice and security for the sex workers and their children. We promise to strengthen and reinforce our struggles for financial security. We vow to make our professional environment more humane. This is a contention for life and livelihood. Another objective is to find urgent longstanding solutions to our occupational problems and evolve appropriate strategies. The committee will resist social injustice and persecution faced by us solely due to our profession. It will also deal with the crucial issues of occupational health and hazards. We will engage in social propaganda and other concomitant exercises to exact legal recognition for our profession. We want to live like any other citizen of this country. We do not ask for much, except to be accepted as human beings. We would like to earn a little dignity and self respect that any ordinary citizen should rightfully enjoy. We aspire to life and occupational security.

We plan to undertake large-scale programs to make the general population aware of sex workers and their multifarious problems, and to present the real picture of sex workers lives at various discussions and forums. We aim to organize publicity campaigns to demand legal recognition for our profession, and to agitate for education and jobs for our children. Efforts will be made to provide adequate health care services to all women associated with the trade. We hope to organize a legal support system for the women of this profession and to arrange alternative sources of income for aged sex workers and for those who are unable to sustain this trade any longer for whatever reason. We will resist all maneuvers to evict sex workers in the absence of suitable rehabilitation programs, and oppose all moves that endanger the social security of sex workers and their children. We plan to start adult education and other vocational training schedules for women in the sex trade, and to develop creches and night shelters for the small children of sex workers. We would sincerely like to develop a healthy interaction with all organizations and enthusiastic individuals, irrespective of their political affiliation. We are hoping for empathy and cooperation from others in the implementation of our aims, our objectives and plans.

18 International Activism Jo Doezema Interviews NWSP Coordinator, Cheryl Overs

Q: What has motivated you to stay working on prostitution for close to twenty years ?

Cheryl: My motivation has changed over the years, which is healthy. But it has always been adversarial, which is probably less healthy. Sheer fury at the anti-prostitution laws were the starting point. But probably a more long-lived force has been my frustration at the appalling way in which the women's movement failed on prostitution and other sexuality issues.

Q: Has the doctrine changed?

Cheryl: Everything has changed. The women's movement is no longer the home of the sex workers' rights movement. The happiest time for me was the late eighties and early nineties when HIV/AIDS brought new links with gay men, and Madonna rose and rose. Our small band of sex worker rights activists suddenly had a new political family. Once a pro-sex feminist theory was articulated we even had new supporters from the women's movement who were listening to sex workers for the first time. Young feminists matured with the notion of sex workers rights as a fixed entry on the women's rights agenda. I enjoyed that because I felt exonerated. It had been hurtful, as well as frustrating, that for many years feminist puritans have said that our demands for recognition of sex work as valid work were a product of false consciousness which blurred our perceptions of our damaging experiences as victims of the sex industry!

Q: Surely, though, the influence of anti-sex feminism is still there. We see legislation which criminalizes clients and services which focus on rehabilitating the prostitute.

Cheryl: Yes, but these are well-established features of the traditional conservative agendas. All that happened is that misguided women loaned credence to them for a decade or two by providing a modern, supposedly woman centered, theoretical basis for maintaining oppression of the sex industry. But I'm not sure how much this matters in the wider schema. Anti-sex feminism may be huge in the United States and influential in some parts of Europe but does not vie with religion say for influence on the popular mindset about sex and sex work. Redefining prostitutes from evil women to passive victim is a blip on the historical landscape. It was never going to affect the actual conditions of sex workers. Criminalizing clients is its greatest achievement!

What concerns me far more is that this brand of feminism had an important role in preventing sex workers from organizing and developing their own ideologies and strategies. The female sex workers' rights movement has been most successful where sex workers set the agenda and then carried it out with the help of other activists and advocates, academics, policy makers, service providers, and lawyers. If all those potential allies are busy protesting against pornography, serving on sexual harassment committees and thinking of prostitution as degrading to women, sex workers have little chance of gathering the resources they need to begin defining and fighting for their human rights. It's most worrying where middle-class educated women in developing countries are taking up the old ideas of western puritan feminism. This is expressed in the plethora of anti-slavery and anti-trafficking organizations who posit the prostitute as victim and call for criminal sanctions to stop her working and moving about freely.

These strategies contrast sharply with the letters we constantly receive from sex workers in developing countries (India more than any other) who are doing absolutely amazing political actions—unionizing, getting elected to local government, and raising prices. This is a far cry from the story we hear from women who represent developing countries on the international conference circuit. They portray prostitutes as poor, illiterate, diseased victims, if not outright slaves, from the platforms where sex workers should be. Their views, the space they take up, and the rehabilitation programs they justify serve only to prevent sex workers from furthering their complex and challenging agenda for emancipation in developing countries. Rich women in poor countries should go to the local sex workers and simply offer themselves and their resources. Supporting sex workers to develop into a self advocacy force would be far better than reworking the drivel about sexual slavery that is produced in American "women's studies" departments and exported in a blatant act of cultural imperialism. For activists in developed countries life is perhaps simpler because we still have one agenda item that dominates—law reform.

Q: Should prostitution be completely decriminalized?
Cheryl: Yes. I can see no justification for any criminal law against any aspect of prostitution. I include in that child prostitution, coercion, and so on.

Q: Do you really believe that all the problems of prostitution would disappear in developed countries with the flick of the legislative pen? It may be that the liberal arguments for decriminalization are too optimistic in a cruel world. What would stop exploitation of young people or a proliferation of street prostitution, for example ?
Cheryl: Complete removal of all laws will go most of the way toward solving the problems and the rest is a question of enforcing proper laws appropriately. Of course all the problems can't disappear immediately. In my view the extent to which they will disappear depends on the skills of the bureaucrats who would be responsible for implementing the myriad of regulations which would come into force to regulate the sex industry in place of the ineffective criminal code. The key to that is good consultation with sex workers.

I remember endless meetings when prostitution was being decriminalized in Australia. As representatives of sex workers, we advised everyone from the tax man to the town planning and workers compensation people. There was impressive commitment to finding ways to bring the sex industry into the fold of legitimate commercial activity. The various departments recognized that they needed information about the industry to do their work effectively. If sex workers had been taxed as other employees there would have been all kinds of problems because patterns of work are quite different. We described patterns of work, the agreements with employers, expenses—and they hunted around for a parallel.

"Fruit pickers and sheep shearers" I remember a grey suit exclaiming. He looked up from his little rule book and it fell into place. Sex workers pay by the clients just as sheep shearers pay tax by the sheep and everyone is happy! Or at least as happy as other taxpayers. This is the kind of sensible and thorough approach we need. I use it as an example. It's possible to work through every aspect of the sex industry in this way. All industries have the capacity to exploit, cause nuisance etc. There are no excuses for out-of-control sex industries in rich countries where systems for regulating labor and commerce are highly developed.

Town planning is a particularly important example of how we protect public amenity but it doesn't apply where commercial sex is illegal. Hence cities all over the world struggle with inappropriately located brothels and "street beats." Brothels, like other businesses, should request to have planning permission. Very small business often don't need a planning permit. Large brothels should only be able to operate where other, similar businesses (say a large gymnasium) are allowed. Small operations which generate less traffic and are open for restricted hours could be located more widely. Planners can chose to have businesses grouped together or disallow it. This is the day-to-day stuff of planning.

I never have difficulty working with residents' groups who activate against prostitution in their area. I think that this is because they, like the sex workers who annoy them, are victims of the law that deprives them access to a process which, unlike criminal courts, could actually solve their problems. Residents groups can be great allies in campaigning for law reform.

The central challenge for governments who could reform the law is to make sure that the way is open for a variety of legal workplaces to develop. This means avoiding setting up traps that discourage women from "compliance" as the regulators call it. A case in point is when high taxes apply in legal workplaces but you can escape paying tax by working on the street—or, if permits are so restrictive and expensive, that only very large brothels are viable.

Sex workers need to see tangible benefits if they are to relocate to legal workplaces. They are very realistic and are willing as anyone else to comply with ordinary regulations and laws in exchange for the same rights and benefits. I know a group of streetworkers, who recently petitioned a politician responsible for reviewing the law, telling her that they are keen to work indoors if the law permitted them to. The politician ignored the petition and announced that her inquiry would not recommend legal brothels because there was no evidence that it would have the desired effect of minimizing street prostitution because sex workers would not comply.

Q: So you are opposed to licensing of prostitutes or brothels ?
Cheryl: Those who expound the benefits of licensing do so most often as a public health measure. But the arguments are so flawed that you can only con-

clude that they must not know the epidemiology or etiology of HIV and sexually transmitted diseases. I used to strongly oppose even the idea of licensing but I don't anymore. I am guided entirely by this principle of looking at other industries. That leads me to ask, which other service providers must be licensed—and why?

Activities with innate capacity to be dangerous are subject to strict regulations enforced by licensing—civil aviation, selling drugs and alcohol, and providing medical services. Is there an inherently dangerous aspect of paying for sex, or taking payment for sex, which should and could be minimized by strict regulation and licensing?

The counterproductive nature of mandatory testing for STDs and HIV is well documented. It presumes that it's possible to identify the pathogens and prevent the sex worker from working while she or he is infected. It didn't work in the old days of "lock hospitals" and it certainly couldn't work as an effective public health measure now that we have an untreatable transmissible virus which can't be detected for months.

The immense popularity of the idea is fascinating. It is invariably the first thing people say in support of legalizing sex work. I looked at this a few years back in a study of issues affecting HIV-positive men and women in the sex industry. I interviewed several professional people with accurate knowledge about HIV and found the majority supported the right of people with HIV to have safe sex. But when questioned about HIV-positive women working in the sex industry, their ideas about mutual responsibility changed. Most thought that the state should identify and remove HIV-positive sex workers from the industry. Few could articulate why the act of passing of a note or a credit card from one partner to another, before the sex, changed the respective responsibilities of the fornicators to such an extent. No one could tell me why the idea that you are responsible for protecting your own sexual health by using a condom during encounters with casual partners changed so markedly in their internal ethical systems when the sex in question is paid for rather than offered for free. It was a very interesting insight into the depth of prejudices against sex work. Some of the respondents even commented that they were surprised to discover their own prejudice as we "unpacked" their reasoning.

Several clients and brothel owners quite openly stated that the consumer has a right to expect a "clean girl" for his money. I think they were coming to terms with the question more intelligently than the other respondents. They were at least honest, if morally bankrupt. They spoke of "health clearances." Of course they had no idea that the government and medical establishment is unable to actually guarantee this supply of disease-free women anyway.

Q: What's the best part of being an activist for sex workers rights ?

Cheryl: My mates in the global village. I can't find superlatives for people sex workers' rights activists. I am particularly lucky as an Australian. Australians are among the few sex worker rights activists who have had a degree of success. Now that I work in Britain I am surrounded by pessimists, and there are even more in the United States where the laws get worse rather than better. I have a "can-do" attitude based on my experiences as a law reform activist in Australia. Colleagues in other countries keep going without any past victories or hope on the horizon to spur them on, which I admire tremendously.

19

Transgenders and Sex Work in Malaysia

Khartini Slamah

Organizing Transgenders

Malaysia is located in the Asian Pacific region and has a population of around 21 million. It is a multicultural, multiracial country, made up of Malay, Chinese, Christians, Indians, Sikhs and many others. The main religion is Islam. Today in our country there are an estimated 10,000 transsexuals, around seventy percent of whom are engaged as sex workers, with another twenty percent employed in the wider entertainment sector. "Transsexual" is a common term we use for transgender people whether they have a sex change or not. What we believe is that the person should feel like a woman and should want to become and act like a woman.

The transgender association *Persatuan Mak Nyah Wilayah Persekutuan Kuala Lumpur* was established in 1987. The initiative came from the Director of the Social Welfare Department and various leaders within the transgender community. The government gave the association a temporary permit to operate and a space to organize meetings, talks and other activities. We formed the organization mainly to gather all the transgenders together and to discuss our particular problems and issues.

The response to the association far exceeded our expectations. It was originally established for transgenders who stayed or worked in the federal territory of Kuala Lumpur. However, we soon had between 200 and 300 transgender members from different states of Malaysia, of different religions and cultures. We were from the outset a multiracial organization. Everyone was pleased because it was the first time that transgenders had their own association and their own activities. We held yearly beauty contests and paper doll shows to fund-raise for our activities. Members also gave personal donations to the organization. We elected members to preside over, coordinate and run the association and its sub-committees. Everyone played their role.

By 1986, AIDS was a hot topic in Malaysia. Every major paper in the country published on the issue. Gay men were the first to be identified as the carriers and the persons responsible for the spread of HIV. At that time, transgenders did not have any access to information about AIDS and nothing was done to ensure that the community received this information. Consequently, many transgenders thought that they were not at risk because they were receivers and not givers, and that HIV/AIDS could only be spread by foreigners. Condom usage was very poor and often brothel owners would provide transgender sex workers with low quality or date-expired condoms.

At that time, around seventy-five percent of the transgender community was in sex work, but with the fear of AIDS, this number decreased. Also, frequent police raids forced a large number of transgenders to turn to alternative jobs, such as show girls, and performers at discos, dinners or birthday parties. This kind of work, however, did not bring in enough money to match the high cost of living in the city. So many turned back to sex work on a part-time basis. The welfare department also gave a small grant for the transgender community to start small businesses, such as a florists, salons and food vending.

In 1989, the government banned transgender organizations because of pressure from religious groups and others in society who believed such organizations encouraged more people to become transsexual and to indulge in free sex. Apart from this, our organization suffered from a lack of experience in management—but this did not stop transgender people from getting together.

In 1992, I was introduced to the gay organization, Pink Triangle, by a nurse who had worked with us on the AIDS issue. She told me about the organization and asked whether I would like to become a volunteer and join in with the training about AIDS/HIV that the Pink Triangle was organizing. Without thinking twice I agreed. Eight months later the Pink Triangle, with assistance from a lesbian volunteer from San Francisco, came up with the idea to hold needs assessment studies among the transgender group, gay youth, bisexual men and middle-class men. I was one of the researchers to interview transgenders and bisexual men. Before starting, we had to do a lot of brainstorming about the kind of information we needed to know from the groups. The studies were based on knowledge, attitudes, practice, and beliefs relating to AIDS/HIV issues. I interviewed transsexual and bisexual men. After three months we held focus-group discussions with transsexuals based on the needs assessment studies. It was found that transsexuals wanted a safe space for getting together, medical check-ups, sex reassignments, hormone treatments, breast implants, legal advice and more accurate information about HIV/AIDS. The focus group discussions gave us important information that we could use to design programs for the transgender sex workers community.

In August 1992, the *Ikhlas Drop-In Center* was opened specifically for transgenders, sex workers, and drug users. The objective of the center was HIV/AIDS prevention. In the Transsexuals Program, we did outreach activities in the brothels, streets and homes of the sex workers. *Ikhlas* also conducted in-house training and an HIV/AIDS retreat workshop for the sex workers. The program identified three female sex workers and two transsexuals to make up the outreach team.

Problems Faced by Transgenders

The reasons transgenders get involved in the sex industry are often because they can not find work in the government sector or private businesses not because they do not have the qualifications, but because of their choice of who they want to be. Transgenders feel much more comfortable dressing like a woman while working, but this is not socially accepted and they are often accused for the failure or unacceptability of the business. Not having many employment options, and in order to survive, many become sex workers. Apart from general societal views, transgenders are also often humiliated because of their sexual preference by their families. They are labeled as *sampah,* or rubbish, because of their appearance, and are seen as sex objects for desperate men who want to satisfy their lust. Consequently, many move to big cities or towns to meet other transgenders, so that they can feel safer and have moral support from friends.

On local television, in newspapers and magazines, transgenders are often condemned for what they do. News about transgenders is often juicy and sensational, and is therefore heavily exploited. This creates more pressure from the community. The most recent propaganda is that transgenderism can be easily passed from person to person through telephone contacts or visiting friends at home. Despite this onslaught, some positive articles have more recently been published in newspapers and magazines due to the networking efforts of the Transexual Program staff.

In terms of harassment by the authorities, transgenders' rights are always abused. Section 21 of the Minor Offenses Act states that a person can be arrested for indecent behavior. The police and the courts interpret this to include cross-dressing although this is not listed in the Act. When transgender sex workers are arrested and they plead not guilty, they are given heavy bails of up to RM1000 (approximately $400) when the maximum fine for any other minor offense is RM25 (approximately $10). If sent to jail, their hair is cut short—this is considered a serious disgrace for transgenders. There are also cases where transgenders have been arrested while asleep or having dinner at a food stall, charged with immoral behavior or soliciting. In a rare occasion when a transgender sex worker does report an incident of violence or a murder of a transgender to the police, the authorities are reluctant to take the case. There seems to be an understanding that because we choose to live as transsexuals we should accept any violence inflicted upon us.

Under the Religious Act, based on Islamic law, transgenders can be charged up to RM1000 ($400) for cross-dressing, and religious groups in many states are currently looking for possibilities to enforce the Act against transsexuals who cross-dress. From this religious perspective, transexuality is not accepted and dressing like a woman is considered a sin. This leads to a lot of confusion and personal agony for transsexuals who themselves are Muslim, and often face the dilemma of whether they should undergo a sex change. On the one hand Muslim transgenders strongly feel that they want to become women, but due to the religious intervention or *fatwa* imposed by the rulers conference it is a considered a sin to have a sex change. Those who have made the decision will go to a neighboring country as it is illegal to have a sex change operation in Malaysia, and the costs are exorbitant—around RM 25,000 (approximately $10,000). Most of the transgenders go to neighboring countries such as Singapore, Thailand or Indonesia for an operation. They do not receive any counselling before or after the operation, and this affects them psychologically particularly in coping with their new role. Furthermore, a Muslim transgender who has undergone a sex change and who wants to get married encounters great difficulties. Their documents still carry their male name—Muslim law does not allow same-sex marriage.

Housing is another problem for transgenders. One of the main reasons is that many landlords/landladies shun them and refuse to rent to them just because they are transgender. The sex workers also have difficulties in getting bank loans to purchase their own houses, particularly if the bank finds that they do not have a legal job or income. They are also always placed as a high-risk category by insurance companies. Now that transgenders are organizing and are beginning to take care of themselves and their future needs, they are finding that agencies existing to provide long-term security for other members of society are not open to them.

Transgenders face many problems, especially with the authorities. They face a lot of harassment during police raids or when they go to the government hospitals to get treatment. Before seeing a doctor there are certain procedures that a patient has to go through, such as registration and contact with a nurse before seeing a doctor. Many times transgenders do not even reach the doctor because they are shunned by the front-line people. Due to this, most transsexuals will go to private clinics.

Because of all these experiences and problems that exist in Malaysia, our vision is to upgrade each and every one of the transgenders with health and other information about transsexuality and their rights, and to reach out to other transgenders in other parts of Malaysia. Most of all, we hope that transgenders have equal rights in employment, medical treatment and other benefits with others in society, and without being judged by their appearance. We want just treatment of transgenders as human beings. Nothing more and nothing less.

20

It's Good to Know The Maxi Linder
Association in Suriname

*Dusilley Cannings, Juanita Altenberg,
Judi Reichart, and Kamala Kempadoo*

What are the origins of the Maxi Linder organization?

    Juanita: Some four years ago a public health worker,
Nicaraguan-American Claris B. O'Carroll, began a female
commercial sex workers project with assistance from the
National AIDS Program in Paramaribo. They knew that sex
workers were a high risk group for sexually transmitted diseases (STDs) and AIDS. So they started a project with registered club women. They aimed at the estimated 450 female
sex workers operating from night clubs. They held weekly
workshops for the women in Sranan Tongo, Dutch, Spanish, Portuguese and English and covered a wide range of
health, medical and other issues. Workshops were also held
for club-owners. After a while they wanted to hire the club
workers to reach street workers. That really didn't work out
because the club women don't like to mix with the women
on the street.

    Dusilley: Women in the clubs think they have passed the
street stage, feel as if they are elevated. Once you go to a club,
you have this kind of bias—you think you are better than
the women on the street. The club accommodations are bet-

ter. They have bodyguards to see that advantage is not taken of the women in the clubs, and so on. But the women on the street are exposed to everything—violence, pimps—and most of them don't go to the Dermatological Clinic [a government clinic which also tests for STDs, HIV, and AIDS]. Mostly in street work you find Guyanese and Surinamese women, and most of the Guyanese are here illegally—"backtrack" we call it. They take a small boat from Springlands (the Guyana border town) and get here faster than the normal launch or ferry.

Well, there was a law at the clinic that says you must have a passport or some form of identification before you could be helped for STD control. Many Guyanese didn't have papers and so they weren't going to the clinics for control. Surinamese women were afraid that their families would find out, so they remained in hiding. They were afraid that family members going to the clinic for other purposes would see them. So they didn't go.

The conditions that they work under are also quite terrible. There are forty-five clubs registered with the Dermatological Clinic, and that's not the full amount in Suriname. There are about twenty or thirty something that are not licensed. In the licensed clubs, they know that sometimes the Department of Health sends people to search the place, but with the unlicensed places the government doesn't know that they are actually brothels. So if you go into them, you see them using one sheet in a room for maybe two weeks without changing it. That's the kind of thing that meets the workers of the street. And that's one of the reasons why women in the clubs separate themselves from the street workers.

Juanita: So we needed a different strategy to get in touch with the street workers, who didn't trust us at all. Workshops were planned, everything was on paper, but it didn't work out like planned. The women promised us to come to the workshop, but nobody showed up. We had to go to the yards. We, in fact, had to "force" them. I went to the streets again and I said, "You promised me that you would come but, I'm not leaving here unless you come with me." I just waited in the yard and I said, "You come even if it is for five minutes or a quarter hour. Come."

Dusilley: They asked, "Why do you want us?" We told them we wanted to help protect them against HIV and AIDS. So when they heard "AIDS" they became suspicious, thinking, "Maybe these people come to tell us we sick." They know the type of work they are doing is risky. You know, most prostitutes here think the only way you can get AIDS is by sex. And some, who are in this business for so many years, think that it cannot happen to them. They were saying, "The government never did anything for us before, so how come they suddenly want us to come to get education?" I think that was one of the barriers—the AIDS approach. When they did come to the National AIDS Program workshop, somebody started a rumor that we had a hidden camera—they quickly disappeared.

Juanita: So we had a special workshop, and we let them search the room, search for a hidden camera. After that they kept coming, one telling the other, and they came.

So Maxi Linder was set up specifically for AIDS education?

Juanita and Dusilley together: No, no, no.

Juanita: No. In the workshops we would introduce different things. Nadia Raveles (a feminist activist in Suriname) would come and talk about self-esteem. A policewoman talked about rights, what their rights are on the street. You know, policemen pick them up, make them pay a fine, take them, and have them sit on a bench until five in the morning, then let them go again. So she would tell them about their rights.

We started a "needs assessment" study, and we wanted prostitutes to have their own peers—to meet and talk with other girls. So we started a training course and realized that many couldn't read or write. Then we did role plays, and a trust began building. When they saw what our goal was—just meeting other sex workers to give them information, showing them things, movies, explaining—they started trusting us.

Dusilley: One of Nadia's talks was on Maxi Linder. She was a well known figure in Suriname for many decades, and still is. We didn't decide to use that image or name. It was only to inform them, to tell them, that even though Maxi Linder was a sex worker, she was proud of herself. She was always neat. You know, when you go to the street women here, you don't always find them smelling so nice or dressed so neatly. So we got this image that Maxi Linder was a proud woman. And women actually started coming to the workshops smelling better and looking better. It was then that we decided to say, "No matter what you do, you must take pride in yourself."

Juanita: The women were not really helping each other on the street. Everybody was there for herself alone. There was no solidarity. Nadia explained that Maxi Linder was organizing women, especially on the Waterkant, the riverside, against the men. That if you have a client, and that is what sometimes happens, you should not run away and leave your friend. You should come back for her, to look out for her. Maxi Linder always helped other prostitutes and she was organizing them. No client got away with beating up a woman and not paying her. She was always there. So Maxi Linder became a positive example.

We did the needs assessment study with interviews of more than an hour. We talked person-to-person for hours. It was after we gained some trust that the study was reliable and honest. It wasn't like going in the street and filling in forms, no, we sat there and they told us their life stories. We found they needed a place to crash, they needed a backbone, a place to belong, a place where they can come with their own problems and so on. So out of the study came this non-governmental organization, and Maxi Linder became the name.

Dusilley: They had problems not only in the line of prostitution, but with their families. Many women have lots of children. And you know, when you see them at work, you know that this is a woman who is doing this thing for her kids. Somebody might say "Why doesn't she look for work?" But it's the only thing that they know how to do. Some don't know how to read and write. The society doesn't accept them—you know once you have started, you get that name-brand. A stigma. So it generally holds you back. People tend to put sex workers in a tainted space—something you cannot touch.

Juanita: So that's why we want this organization to help them, give them skills (socially and economically), all kinds of skills to let them develop their potential and lead a fruitful life.

There are quite a few projects in different places in the world which encourage women to leave sex work. How do you feel about that?

Juanita: We don't bring that up.

Dusilley: I was a sex worker. And I said that if we are going to have this center, I intend to see people's lives get changed. But we don't tell them that things have to change. We have to give them something to do.

Juanita: Some other opportunity, something to do in the place of what they are doing. Then they can decide. You see, most are trying to make a living for their families, and they take risks. For example, if they don't have anything to eat at home, they take the risk of not using a condom. If they have something besides this to upgrade their social-economic level, then they will start thinking about responsibility.

Dusilley: I realized that a lot of the women want *out*. They really want out. But then society does not give them a chance to really get out of what they are doing. So, I hope that this works, I hope that this center will do those kind of things.

A woman falls into this work. Say the street is giving SF5,000 (roughly $12), she gets SF5,000 on her first night.[1] Maybe it looks like she's making good money. Okay the first time she's on the street she gets five, she goes for seven nights: seven times five. And then the next week she's broken, worn out. Or the next week there's nothing, maybe SF1-2,000 (between $2–5). Or say, she works for SF10,000 now (approximately $25). Tomorrow morning she gets up, she sees a pair of shoes for SF9,000, she buys it, because she says to herself, "Okay, maybe tomorrow I get another SF10,000." But maybe there's nothing the next day.

So if she has a job where she's working for herself, with a steady income, and she knows that at the end of every week she has say, SF2,000 (roughly $5), then she can start living to meet that amount. If she really wants to get out—and I am not speaking about ones who say "I like this, this is my lifestyle"—you cannot put her in an office where other people are saying "Oh, she was a hooker, she's going to take your husband." People do make these nasty remarks. She has to be doing something that she really likes, having her steady income, seeing that her children can eat from it, and that she can survive. Then she will stay out.

How many women are with Maxi Linder?
Juanita: Right now about 100–150. The core group changes, but we have a steady number of about forty that come every time to meetings.

Are they all sex workers?
Juanita: Yes, this is for sex workers. And they are very critical about it. They watch out, and point out if another woman comes here and is not a sex worker. We know that other groups of women still have a difficulty in associating with sex workers. And they know that. Even the nurses who test or treat sex workers have problems.

What are the ages of the women who come here?
Juanita: The oldest is sixty-four, and the youngest is fifteen.
Dusilley: There were a few girls. I had to interview them, and I thought, "What are they doing here? I cannot interview these young women, I have to counsel them." One seventeen-year-old told me that her parents were in New York and that she wanted money to go there and do hairdressing. We talked about it. She's now going to the Fashion School here, doing sewing classes. The other is in English night classes and the two youngest are back in school.

Do the women have other sources of income? Or are most just involved in sex work?
Dusilley: No. We have it another way. A lot of them tell their families that they are going to do other work, so they go to these houses (saying they are domestic workers) at seven in the morning, and around twelve-thirty they leave to go to their homes. So when people ask where they have been, they say "I have been to work." But it's sex work they've been doing, so its the other way around.
Juanita: Some never leave their home at night. So even the children don't know.
Dusilley: We have cases of somebody working at an office, and at night they go out.
Juanita: A couple of women are in the government, and they are hustling the

streets at night. It's even so that some sell on the market—women from the market places who are selling their goods. They have a client, leave their stall, and the woman next door takes care of her goods and sells for her. She has a client, then she comes back.

Can you say something more about the working conditions?
Juanita: Women on the street operate in the yards which belong to somebody in a house in the yard. People just rent rooms for them, and the rate of the room depends on what street it is—it differs.

What are the price variations?
Dusilley: You can find from SF250 (60¢). There are one's who work for less, but I know of sex workers who tell me they get sometimes SF1000 ($2.5) in the streets.

Is that for sex, or just the room?
Dusilley: No, for what they are doing. For the room, it's now 200 guilders (50¢). Just a few days ago one lady locked her gate because the girls refused to pay the SF200. They said it was too much. She used to ask SF75, now she wants SF200. So she locked the gate and, because in central Paramaribo there are not so many places like these, the women had nowhere else to go.
Juanita: They have to pay in the end. They have to agree to the bad accommodations like dirty sheets, no water, etc, etc.

But what happened in this case?
Dusilley: Well one woman told me that two of them went to another person's yard. So what you find? The Guyanese were operating on one side and Surinamese on the other side. When the one who had the Guyanese house raised the price, they went to another place where they can operate day and night, and the price is still SF75. I think there are about four places in that neighborhood,

Do you know of any cases where women have been forced into prostitution?
Juanita: No.
Dusilley: But first in Suriname, they used to bring the Guyanese Indian girls [descendents of indentured laborers from India]. They would tell them they would bring them here to make roti in the roti shops, and then when they came here. . . . At that time you had Solo Club and El Paraiso. It was about seven to eight years ago.

Guyanese coming "backtrack" are undocumented, but how long do they stay?
Dusilley: As long as they like. They could be here for years. But now they're

going to French Guiana. At this moment, because of the economic situation, you find there are not a lot of Guyanese here, just a few. Most of them are going to Cayenne.

So what is the nationality of sex workers in Paramaribo today?
Dusilley: The largest group is Brazilian, and they live in the clubs.

There is quite a separation between street workers and "club girls". Do the women who work in the street ever move into the clubs?
Dusilley: Not into the Brazilian clubs, because in Suriname these club owners have their own style. They have their grades—what must I say! Listen. If I am outside. If I am a sex worker and I want to go to certain club where the Brazilians operate, I cannot enter. They don't allow that. If I go with a guy, they would allow me to go inside, but not into the rooms.
Juanita: So you can have a drink.
Dusilley: If I get a friend to take me inside to find a guy to come out, okay, no problem. But not on my own. Every club owner thinks his club is the best, even for the Guyanese.

Do Brazilian women know they are coming to the clubs here for sex work?
Juanita: The club owners are not tricking them. The women know exactly what they are doing. I think they don't know the conditions, and how hard the work is. They have to pay back their ticket and money to come into the country, which can easily amount to SF400,000 (approximately $1,000). That is very hard.
Dusilley: In a "Grade A" club, a woman can ask up to SF15000.
Juanita: That is for overnight.
Dusilley: And most men, you find guys from the ships and high society, pay in dollars too.
Juanita: It's not only guys, you have also women picking them up. Women clients.

Are there any female club owners?
Juanita: I don't know, I'm not so familiar with the clubs.
Dusilley: One woman, yes, there is a woman. She has clubs in Holland. She goes to a club here in Suriname, for instance, a high income club like Diamond. She goes there and selects some girls. She checks the girls, checks their skin, checks their body and takes a couple of girls. It's really a business, because you have files and passports, more photos, and then you have a contract for three months and then go to Holland to the clubs, stay there for three months, then come back. Some hide there. But after three months they are supposed to come

back and another group gets "the chance" to earn money. When I interview them, I get the feeling that they think the club owners give them a chance to earn money, but really it is the owners who make money.

What about male prostitutes?

Juanita: Yes, there are male sex workers. We know that there are a lot of male sex workers, but we don't have any program yet for them. There are clubs for male sex workers—houses, they call them. "Castles." We had one meeting with homosexuals, and they explained to us that to enter this network would be difficult. There are houses in residential areas and poor ones, but they mix. Some men from the poorer houses go to the richer houses. And you have different ages also.

Another group we know about are women who don't tell that they are doing sex work. They don't consider themselves sex workers. We have these cards that we give to them and we have an agreement with the Dermatological Clinic that the staff doesn't ask for any papers, just the visiting cards. The card is anonymous—there is no name on it. You can give it to your friend and she can go for a check-up. So, even if you're illegal or underground, you can have your check up.

Can you give us any idea of the number of women who are involved? Registered and unregistered—in the clubs, in the streets?

Dusilley: It's really difficult because of the migration. They move around so much.

In 1994, there were around 3,000 who were registered. Something like that. In 1993, 2,334 Brazilians and 1,268 of other nationalities were registered.

What kind of projects is Maxi Linder developing? And what are some of the needs of the Association to be able to continue to grow and strengthen?

Juanita: We try to educate sex workers. Teach them skills, like to read and write, catering, sewing, handicrafts. We want to develop a well organized outreach service. We have acquired twelve acres of land for agriculture and poultry as a pilot project.

Is that to grow food for their own consumption?

Juanita: First, and then they can sell the surplus. We are trying to get funding for this project. Right now we are working with an international foundation for small agricultural projects. They contribute by teaching the women skills, training, everything they need to know for agriculture, while continuously training them and helping them to plant. That is their contribution—they don't give money, but give the know-how. We are still in need of a pick-up truck to help us with this project. We are also continually in search of funding which will help pay for trainers of the cooking classes, for literacy programs, for counselling and, of course, for the everyday running and up-keep of the center.

And part of Maxi Linder's work is to try to encourage sex workers to become peer educators and counsellors? You are the first one Dusilley?

Dusilley: Yes. I tell them so much about HIV and AIDS. Try to help when they are going to make the step to be tested an so on.

Juanita: I counsel too, but Dusilley does it mainly. I know that they like me a lot. They trust me, I'm there for them. But when they are in real trouble, it's not me whom they go to, it's Dusilley. They are not ashamed of showing anything about their bodies to Dusilley, but they still think that I won't understand. They can ask me anything, but when it comes to very intimate things. . . . We started a support group for HIV-positive women with Dusilley. There is that subject again: of the peer. Peers for peers. I have been in so many discussions. Every time I come up with the solution for a problem, I discuss it with Dusilley. She has a different approach to the problems of HIV-positive people. I may think that this is a good solution, and she looks at it from a different angle. You need somebody who is HIV positive to lead such a support group.

After Dusilley said publicly that she was HIV-positive, some sex workers approached her and told her that they knew that they too were HIV-positive. And now we know that there are women joining this program because they are infected. So now, Dusilley has started a support group for HIV-positive sex workers. We also try to do some day care, for the mothers who bring their children along to the workshops. Because of the economic situation in Suriname, however, we are short on food for the children, and need a regular supply of basics such as milk, cereal, cocoa, tea and vitamin tablets, especially vitamin C, so that we can distribute these to the women and their children.

Dusilley: We also work with the club owners. There was this one guy who operates one of the highest rate clubs in Suriname—Diamond Club. The problem was that he thought that when he sent one of his girls to have an AIDS test, she could go back to the club and do what she wanted—that she didn't have AIDS. So when we had the workshop, I gave them my story. Afterwards, a lot of them came to me and said, "Dusilley, thank you, because we never knew that this HIV/AIDS was such a dangerous thing." I said, "One of your friends could come into your club and you don't know he's infected, and he can do the same thing. And then the next thing you know, your club is gone tomorrow." So this club owner started taking the thing serious. He now buys condoms by the big boxes. We told him, "Come on, you can give the girls condoms for free." So, he started buying them. Now, when we have a workshop, he always sends his girls.

Do the club owners want you to counsel?

Juanita: They agreed. It's not necessary for them. But now they know that we think its necessary for the women. If it was up to them, you just go there, take your blood and that's it. Counselling wasn't important. But now they know that the girls get counselling.

Is it true that women in clubs have a steady friend outside?

Juanita: Oh yes, they have. That is the problem. That is what Dusilley is always explaining to them that they all have a boyfriend with whom they have risky behavior.

They think its safe to have sex with him without a condom?

Juanita: Even if they don't think it, he's seen as "special" so they don't use a condom.

Dusilley: Yes, and one of the problems here is the client, especially with the high grade clubs. The clients treat the women so rough, you know, and they want to do the impossible. But with a boyfriend, they can have an orgasm. So then they would get rid of the condom and say, okay, now he's going to make love to me. Its not going to be like at the club.

There's a very clear distinction between love-making and sex work?

Dusilley: Of course. Some men would try to make love to a body. Some would see a woman and really want to make love, but then the sex worker makes up her mind that she's not going to have an orgasm with him, not going to kiss him.

Juanita: And they check the time. Fifteen to twenty minutes.

Dusilley: Ten minutes. And when you have a boyfriend you can go out, enjoy yourself.

You know, I was a sex worker who met a special boyfriend and he took me off the streets. We were living as man and wife. That man was infected with the HIV virus and he never said a word about it—he got me infected and he died. Amen. I've heard so much about AIDS, read a lot. I went to a conference in Sao Paulo, Brazil, I met other people who are involved in the same kind of programs in different countries. But I think that there is only one way to be successful: we have to use peers. That is the only way to have positive results, to try to hire or recruit sex workers to educate others.

What kind of responses have you had to your "outing" as sex workers?

Dusilley: On World AIDS Day in December 1993, Maxi Linder members participated in the annual health march. We displayed our banner with the slogan "No

Condom, No Pussy." We wanted to let the public know that using a condom is not a problem for sex workers and at the same time give a direct message to the clients. There was no discrimination shown to our walkers by the public.

Would you say your program is successful?

Dusilley: Our program is working. When it started the women were still biased, they tried to play smart with us. Now they are at each other's backs to use a condom.

Juanita: They're keeping an eye on each other, and we give them free condoms.

Dusilley: And when they want extras they go all the way to the National AIDS Program to buy, or send somebody to buy for them. By the boxes! It feels so nice. Men are giving them money in their hands, and they ask "condom?", and if the men say, no, they give the money back. It's good to know.

Note

1. At the time of the interviews, in late January 1995, the rate was SF413 (Surinamese guilders) to US$1. SF5,000 was then roughly equivalent to US$12.

Part Four # AIDS Prevention and Sex Workers' Empowerment

Introduction

AIDS prevention work is an important basis for activities with and among prostitutes, leading in some instances to the emergence of new sex workers' rights groups and organizations. In this section, four different AIDS-prevention projects are described, for Brazil, Senegal, the European Union, and the Dominican Republic, all of which have as their aim the empowerment of sex workers. Each chapter points out some of the contradictions and difficulties with State involvement in AIDS prevention work for sex workers, making the case for community-based interventions and support. The various successful intervention strategies provide valuable models and examples for future work in this area. One of the most striking aspects of all the methods described here is the central position that sex workers hold in the projects and the sustained involvement of the project with sex worker communities. In Brazil, Senegal, and the Dominican Republic, these projects have all given rise to new autonomous sex workers organizations, such as those described in the previous section, which are beginning to make their own voices heard in the international arena.

Paulo Henrique Longo's chapter describes the Pegação program among young male sex workers in Rio de Janeiro in Brazil. The program began due to the high HIV-seroprevalence signalled among male prostitutes in the city in the late 1980s. From a government initiative for AIDS prevention in 1989, the Pegação program quickly broke away from the State and in 1981 became a part of the non-governmental orgnaization NOSS (Núcleo de Orientação em Saúde Social). The program works among *michês* in Rio, young male street hustlers, who commonly sell sex to men. Longo points out that despite this same-sex activity, the young men do not define themselves as "gay" or "homosexual," and describes how this particular construction of masculinity and manhood is experienced in Brazil. He goes on to detail the methodology developed over the years, describing both the positive results as well as the problems the organization faces. Even with self-reported safe-sex practices among *michês* increasing drastically, and a sense of empowerment growing among the young men, because of its advocacy work and on-going commitment to the young street boys, the program has not gained the financial support it requires to function easily. Nevertheless, today the program is embedded in a network of AIDS prevention activities in the country, and serves as an important model for effective community-based intervention.

In Senegal, the SYNFEV (Synergy Women and Development) program, as part of ENDA (Environmental Development Action in the Third World) has been in operation since 1987, including in its program research and activities on prostitution. Oumar Tandia describes here some of the general conditions in Dakar, the capital of Senegal, for working women, the SYNFEV activities and some results of their interventions. Important in the situation in Senegal is that it is a country that has legalized prostitution, one of the few African countries to have done so. Forced prostitution is not known to exist in the country and sex work is almost always a careful negotiation between prostitutes, clients and intermediaries. Women become legal prostitutes through registering with the government's Institute of Social Hygiene. Such registration requires them to undergo regular health checks, carry a health pass and attend lectures and meetings about health matters. In the past, such requirements were considered a threat by the women, and hence few sex workers actually registered with the authorities. SYNFEV has intervened to try to ease the relationship between prostitutes and the state institutions, in an attempt to ensure safe-sex practices amongst all sex workers. It has furthermore, conducted peer-education and organized informational campaigns and meetings. The main activity of the program in the last few years has been to establish a house for sex workers which functions as a drop-in center and a place for exchange of information and solidarity among the women. The SYNFEV activities have begun to result in the emergence of an articulate leadership among Senegalese sex workers, a change in attitudes towards their work, and an increase in safe-sex practices

Licia Bussa's chapter presents the results of the four-year TAMPEP project: an AIDS/STD prevention program among migrant sex workers in four countries in the European Union. Migrant sex workers from a diversity of Third World and Eastern European countries are the majority of the sex working population in Western Europe today, she explains, yet remain largely outside legal, social and medical structures due to immigration and prostitution laws. The chapter describes some of the varying conditions for migrant sex workers and points out that great diversity exists in the countries between nationalities of sex workers, duration of stay in a country and length of time they are engaged in the sex industry. The TAMPEP project has attempted to work with this diversity and has constructed an appropriate methodology. A starting point is the development of programs that are based in already existing non-governmental organizations (NGOs) that have established contact with migrant sex workers, thus building upon existing access, insights and knowledges. The project employs a continuous process of research, production of informational materials, implementation and evaluation and has enabled the growth of community-based activities that meet the specific needs of the local populations. It relies on the identification and training of cultural mediators and peer educators, the former who act as interpreters between the migrant community and institutions in the host countries, the latter who are migrant sex workers themselves and advocate the interests of their specific group. The TAMPEP project aims to boost cohesion among migrant sex workers, promoting self-confidence, self-efficacy and overall empowerment in their dealings with clients, pimps and brothel owners. The program has made an successful start with creating a network of peer educators who move throughout Europe, in a climate of increasingly repressive laws and polices towards immigration and prostitution.

AIDS prevention work in the Dominican Republic among prostitutes started in 1985, through the government National AIDS Program. By 1987, the NGO COIN (Centro de Orientación Integral) was established for this work. COIN's main outreach work is conducted through teams of peer workers: "messengers of health." It also publishes a newsletter for sex workers, has a theater group, distributes condoms, has developed informational materials for the peer workers and participated in making a film on the trafficking of Dominican women to Europe. The organization has also conducted various surveys among sex working populations in four different cities, resulting in extensive information about demographics of the populations, and motivations, attitudes and migration patterns among sex workers. COIN held its first sex workers congress in 1994 through which the participants formulated various resolutions for the improvement of working conditions for sex workers in the Dominican Republic. It is also through COIN's work that the empowering term "trabajadora sexual" (sex worker) has been introduced into the national discourse on prostitution. As a result of all this work, in 1996 several of the messengers of health formed their own independent sex workers organization: MODEMU (Moviemiento de Mujeres Unidas).

Kamala Kempadoo

21 The Pegação Program Information, Prevention, and Empowerment of Young Male Sex Workers in Rio de Janeiro

Paulo Henrique Longo

Introduction

Rio de Janeiro is the second largest city in Brazil, with approximately eight million residents. The city is divided into four zones: north, south, downtown and the suburbs. Tourism is one of the most important sources of income and is restricted to the south zone, where the famous beaches such as Copacabana and Ipanema are located. The business and commercial district is concentrated in the downtown zone, where there are also cinemas and bars. Early in the evening, such areas are generally overcrowded.

It is estimated that approximately two thousand male prostitutes are currently working in the streets of Rio de Janeiro in the two main districts—the center or downtown area and the neighborhood of Copacabana. A study by Cortes (1989) established that forty-three percent of Brazilian male prostitutes were HIV-seropositive. Given the extent of male prostitution, with prostitutes making approximately forty new contacts each week (Longo, 1990), coupled with the high seroprevalence level that has been reported, the situation in Rio de Janeiro is the cause of considerable concern. As an initial response to the potential risks involved in this situation, a team of outreach workers was formed in July 1989 to provide counselling, education, and to distribute condoms for young male sex workers (Longo 1990). Over the course of more than six years, this team has taken important steps in developing an innovative intervention program aimed at reducing the risk of HIV transmission within the context of male prostitution.

Hustlers in Rio

We began working with young male sex workers because there were no AIDS prevention programs geared towards this group. During the first three months of the project, we went to different male prostitution areas to identify character-istics that could be relevant to the design of an intervention project. During this period, a large number of young males involved in prostitution were inter-viewed, with the aim of assessing their interest in such a project and to get them involved in the design. Some of these young men made important contribu-tions and suggestions, especially about where it would be best to work. They also suggested the name *Pegação*, a slang expression in the Brazilian homosexual scene which means *to seduce* or *search for a client*. Initially they thought that we were in the areas with the purpose of searching for either a "hustler" or client. So when we were thinking of a name for the project, they immediately suggested *Pegação*.

To be a "hustler" or *michê*, on the streets of Brazil is to belong to the fringe, and quite often to be a part of the cycle of drug abuse as well. There are some who would insist that to be a prostitute means that you are poor: you are first and foremost a victim. And if you are a male prostitute, then you are not only poor but you are also homosexual. The stigma sticks. Our experience has shown that poverty cannot be used as the only justification for prostitution. In our day-to-day work at *Pegação*, most of the boys approach us first as potential clients. As time goes by, and the relationship gains more intimacy, we hear things like "With you I would have sex for free, 'cause I like you a lot." The mask falls away. This mask is what the client usually wants: a young boy, seemingly macho. Never ask a male sex worker if he is gay. The reaction might be more than you bargained for. In our culture, to be described as a homosexual is an insult: "Me, gay? What are you thinking of? I'm a man, I just come here to fuck some queers for money." It is also common to hear gay men tell a hustler with whom they have just had sex: "If you had sex with me, you must be gay as well." This gener-ates tension within the relationship, because the client exposes what the boy does not want to hear.

In a society where the macho figure is seen as the cornerstone of masculinity, anyone who is not macho is rejected. So the hustler feels he has to be seen as macho, paid to fulfill the wishes of the "almost-female." Hustlers adopt false names which act like registered labels to help sell the product. Off the streets, things are different. We have a proverb in Brazil which says: "Within four walls, anything goes." Protected by the secrecy of a room and the anonymity of the partners, the macho mask can fall. It is difficult to be gay, but it is not difficult to have gay practices in bed. The concepts of "active" and "passive" are much more important than how the individual defines himself. That is why the hustler will approach the client saying "I don't get fucked, I fuck." And the boys can use their lack of money as an alibi for an extremely repressed homosexuality, with the excuse "I don't like men, I do it for cash." Neither party has to reveal what goes on "within four walls." The mask does not stay on in the face of an offer to have sex with the educators of the *Pegação* program for free. Most of the boys we encounter in street sex work will begin by telling us that they hate what they do. Many pejorative terms are used to define the clients, such as *veado sujo* (dirty queer), *engolidor de cobra* (snake-swallower), or *chupador de pica* (cocksucker). However, the attempted seduction of the *Pegação* educators by the *michês* shows that money is a secondary rather than a primary objective. There is also some pleasure in their activities.

Hustlers face violence from police and their clients, and many boys bear the scars of such violence on their bodies. *Michês* in Rio de Janeiro have developed a strategy to protect themselves from such violence by, for example, using public telephones. In Rio, not all telephones can receive incoming calls, but there are some in public areas which are used by taxi-drivers. So when a *michê* goes with a client, he will arrange for colleagues to stay near to one of these phones. If they don't call in half an hour, then the other *michês* will search for them, first in the agreed place, and then throughout the hotels of Copacabana and downtown Rio. They make this arrangement within earshot of the client, and so far it has worked.

Little by little male prostitution is coming out of the shadows. This may not improve the way that it is viewed by others, but it does reflect an internal change. Until now, in the few academic papers, in the press and even in social debates, male sex work is not considered alongside female sex work as "the oldest profession." *Putas* (female prostitutes) are recognized, sometimes even being given the title of "public utility professionals," but the combination of homosexuality and prostitution is often too much for many Brazilians to contemplate. Even within the gay community, where most of the *michês'* clients come from, they find female prostitution more acceptable than male. Many would rather deny themselves sex than pay for it. People involved in health care say that hustlers are hard to reach, and use this as an excuse to deny them health services. At *Pegação* we believe that *michês* are hard to reach because they are difficult to pin down as a homogeneous group. Unlike *putas* they do not dress in a particular way for work, they do not fit into a particular category, and are quite likely to earn their money in other ways as well. They might be office boys, street kids or they might work in the informal economy as peanut vendors or shoeshiners. *Michês* working on the streets in Rio are generally very young, between eleven and twenty-three years old.

One of *Pegação*'s objectives is to prevent the spread of HIV. In order to do this we have to persuade the boys to want to protect themselves. We work constantly on their self-esteem. When *Pegação* first started in 1989 most of the *michês* were not interested in hearing about AIDS. The official prevention campaign usually stressed the message "AIDS kills," so when we came to talk about it, we often heard "Don't talk to me about AIDS, OK? I already know that AIDS kills. So what? Other things also kill. Police kill, hunger kills, other diseases also kill. Even parents kill their children. . . ."

It was clear that death was a theme that would not have an impact. In addition, the boys were not used to people offering them anything related to their health and well-being. Furthermore, AIDS was seen as a gay disease, and as most boys did not consider themselves to be gay, they didn't see it as their problem. It was also clear that our project needed to consider self-esteem since even basic hygiene depends on self-respect.

The Pegação Program and NOSS

Pegação's work is based on regular personal contact with the hustlers: a group of educators goes to different areas of town known for prostitution and discusses a range of issues. Life stories are debated on the streets. The regularity of such contact builds a relationship and opens up more intimate discussion. It also reinforces positive messages about health. Another important dimension of the work is related to the boys' identity. Since they consider themselves neither professional sex workers nor homosexuals, it is clear that we must talk about sexual practices rather than of sex work as a profession. We have to emphasize the need to also protect their girlfriends and female lovers, considered by them to be much more important than their gay clients.

The project also realized that it needed to advocate the rights of *michês*, from the rights to have health care to very simple issues like asserting their rights to be served in a bar. In 1990, the coordination and team of *Pegação* felt a necessity to create our own organization, and in January 1991, together with representatives of other social movements, we founded NOSS—Núcleo de Orientação em Saúde Social. It is a non-governmental, non-profit organization with the aim of providing health education to socially marginalized groups. But it was not until 1993 that the first meeting of *michês* in Rio took place. It was also one of the first in the whole of Latin America. Together in a bar, after a picnic on the beach, we discussed the subjects which really interested us. Topic after topic came up that we would never normally have raised. We discussed desire and pleasure, and it was all right to say that you liked men. This has led to new "romances" among some of the boys who came to the meeting. They are now beginning to combine their desires with their needs. It is now less of a problem for many of them to recognize that they are working when they sell their bodies. Some of the boys are planning a proper organization with regular meetings.

NOSS also includes the Tereza project, which started in 1991 as an HIV/AIDS and STDs prevention project with incarcerated people in the State of Rio de Janeiro. The team has similar activities as those in the *Pegação* program, providing services and counselling. NOSS has furthermore generated a bi-monthly newspaper with information about STD's and HIV/AIDS for the gay community throughout the country. The newspaper also contains other useful information, such as legal aid and more general matters of interest. It is distributed and sold in eighteen states in Brazil. A third project is *Alerta*, which provides training to people living in poor communities to enable them to become health care agents. This was initiated to address the lack of health care campaigns and education in slum and peripheral areas of the city. Finally, we broadcast a weekly fifteen-minute national radio program. The transmission is live, allowing people to call in with questions while we are on the air.

Pegação Methodology

Since the beginning of the *Pegação* program, a team of four outreach workers have been in personal and regular contact with male street working prostitutes in metropolitan Rio. Contact points have been established in the center of town, at the central train station and the cinema district, as well as in Copacabana at Maxim's bar and Galeria Alaska. Approximately 9,000 face-to-face contacts are made with these young male prostitutes every year. At each contact, information about HIV/AIDS and other sexually transmitted diseases is provided. General health care topics are also discussed with the aim of reinforcing better basic personal health care and safer sex practices. Condom-use is strongly encouraged and the boys are shown how to properly use condoms. The outreach workers form a personal relationship with the boys and encourage discussions. They counsel the boys not only about HIV/AIDS, but about other social and personal problems.

Given the limitations that have been found in existing written or published educational material, the *Pegação* program has placed central emphasis on a range of more interactive educational activities. Face-to-face discussions, games to explore safer sexual practices, and meetings between prostitutes, outreach workers and health professionals are among the activities. The program also maintains links with public service agencies for psychological counselling and legal aid matters for prostitutes.

Based on the records kept by the outreach workers during their work in the streets, it is possible to compare pre- and post-intervention results. In the beginning of the program, only fifteen percent of the young men declared to always use a condom. After a period of six months this had increased to sixty-five percent and one year later to eighty percent. The reported "never use" has declined as dramatically. In June 1989, none of the boys sought periodic medical assistance. This situation had improved to forty percent by January 1990, and today the percentage is around seventy-five percent. Self-reported safe sex practices in June 1989 were around nine percent, rising to seventy percent in recent years. Cases of STDs reduced from seventy-one percent to thirty-two percent in the first six months.

Another important result that must be considered is that approximately eighty percent of the new contacts are made with young males who are referred to us by others who are already part of the program. This trend underscores the finding in a study on male prostitution and HIV-transmission (Longo and Parker 1992), that the most useful sources of information for male prostitute street workers were "specific intervention projects." Some of the young men attended by the program were integrated in prevention activities after regular contacts with outreach workers. Three boys have, on their own initiative, begun distributing condoms in the communities where they live.

There are a number of probable reasons for the success of the *Pegação* program. First, the boys are seen on an individual basis and their life stories taken into consideration in the prevention work. This personal information helps the educator to concentrate on building the young men's self-esteem and awareness of health. Second, most of the boys have no other person to turn to other than the street educators. Strong relationships in which trust and intimacy play and important role, are fostered through this. Third, the educators are visible in the male prostitution areas everyday. The young men know where to find the educators and the services provided by the program. A fourth reason is that since the inception of the program, regular evaluations have been held, allowing continual assessment and adjustment. Finally, the integration of a growing number of young male prostitutes into the projects activities have strengthened the program. Taken together, *Pegação*'s activities carried out on an on-going basis, have contributed to the development of more accurate personal risk assessment and provide a context of social support for young male sex workers.

Pitfalls

Among the problems encountered, the lack of infrastructure—such as an office—has been significant. Team meetings and talks with others interested in the project, as well as the press, take place in bars or at the coordinator's home. A room was lent to the project by the government, but could only be used as a storeroom for condoms and other materials.

During the first year and a half, *Pegação* program received funding from two Dutch agencies interested in supporting health work with street youth. This was received through an umbrella organization with which the program was affiliated. However, serious ethical problems caused our program to leave the organization and create our own institution, NOSS. Since then we have had to face a severe lack of funding.

The original objective was to set up a place where young male prostitutes could meet, talk with educators and other health care professionals, where we could hold training sessions, etc. This goal was not attained because of a lack of funding. Our plan to expand our methodology and project activities to other male prostitution sites and other states was also hindered by inadequate financial support. It has also prohibited us from hiring new educators, providing training to other organizations and to the boys. We have come to realize that this kind of project, whose emphasis is not on producing a large quantity of printed material does not interest many agencies. They do not seem to be interested in financing a project whose methodology is based upon the relationship between street educators and the target audience. We do not stand alone in this matter. This particular method of outreach is poorly regarded in many countries, mainly because it involves salaried personnel. This prejudice is a serious drawback and hindrance to our development.

Lessons

We can identify a number of trends which appear to be important for working with marginalized social groups in a country like Brazil. From the start, it is extremely important to always hear the target audience and to listen to their objectives, beliefs and wishes. An outreach intervention will only be successful if it is able to consider aspects that are relevant to the group and can only find this out by listening closely. Secondly, any outreach work among a marginalized group must be based on regular and long-term contact with the group. Male prostitutes or street kids are not accustomed to interventions that respect them. People generally visit for a short period, develop research, produce some printed material and leave without any further regard for the population. If the young people are able to see a team of outreach workers constantly in their neighborhoods, get to know the services provided, and discover that there is someone willing to hear what they have to say, a strong relationship can be established and this is very useful for promoting health care.

Another lesson is that it is as important to concentrate on efforts to increase the boys' self-esteem, as it is to create and generate a desire to protect themselves against AIDS/HIV and any other disease. Furthermore, these sex workers do not usually consider their activity as a profession, so the emphasis must be on sexual practices. It is also necessary to emphasize the protection of girlfriends and female lovers, since these relationships are considered to be of more importance by the boys than those with gay clients. Factors which induce young men to undertake safer sex vary, and are most likely discovered through intimate and regular relationships. A strong bond between educator and sex worker is therefore very essential part of the work. For some boys, providing information seems to be sufficient, for others emotional factors are of importance.

On a more public level, we have realized that after three years of being the only intervention program among male sex workers in Brazil, our *Pegação* program had generated interest among other non-governmental organizations, community based organizations as well as health and education professionals in different states. And finally, since the inception of the *Pegação* program the issue of teenagers and child prostitution has been raised more often in the media, contributing to a social debate on the subject. Both are encouraging trends.

Future Developments

The main objective is to maintain the activities that have been going on since 1989 and supporting the outreach work of the four educators. For that it is very important to secure continued funding for the program and to create a better infra-structure for the project. As there are many young male prostitutes becoming involved in prevention activities, one objective scheduled to begin is a formal training for peer educators. We can see that such boys may become important health agents within their own communities. A large number of "hustlers" usually say that it is very difficult to practice safe sex with their lovers/partners inside the communities where they live because of the prejudice that associates condom-use with promiscuity. Some boys say "I can't use a condom in my community because people may think that I am ill or that I have some special reason to use it." Experience has shown that when one of these boys becomes a peer educator, the results can be effective, especially within same-age groups of both boys and girls.

After *Pegação* became an NGO aiming at AIDS prevention with marginalized groups, important political steps were taken. Our organization was elected among others to represent the community-based organizations as a member of the State Commission on AIDS, responsible for promoting all the AIDS-related policies in the State of Rio de Janeiro. Politically we have the support of the government and other NGOs fundamental for prevention activities. That is also important as a stand to defend the rights of male sex workers. Representation in the National AIDS Commission since 1994 also creates a possibility for influencing national policies.

The *Pegação* program offers an important example of the potential for effective community-based interventions aimed at AIDS prevention. The accomplishments of the project prove that it can serve to stimulate and develop similar projects in other settings.

22 Prostitution in Senegal

Oumar Tandia

Translated by Maritza Paul

ENDA (Environmental Development Action in the Third World) is an inter-active and non-profit international organization based in Dakar, Senegal. Our focus is on issues relating to the environment, development, and the fight against poverty. The institution comprises twenty groups, among them, the SYNFEV program (Synergy Women and Development), that was founded in 1987. SYNFEV prioritizes women's issues as they relate to socioeconomic growth, health, particularly sexual and reproductive, and the right to exercise greater control over their sexuality. In 1991, we initiated a study of prostitution as part of the SYNFEV program. The reasoning behind this focus was that we believed that the problems that prostitutes experience reflect the conditions that all other women suffer, in addition to some that are unique to sex work. Against this premise, we thought that if we could identify and address some of these problems we would be responding to women's problems.

The Contemporary Situation

After much careful consideration, bibliographical research, local and international investigations into the subject,

SYNFEV carried out fieldwork in the city of Dakar. A first phase of canvassing in the districts allowed us to have informal contact with women practicing prostitution in different contexts.

In Dakar, clients are recruited in the street, then the client takes the prostitute to a hotel or they go to her house. There are also special places that accommodate prostitutes in the most rudimentary fashion. The same method of recruitment occurs in other cities, such as Kaolack. Residents of these areas have been known to "purge" or burn down these sites, to drive away the prostitutes. Prostitutes can also solicit clients by picking them up in front of hotels. There are places set up, exclusively or secondarily, for that purpose (salons, special nightclubs, secret bars). Prostitutes also work in nightclubs, casinos, near military bases, industrial sites, harbors, probably also at bus stops. There are also houses that recruit foreign prostitutes, in particular English-speakers such as Ghanaians and Nigerians, that are run by a responsible and older "mother". It appears as if these places that house foreign prostitutes also have a special inside organization with leaders who assist them in managing their problems. Other segments of the population also practice prostitution on an individual basis, such as college students, high school students and civil servants. However, it is difficult to approach these other categories.

There are no brothels per se in Dakar. There are no naked women dancing on tables, but there are those who attach themselves to particular bars. Nowadays, there are certain bars whose managers arrange passes for clients and prostitutes, and act as intermediaries as far as making the contact and payment for services rendered. Some of the girls work as hostesses. They coax the customer into buying drinks and are paid a certain percentage of the drinks consumed, plus a bonus and must remain on the job for a specific length of time, without actually selling sex during that entire period.

Women who work independently choose their hours and are paid directly. The women who work through intermediaries negotiate with them as far as conditions of work, in a way that is fairly flexible. Their schedules and methods of payment vary according to the clientele. We cannot say that forced conditions of prostitution exist, in any systematic way. Generally, the prostitutes do not perceive themselves as having schedules, work conditions or intermediaries forcefully imposed upon them: all is negotiated. We have not yet come across any situation of forced labor. Dakar is also a central port of attraction for prostitutes from Ghana, Nigeria, a few from Chad and regions from within Senegal itself. Other cities attract prostitutes from Gambia and Guinea Bissau (Kaolack, Ziguinchor). We know a few instances in which people leave Senegal, for the Ivory Coast and Gabon. Foreign prostitutes who migrate to Dakar (mainly Ghanaians and Nigerians) live on the fringe of Senegalese prostitutes. Their position of marginality is due to a problem of language as well as one of non-integration. They have almost the same clientele, but they operate in their own communities, and do not regularly frequent other locations. In reality, all prostitutes are stigmatized by every sector of the Senegalese population, the clients included. They are generally considered to be the object of social disgrace.

Prostitutes and the State

With regard to relations between the police and prostitutes, we can draw two specific conclusions. In the eyes of the prostitutes, the maintenance of public law and order by the police force represents an element of repression through the repeated efforts to restrict and control the women's practice through making the possession of a health pass mandatory. The police conduct interrogations into public soliciting, impose fines and issue court summonses which could result in prison terms. On the other hand, certain members of the police force maintain fairly amicable relations with prostitutes, and assist them in handling any problem that the latter may bring to their attention.

Senegal is one of the few countries in Africa, (if not the only one), to have legalized prostitution since its independence. Any woman who is older than twenty-one, and is registered at the Bureau of Health and Social Services of the Institute of Social Hygiene, is legally recognized as a prostitute (the law does not foresee males applying for this job). When the applicant goes to register, a social worker conducts an inquiry at her residence; she is asked to give the reasons behind her desire to become a prostitute and is tested for any sexually transmitted disease. There is clearly a connection between a police file and a health file, initiated by the institute of public health. When the woman has met all the requirements, she is issued a health pass. She can then practice, but may not engage in any public solicitation. She must also make regular appearances (every 45 days) for the purpose of health checks. There, she undergoes a bacteriological test, for which blood and vaginal cells are taken. If she tests positive for any sexually transmitted disease (STD), her health pass is taken away, an action which makes it legally impossible for her to practice. She is given a prescription that she must fill at her own cost and her health pass is suspended until the time that a subsequent visit shows that she is completely cured. With respect to these mandatory medical appointments, any late show results in a suspension of the health pass, as a form of penalty.

Informal lectures are arranged by the Institute of Social Hygiene. If the prostitute misses a session she is further sanctioned by way of a three-day pass suspension. The informal lectures treat the subject of STD and AIDS. They are

conducted by a social worker and several group leaders. The sessions are organized into groups, each presided over by a female leader. As far as the mandatory
consultations, the women complain profusely about blood tests, the results of
which they never know, and about the fact that, although they possess health
passes, they are not sufficiently protected against the police who can falsely
accuse them of public solicitation. They are frustrated because they are given
these prescriptions for which they have to pay out of their own pocket, without
understanding why the medicines are prescribed in the first place. They are dissatisfied with the lectures, whose themes they find redundant, and with the
penalties that they endure when they miss the lectures, because they learn
nothing new and are only inconvenienced as far as their work schedule. In addition, they deplore the lack of courtesy and sensitivity on the part of the staff that
work at the Center. In any event, the Institute of Social Hygiene has not registered more than 1,000 women, and therefore large numbers of prostitutes work
undercover.

SYNFEV Interventions

Part of the role of SYNFEV is to make contact with the health authorities
(the Institute of Social Hygiene), the police (the Vice Squad in charge of Morals)
and officers of the law (Regional Tribunal). Initially, at the Institute of Social
Hygiene we were seen as a threat, because of the difference in our approach to
prostitution. Currently, the relationship has improved because it has been possible for us to collaborate our efforts in certain situations. The Institute has
come to realize that involvement in matters of prostitution is not its exclusive
right, but that with different strategies, each activity could in fact complement
the other. Now the Institute offers services (consultations, examinations and
educational activities). We have women who are actively engaged as co-workers
in efforts to raise public awareness and share information, and we support and
reinforce women's right to control their own sexuality. Several branches of the
police solicit our input in cases involving child prostitution, in order to work
with them at finding solutions to these individual cases. The main problem with
the police is their relentless pursuit of prostitutes, which is an issue we need to
formally take up with the Vice Squad.

On the level of public awareness, there are three types of activities which we
conduct: a) lectures, slides, films on the provision of contraceptives for the
group; b) personal communication, peer education, distribution of AIDS literature to prostitutes who are not part of the group, but who work in the same
places, and to bar owners and clients; and c) public campaigns aimed at mass
public awareness such as evening open-air sessions where we present films,

sketches, songs and dances. Our main activity has been the setting up of a meeting place, under the guise of a home. That is to say, a one-room dwelling in a rented building located in the district of Grand Yoff, a popular residential area that conducts illicit economic activities. The tenants form a community composed of recent immigrants from rural districts, who remain fairly mobile. The room is sparsely furnished: a table, chair, some benches and mats. Based on need, we bring a VCR and television to show films on AIDS and STDs, and examples of women's economic activities. In this setting with the women, we have conducted sessions aimed at educating, spreading information and raising public awareness about prevention of STD and AIDS. In other words, promoting safe sex. A group of about seventeen women who know each other meet in the home regularly to discuss their situations. The composition of the group changes with time, depending on the presence of newcomers.

With the women we identify a number of situations relating to their experiences: social marginalization, society's perception of them, their own self-perception, relations to their surroundings, their family, the police, clients, and health services. In regard to their economic situation, we discuss the responsibility that they assume for their family, and how they manage to meet these demands, given the pressures they are under. Together we think of alternative solutions, for prostitution does not guarantee them a living. We are considering launching some economic projects such as a hairdresser's salon and a restaurant (a food section and a refreshment bar for the sale of drinks) to generate alternative income for the women. The problems relating to this project are specifically linked to the issue of internal organization, and also to the lack of resources.

Two other groups have been formed in the same district; they meet at the home of one of the members, but are less structured, and operate on an informal level. We have been unable to become actively involved with English-speaking prostitutes, since the social worker who conducts the fieldwork does not speak English.

Project Results

Since the start of this activity, we have noticed changes on three levels. Firstly, the women demonstrate more expertise and ease as far as group interaction and activity and we have noticed the emergence of group leaders who are able to articulate the objective of their group. Second, there seems to be an growing awareness of responsible sexual behavior. Many of the women admit that in the past, they either did not, or rarely, used contraceptives, and that at present, they use them almost systematically. Third, many have been able to free themselves of their inhibitions that resulted from the stigma attached to being a prostitute.

Now they manage to speak openly in public about health issues relating to prostitution and regard themselves as professional experts on the subject of sex. We have also noticed a tendency of a stronger self-esteem and better attitudes in response to questions about sexual health, particularly in the context of their marginalization and disadvantaged economic position. We observe this level of progress in their speech, in the way they handle certain situations and in problem-solving. A certain sense of internal solidarity manifests itself concretely, even as far as their ability to analyze situations and their willingness to take charge of problems.

The SYNFEV fieldworkers are now consulted by those who work on prostitution in Senegal on the basis of our expertise in work-related matters in the field of prostitution. The fact that we have visibly realized certain objectives has served to strengthen our faith in our project.

23 The TAMPEP Project in Western Europe

Licia Brussa

Migrant Prostitution

This chapter[1] describes the work of a transnational AIDS/STD prevention project among migrant prostitutes in Europe (TAMPEP). The project combines research and active intervention, promoting awareness on HIV/AIDS and STDs among migrant sex workers. The target groups of our interventions are a varied group of women whom we define as "migrant prostitutes." Prostitution in Europe should be seen as an international phenomenon, involving an increasing number of women and men, from other European countries and from other continents. There has been, since the 1970s, a noticeable influx of persons involved in the sex industry who have migrated from Asia, Africa and Latin America (Brussa, 1991). In addition, and more recently, the industry has seen a constant increase in the number of Central and Eastern Europeans who have crossed into Western Europe, and have been initiated into or continue to practice as sex workers. Interviews performed during the course of TAMPEP activities have made clear that many of the individuals to whom our intervention is targeted had no previous experience of sex work in their country of origin, and had no intention of engaging in this trade when they moved to Europe. The majority of women had no realistic information on the working conditions and possible earnings. It should also be stated that many of those involved in the sex industry do not identify themselves as prostitutes, and think of their work as only temporary.

Both female and transsexual sex workers have been contacted as part of our work. In our work, we respect the gender identification with which transsexual sex workers present themselves to us, and do not consider them a third gender. We refer to transsexuals here as women, since the majority present themselves in this way. They have specific medical and social needs requiring special attention. Such differences are beyond the scope of this discussion, however, and will not be referred to again here.

Prostitution involving migrant sex workers occurs in all countries of the European Union (EU). Groups are becoming increasingly mobile, both within single member states and within the larger community. In a phenomenon which merits particular attention, this mobility has activated a structural process of serial or chain migration, in which an individual who has already found employment in Europe may arrange for friends in the home country to follow. It should be stressed that migrant prostitution is not a temporary or a static phenomenon, and that parallels need to be drawn with the experiences of other groups who migrate to Europe in search of employment.

In many areas within the EU, the number of migrant prostitutes active within the sex industry is greater than that of local sex workers (EUROPAP 1994). However, migrant sex workers frequently remain outside of legal, social and medical structures, and therefore face enormous difficulties in gaining access to information and resources that could improve their quality of life. This marginalized position also leads to victimization of migrant prostitutes in criminal activities and illegal trafficking of women and men, as well as to isolation and dependency (Brussa et al., 1994).

Existing services in the European Union have little contact with members of this target group, and it is for this reason that the TAMPEP project originated in August 1993 in the Netherlands, Italy and Germany. Austria joined the project in its second phase. The coordination of each of these sites has been the responsibility of the Mr. A. de Graaf Foundation in the Netherlands, the Comitato per i Diritti Civili delle Prostitute (Committee for the Civil Rights of Prostitutes) in Italy, Amnesty for Women in Germany, and LEFÖ/ Lateinamerikanische Exilierte Frauen in Osterreich (Latin American Migrant Women in Austria). The objective of the project is to develop, in collaboration with migrant sex workers, more effective strategies to facilitate contact with the target group, as well as new materials. The four organizations involved in the project had already played an active role in the field of prostitution in their respective countries, and functioned as a reference for migrant prostitutes. This previous work in the field determined the philosophy and conduct of the project, and facilitated making contact.

The TAMPEP Project

The creation of TAMPEP was initially motivated by three factors. First, there was the lack of HIV/STD information available in the native languages of the target group. This lack impedes the development of educational and preventive programs concerning risks linked to the professional activities of the sex workers. In addition, it makes it difficult to improve their working conditions and, consequently, poses an obstacle to opportunities for improving physical or psychological well-being. Second are issues linked to the living and working conditions of migrant sex workers. Some sex workers live in conditions of great need with regard to health and hygiene. The general conditions prevalent in establishments or venues where migrant prostitutes are professionally active also create such needs. Third, it is important to facilitate direct contact between migrant sex workers and institutions active in the social and medical fields. This contact should allow for cultural mediation while not compromising the delivery of an efficient service. From the start, TAMPEP conducted experimental outreach work in very diverse regions. The respective countries and/or regions differ in immigration policies, in application of laws relating to prostitution, and in the ways in which sex work is organized and practiced. The sites also differ in health care structure, and in the organization and implementation of health promotion activities, especially those targeted towards HIV/STD prevention among sex workers. Finally, activities were conducted with sex workers originating from a very wide range of cultures. It should be clearly stated that the project did not set for itself the objective of creating a network of services capable of covering the needs of entire countries but to stimulate these services in this area.

There are many different forms of prostitution. The forms of the sex business in which migrant prostitutes most often work are street prostitution, sex clubs, shop windows, and private apartments. Each of these has its own specific working conditions, but what they all share is the fact that the population of sex workers is very international, and that the concentration of any specific nationality varies from country to country. There were a total of twenty different nationalities among our target group, from Latin America, West Africa, Southeast Asia, and from Eastern Europe and the Balkan countries. In the following, a few of the various different situations covered by the project, are described.

The Shop Window in the Netherlands

Most of those working in shop windows are migrants, from the Dominican Republic, Colombia, Venezuela, Ghana, Benin, Poland, Russia, the Ukraine, Lithuania, Serbia, Croatia, and the Czech and Slovak Republics. Sex workers pay rent for the windows, about ƒ150 ($90) a day, although this varies. The woman waits for clients in a room with a window that looks onto the street. The room contains the bed where she works, lives and sleeps. In some establishments two sex workers may share a kitchen, a room for eating, a bathroom and toilet. At some sites the buildings comply with general sanitary and administrative rules for the municipality, security is assured by men patrolling the street, rents are fixed, and neither minors nor trafficked women are officially allowed to work. In others, up to four women may use the same window room, share a single toilet, an improvised shower and no kitchen. In some cases workers receive one towel and two sheets for use throughout the week. On the average, the sex workers interviewed work between twelve and seventeen hours a day, receiving from ten to twenty-four clients, at a usual charge of ƒ25 ($15) for fifteen minutes of work.

Sex Workers in Hamburg

In the last two years the sex industry, both in Hamburg and in other parts of Germany, underwent important changes due to a significant increase in number of women coming from East European countries. According to an estimate of the Hamburg police department, there are today around 6,000—8,000 sex workers in this city. About seventy percent are migrant prostitutes and one half of those are East European women, coming mostly from Poland, Ukraine, Bulgaria, Rumania and the Czech Republic.

As for their living and working situations, the majority are strongly tied to pimps and therefore, quite difficult to contact. They find themselves in very isolated apartment-brothels controlled by the so-called "Russian mafia organizations." As a consequence, they are often forced to move from one city to another, suffering from very bad working and living conditions.

The second largest migrant sex workers group in Hamburg comes from Latin America. Here, in addition to genetic women, there are also both transvestites and transsexuals. The genetic women come mostly from the Dominican Republic, Ecuador, Colombia, Venezuela and Brazil. While Dominican women work mainly in apartments, those from Ecuador work on the street and the others in bars and cabarets—all of them as "free women." The transgenders are mostly from Peru, Colombia, Venezuela and Brazil, and have already worked in prostitution in their home countries. In Hamburg they work in bars and on the street.

Female Sex Workers in Austria

As in the other European countries, in Austria there is a large number of migrant women working as sex workers. The massive presence of migrant sex workers began in the eighties, mainly from Latin America, Southeast Asia, Ghana, Kenya, Brazil, and the Dominican Republic and in the nineties from Central and East European countries (Poland, Russia, Hungary, Czech Republic). They work throughout the country, in big cities as well as in small towns and villages. The majority of migrant sex workers are in bars and night clubs as dancers and entertainers, and are not registered. A small number work on the streets or in private apartments. A great number of Latin American sex workers have a regular migrant status as dancers and artists in Austria , although this does not allow a regulated working permit as a sex worker. The working conditions of migrant sex workers are characterized by poor sanitary conditions. Often they work and live at the same place and they pay huge amounts for rent and other services. Although some women come to Austria in the hope of getting a job and earning money to support their families at home, some of them also hope to marry in order to be able to stabilize their immigrant status in Austria and improve their economic situation. Often they marry someone who is related to the sex trade. Lack of immigration rights, legal and economic dependency, and social discrimination cause a situation of isolation, violence, marginalization and extreme psychological pressure on the women.

Sex Workers in Italy

Although soliciting and the exploitation of prostitutes by third parties is prohibited by law in Italy, a number of clubs and discotheques engage "entertainers." "Talent agencies" arrange to have women hired as dancers, and transferred from club to club every two weeks. When their visas expire after three months, the workers either return to their country of origin or go underground. Those engaged in sex work in night clubs, and who are in the country illegally, are vulnerable to exploitation, including trafficking. The official duty of the women working in the clubs is to eat, drink and dance with clients, and they earn a commission on the number of drinks consumed. Anything earned from sexual activity with the clients tends to belong exclusively to the women. Women involved in this area of the Italian sex industry come from several regions, including Latin America, Southeast Asia, and Eastern Europe. Relations between prostitutes of different nationalities in the same circuit of sex work are almost non-existent.

The biggest prostitution area is street prostitution and the greatest proportion are Nigerian women. Next come Albanian, Russian and Ukrainian women and the rest are Latin American women and transsexuals. This kind of prostitution has been controlled by pimps during the last years, and this type of pimping has two natures: the pimps who have the same nationality as the women and who exploit the women; and the mafia organizations that control the streets as godfathers. Very typical for the Nigerian community is the presence of madams, who are prostitutes or ex-prostitutes.

TAMPEP fieldwork revealed that in all countries where the project operated there was a stratified population of migrant sex workers. One distinct category resides in the host country for an extended period (at least five years) and engages at most in internal mobility within the host country, or work for very brief periods in other European countries. A second category is that of transients, who move continually throughout various states, and whose presence in each is always of short duration. There is a difference, then, between sex workers who choose to emigrate more or less permanently to one of the four countries and who constitute a rather stable group, and those who represent a new wave of trans-European migration. Migrant sex work is characterized by constant changes in the make-up of the target group, with frequent variations in the concentration and number of such workers in any of the four countries participating in the project, in the nationalities represented, and in their degree of mobility.

The variety of policies concerning immigration from outside the European Union, and differences in possibilities for obtaining a residence permit, influence the living and working conditions of migrant sex workers. These differences also increase their marginalization, and facilitate possibilities for exploitation, dependency, and control by criminal organizations. In particular, the severity of regulations recently enacted in Europe against non-Europeans directly influences the basic living and working conditions of clandestine migrant sex workers. Those who are clandestine and work in closed prostitution (apartments, window brothels, sex clubs) remain constantly within the same milieu. Since they rarely, if ever, have an opportunity to leave the context of work or of the sex industry, their lifestyle is one of severe isolation and marginalization, with damaging consequences to physical and mental well-being.

Strategies of Approach

The method used by TAMPEP, applied in all four partner states, involves active and direct participation and collaboration with the target groups. Sociological investigation and practical interventions for AIDS prevention were developed in a continuous cycle of gathering information, organizing activities based on the data gathered, creating new materials, and evaluating results. Provisional findings from the evaluations were then put into practice in new activities. This continuous process of investigation, production of material, implementation and evaluation has permitted the development of grassroots activities tailored to each group and sub group. It has allowed us to work towards positive interventions to improve the health of sex workers.

The concrete activities of the teams are multiple. They have been to conduct interviews to gather general information concerning migrant prostitution in Europe, to conduct an initial needs assessment with sex workers, test and adapt existing materials, develop new materials in collaboration with the target group, and to hold workshops. The teams provide individual consultations, encourage the development of adequate services by governmental institutions, mediate, refer and accompany sex workers to service providers and train peer educators. They continuously evaluate the effects of the activities, focusing on levels of knowledge and attitudes towards health promotion, and behavioral changes regarding safer sex and other health behaviors. Finally, they identify structural impediments to achieving the above.

The target group for our project has characteristically been hard to reach. As with other marginalized populations within society, there is an increasing recognition of the influential role of informal peer educators and supporters in facilitating access to information about and for the community. Interventions have thus been developed through the use of these two types of intermediaries, cultural mediators and peer educators.

Cultural Mediation and Public Health Services

"Cultural mediators are a go-between who know the reasons, the customs and the codes of a majority culture and the host country, as well as the conditions, social ethics and the scene in which a minority group finds itself" (Brussa et.al. 1995: 78). Cultural and linguistic mediation can help stimulate new models of intervention. It may also serve as an example for integrating immigrants into a particularly important arena, that of public health services. In their contact between clients and service providers, cultural mediators serve as a bridge, proving the need for raising awareness, and verifying the perceptions of both sides. Their work is with the many factors intervening between a migrant group and those who provide services for international clients. At the same time, they can facilitate contacts with a population seen to be problematic and burdensome.

Cultural mediators are not social workers, health assistants or exclusively translators. In the TAMPEP project they are individuals capable of eliciting the trust of the target group, and of the same ethnic group or nationality as the sex workers, thereby being capable of recognizing and appreciating the cultural and social mechanisms influencing their behaviors and choices. Cultural mediators are also educators and trainers, with a mandate to pass on knowledge and experiences in the field of STD/AIDS prevention among sex workers. They are recognized as such by the target group. Cultural mediators belong to a "different" culture, interacting with, and reacting to, the dominant culture of the host country. They facilitate communication between members of an immigrant community and those of the dominant culture, as well as with other individuals or groups who in some way have contact with the migrant sex worker. They serve as a point of reference since they have experienced migration and, in some instances, experience within the sex industry.

In their work linking migrant sex workers and service providers, cultural mediators seek to explain host country health systems to people whose ideas and experiences with public health services in their own countries may be quite different. They negotiate and illuminate a variety of non-verbal messages in the way in which the clients address themselves to the service providers. They intervene in the many factors which hinder the access of migrant sex workers to health systems. These factors go beyond the obvious problems of language, and include problems related to specific cultures, to the general situation of the migrant sex worker in the host country, and to levels of education and to the sexuality of the worker.

Mediators must be able to maintain a position of autonomy and neutrality. Their responsibilities go far beyond linguistic interpretation: in the course of their work they translate cultural concepts rather than mere words. The role of cultural mediators in the TAMPEP project is thus a very complex one. On one side, mediators may be perceived by sex workers as healers. On the other side, they may be seen as advocates for the services themselves, rather than for the target group. In this case, the risk is that cultural and linguistic mediators may be perceived as accomplices of the services, thus in part responsible for behaviors which cause dissatisfaction among the target group. Mediators inevitably find themselves trapped between two sides: service providers who may have unrealistic expectations about the effects of cultural mediation, and sex workers themselves who may nurture unrealistic expectations concerning mediators' possibilities to improve health services. It must be made clear to both parties from the outset that cultural mediators cannot provide guarantees to either party.

Cultural Mediation

Merely offering free, anonymous testing or screening does not in itself guarantee access to many of those who most require such services. Just because a door is open does not mean that entry is any easier if one does not know where the door is located, or even that it exists. Just getting in a door does not mean that one necessarily enjoys the room in which one finds oneself. For example, although there are no policies of mandatory STD screening in Hamburg, and no direct control is exercised over prostitution venues to ensure regular medical check-ups, in the minds of many sex workers public health services still connote institutions characterized by repressive measures and attitudes. Many of the women have professional experience in other areas of Germany in which mandatory screening is conducted by the municipal health service. It is obvious, therefore, that many migrant sex workers are not in a position to percieve visits to the public screening and treatment center for HIV/STDs as anything but coerced controls conducted with the complicity of pimps. In a situation fraught with ambiguities, one of the challenges of cultural mediation is to promote the center's vision of medical care and check-ups as a tool for health promotion and self-esteem.

Peer Educators

In contrast to cultural mediators, peer educators are members of the target group, and therefore identify themselves completely with the group. They play the role of leaders, and articulate the interest of their peers. The experience of the TAMPEP project with peer education targeted towards a specific group of sex workers (mobile migrants who are frequently marginalized and in a position of dependency) has provided insight into the advantages and limitations of the approach, and pointed to certain modifications which may need to be introduced in applying concepts of peer education.

Our experience has shown that there are some preconditions for effective peer education. Generally speaking, peer educators must have a base in the community, and must be recognized as leaders by the community base, while being representatives of the particular project. Experience has shown that the success of peer educators depends more on their self-identification with the role, and on their acceptance within the community, than on their specific position within it. Peer educators must also be clear about their role both within the group and within the project. Peer education implies a didactic role, influencing changes in behavior. Educators should be able to raise awareness among their colleagues, and to organize and conduct workshops on various themes related to prevention and safer sex practices in the field of AIDS/STDs. Their role implies a certain distancing, which facilitates the assumption of a student/ teacher relationship. While they have the role of imparting information and knowledge, increasing responsibility and self esteem, peer educators must also make distinctions between their community work and their own and other sex workers' private lives (their romantic involvements, professional contacts and career). They must also be able to apply the concept of peer education with a community that is extremely mobile. As opposed to cultural and linguistic mediators, peer educators do not need to have to have either a relationship of confidentiality or a "mandate" from the group with whom they identify. Their primary focus is on mutual support among colleagues for sustaining behavior changes in adopting safer sex.

Training Nigerian Sex Workers in Turin

The creation of a drop-in center for Nigerian (and other African) sex workers in Turin is a concrete example of how coming together around a common idea and a shared base serves to mobilize a community, and can lead to further activities. A group of fifteen active and recently retired sex workers who had participated in the development of the drop-in center were successively trained and functioned as peer supporters. They collaborated in the development of material, translated, and promoted the project's activities. Once this structural base was established, the workers identified twenty additional Nigerian sex workers from five different ethnic groups who, in turn, underwent structured training courses on AIDS, STDs, and the female reproductive system. These peer education courses have been repeated three times, each time with a new group of participants.

Using Mobility

A travel route is formed by a network of contacts among fellow nationals who inform others of work opportunities, with a snowball effect. Other networks are formed by individuals who channel women within a circuit managed by people external to the sex industry. In both cases a sex worker's period of residency within a country may be extremely brief. This form of mobility is inherent to migrant prostitution, and what at first glance may seem as a handicap may be taken as an opportunity. The fact that frequent mobility may limit possibilities for repeated contact with the target group should not detract from the equally valid fact that said mobility can contribute to a further dissemination of health promotion messages within the same circuits: it should be possible for those involved to become health messengers. So far the project has been able to use this phenomenon only to a limited extent, but that the possibility exists is demonstrated when sex workers interviewed as a control group, who had not had been involved with the project's activities, had already heard of TAMPEP through colleagues encountered in the new workplace or through fellow nationals before they left.

Preliminary Results

Because of the extremely marginal and vulnerable conditions in which migrant prostitutes live in Western European countries, and through the experience gained during the first year of the project, both by the direct contact with migrant prostitutes and by an assessment of their living conditions, we have concluded that STD and HIV/AIDS prevention for this group must be included in a broader framework of general health promotion. The development of such a framework should be recognized as a priority. It has also become clear that more than 10,000 migrant sex workers in certain areas of the Netherlands, Italy, Austria and Germany have been in contact with the TAMPEP project resulting in more than 140,000 interactive contacts. Group activities like workshops have been attended by 400 women and 150 transsexuals. Of them, 200 women and 20 transsexuals are collaborating in the design and implementation of the activities as TAMPEP peer educators. We are now working with these individuals. Another important observation is that, although many projects employ strategies and materials designed for "Western" eyes, women from different cultural backgrounds need totally different approaches, strategies and materials. That was the basis for the methodology of TAMPEP.

The production and use of materials for the project was considered a tool for our work and not an end in itself. The materials were created and developed together with the target group during workshops, streetwork and other kinds of regular meetings. They were an important didactic material for training the peer educators. The aims were to produce materials for learning purposes as they were done for and with migrant sex workers and to observe and incorporate the specific cultural differences within each group. The different materials were useful in terms of increasing awareness on STDs and AIDS as well as supporting the other activities implemented through the project. This material was not only disseminated in the regions where TAMPEP works, but is also used in other countries in the European Union and in the women's countries of origin.

After four years of the project, we have found that social control and social cohesion are important factors in increasing the capacity of sex workers to challenge clients who are unwilling to practice safer sex. We have thus attempted to boost group cohesion among migrant sex workers in an attempt to positively influence their articulated and implicit codes of conduct. These strategies will improve both the initial bargaining position of sex workers and their negotiating techniques. We believe that it is necessary to focus on augmenting the self-confidence and, consequently, the self-efficacy of the sex workers. Women must be supported in their efforts to gain control over their working and living conditions. By building on naturally existing contacts, peer leaders and educators have a crucial role to play in this process. A broad spectrum of community-based initiatives directed at empowerment of migrant sex workers can have a major impact on primary prevention in that it allows sex workers increased scope in their negotiations with clients, brothel owners and pimps.

Conclusions

It is not only cultural diversity that creates diversity in attitudes. More important is the particular context of the sex industry in which migrant prostitutes are employed, the structural factors regarding prostitution in the host country; and the health policies that have a direct impact on the social and working conditions of sub-groups within a targeted population. Moreover, the possibilities for sex workers to have optimal control over their sexual services and the promotion of their health in general, is determined more by the control they have over their working and living conditions, and by their legal status in Europe, than by their cultural and national background. There must to be constant collaboration with the sex workers, in which a space is created to allow them to define their own needs and priorities, to create their own materials and activities, and to make their demands within the ambit of European prostitution.

Those who work with migrant sex workers should ideally be of the same nationalities and cultures as the migrant sex workers themselves. This allows effective and direct dialogue, and working group members can function as cultural mediators between the prostitutes and all possible service providers. Partial results, effective implementation of activities, ways of adapting existing materials and methods, and ongoing evaluations need to be periodically reviewed in order to make them as effective as possible.

Leaflet distribution alone is insufficient to bring about behavior change. The basis of the work must be in continuous and intensive fieldwork to establish trust. Individual and group counselling (including social, legal and psychological matters) is necessary to facilitate behavior changes. Supporting migrant sex workers to empower themselves in other aspects, such as in improving working conditions, in the social sphere, and in their legal status, must also be part of any intervention, as this will enable them to control their own lives.

Continuous collaboration with health services is crucial in ensuring that information on safer sexual behaviors reaches migrant sex workers. The role of the program in this should be focused more specifically towards that of mediating between the sex workers and the medical services, shaping and gaining official backing for co-operative models to be adapted according to local circumstances in each country.

Interventions promoting safer sex practices alone are not sufficient. Informing migrant sex workers about the right brand of condoms, instructing them in proper use, and teaching negotiating skills need to be supplemented by direct field work—actual assistance in going out to buy condoms, or creating the conditions so that they are supplied condoms that are adequate. Similarly, informing sex workers of the value of regular preventive medical attention must be complemented with referral to addresses of empathic doctors. In other words, campaigns to give information and to promote health without connecting these campaigns to service provision will not be effective.

The mobility of migrant sex workers within Europe requires that concepts of "peer education" be adapted. This mobility can be used in a positive way: when peer educators are trained in the fundamentals of safer sex and health promotion, they can function as "health messengers" as they move through Europe. Ideally, they should be supported by an international network of intervention projects. On the other hand, the possibilities for non-European prostitutes to create an autonomous organization and to work together in a community-based model focusing on human rights and advocacy is limited by the legal status of clandestine migrants and by the marginalization to which they are subjected. A further limitation to group work stems from the fact that for the majority of foreign sex workers, prostitution represents a means of survival, an activity practiced out of economic necessity. It is seen as temporary work, and not as an identity.

The project has developed a number of leaflets, and one might have the impression that now that these have been developed, future work can restrict itself to distributing them among new groups. This would be to miss the most important aspect of the method: the process of making the leaflets is important in itself. Making materials stimulates discussions of their needs amongst the women and men involved, and fosters group cohesion. Thus each activity with a new group should include the production of new leaflets: each particular situation calls for new items, and is in itself a very important educational activity. Moreover, leaflets serve as a written reminder after a working group session or an individual communication, but they cannot function as an information tool in themselves.

It is necessary to establish a network of contacts both within the sex work milieu and within the broader community. Proprietors of prostitution businesses obviously often play a decisive role influencing working and sanitary conditions in their houses, and affecting the possibilities of practicing safer sex. TAMPEP has now found that influencing proprietors, with the support of medical and health authorities, is a powerful tool in changing structural circumstances.

The presence of migrant sex workers in the European sex industry constitutes a phenomenon which has changed all aspects of the market. Current European policies in the areas of prostitution, of migration, and of AIDS prevention do not reflect this. The effects of the policies are at the moment counterproductive: migrant sex workers are not stopped at the border, but are more and more dependent on, and under the control of international criminal organizations. This clearly does not serve the interest of either safer sex or of public health. The problem is that we have to recognize that the policies concerning immigration and prostitution have a direct influence on the living and working conditions of migrant sex workers and that these policies carry the responsibility for making migrant sex workers vulnerable to exploitation and dependency, through marginalization and isolation. It is not a matter of preventing migration and/or prostitution, but to prevent all kinds of situation in which women can become dependent.

Note

1. An earlier version of this chapter was published in *Crossing Borders: Ethnicity, Migration, and AIDS*, edited by Mary Haour-Knipe (Taylor & Francis 1996).

24 | COIN and MODEMU in the Dominican Republic*

Kamala Kempadoo

The COIN Organization

COIN developed from a national concern in the Dominican Republic with the spread of AIDS and the HIV virus. From 1985, various steps were taken by the government to reach and educate sexual workers about HIV and AIDS and to improve public health. Surveys were held to assess the sex workers population in the capital of Santo Domingo, a peer out-reach group was established for preventative health care work among sex workers, and doctors and nurses in fifteen hospitals in four different cities were trained. The activities rapidly grew under the auspices of the National AIDS Program. In 1987, the peer out-reach program disengaged from the government agency and established itself as the non-governmental organization COIN (Centro de Orientación e Investigación Integral). The organization developed its specific intervention model with a focus on preventative health care work, support for HIV-positive and AIDS patients, finding alternative work for sex workers and distributing condoms. The peer workers were christened *Mensajeros de Salud* (Messengers of Health) and their

*This chapter is based on translations of several COIN publications, edited by Kamala Kempadoo, with assistance from E. Antonio de Moya.

work extended to various cities and tourist centers. By 1994, the network of "messengers" consisted of twenty-four paid team leaders and 387 volunteers.

Other activities sprang from COIN's central work. For example, the theater group "Avancemos," designed by the Messenger of Health educators has performed and held training sessions in prostitution venues for workers, customers and sex business owners about safe sex practices. In 1993, COIN started publishing the newsletter *La Nueva Historia: Periodico de la Noche*, a monthly bulletin created by and directed at Dominican sex workers. Approximately 5,000 bulletins are distributed monthly in different parts of the country. The organization has also produced a number of instruction manuals for peer educators, comic books about conditions that prostitutes must deal with, and a film "Me Duela el Alma" on the trafficking of women from the Dominican Republic to the Netherlands for sex work. By 1995, street-corner work among young male sex workers and a collaborative research project among 354 male sex workers in Santo Domingo was underway (De Moya et al. 1996).

COIN's activities aroused a debate in the country about the nature of prostitution, and led in 1988 to the introduction of the name *trabajadora sexual* (female sex worker). This redefinition was considered necessary to adequately address the situation in which women who exchanged sex for money understood themselves to be involved in the trade, and as a way to dispense with the stigma and negativity associated with the traditional definition *cuero* (prostitute). According to the journalist, Luchy Placencia:

> If sex workers had not begun publishing a newspaper in which they do not call themselves "prostitutes" and do not think of themselves as victims, it would probably be true that the media would have continued to call them "prostitutes" or "cueros." . . . *Trabajadoras sexuales* is a term that gets rid of the false morality and as a consequence reflects reality. It helps to define a woman who earns a living performing sex work (Placencia 1995).

Nevertheless, this definition remains contested by conservative groups which deny the right of women and men to earn a living through sexual activity. The editors of COIN's first congress report advise that the debate around the term prostitution is "incomplete and contradictory" since it reflects the idea that prostitution is a form or labor around the exchange of sex for money and, simultaneously, the notion that prostitution is forced (*Juntarros* 56).

Research into the Sex Industry

A large part of COIN's foundational work lay in researching the sex trade in the Dominican Republic for the creation of educational materials and out-reach methods suitable for the working populations. Various studies were also made resulting in a report, published in 1994 entitled *La Industria del Sexo por Dentro* (Inside the Sex Industry). The first study was conducted, in two phases, in 1992. The first phase was held among 300 female sex workers in Santo Domingo and 126 in Puerto Plata and the second, among respectively 304 and 202. A second study was held in the same cities, among respectively 302 and 126 female sex workers. The third study surveyed 98 male owners and managers of sex businesses in the North and East zones of Santo Domingo, and a fourth and last, held in May 1993 among 288 female sex workers in Santo Domingo, San Francisco de Macoris, and Vicente Noble. This final study addressed issues not previously included in the earlier surveys concerning reproductive health matters, levels of violence, knowledge of civil and human rights, travel experiences and attitudes about organizing among the women. The surveys were conducted by the "Messenger of Health" workers to facilitate communication, sensitivity to sex workers issues and to identify the pertinence of the research questions and assumptions (COIN 1994:8). Conclusions of the report state:

> The sociodemographic characteristics shows a profile of women between the ages of 15 and 45 years, with an average age of 23–25 years and an educational level below the eighth grade in 80 percent of the cases. Seven or more out of 10 are mothers who work in different locations than where they live, 51 percent of whom do not receive financial assistance from the biological fathers of their children. Twenty percent have an additional income to sex work. Contrary to the myths about the causes of sex work, less than 10 percent of these women are victims of abuses or maltreatment by their parents. . . . The age when they begin sex work for money is the most consistent finding in the studies, motivated principally by economic needs, beginning, on average between the ages of 18 and 20, approximately three to four years after their first sexual contact and for the most, after having had one to three children. The number of clients depends on the place of work, with the majority working in bars and hotels and where, on few occasions, there is more than one client a day. . . . This confirms the notion that sex work in the Dominican Republic is for basic survival, a means for a woman to provide and feed her children and to resolve an immediate economic problem, and not for accumulating capital or saving money.

Information gathered in the final study about migration clarifies ideas about the movement of women into sex industries elsewhere. Around half of the women interviewed in the fourth study, for example, said that if they went abroad, they would continue with sex work. The other half aspired to doing something other than sex work. For eighty percent of the women, working in another country was seen as a way to financially support their family. The majority of the women interviewed hoped to be better accepted by their local communities once they returned home (COIN 1994: 38–39). Of the fifty-two women who had traveled and returned, Greece, Haiti, St. Thomas, Curaçao, Aruba and Spain were the most visited countries (see also Rosario et al. 1996). The average age to make their first trip was around twenty-two years. Approximately half of the travelers had been assisted by family and friends, nineteen percent were recruited by "men and women who prepare trips" (i.e traffickers), and four percent made it on their own. More than half—fifty-six percent— were aware of the type of work they were migrating for. Twenty-seven percent stated they did not realize what the consequences of the trip were. Approximately half of the women in the study had worked exclusively in prostitution once abroad, others were engaged as hotel workers or dancers while a few had been involved in the garment trade (COIN 1994: 39).

Return home was conditioned by various factors. Among them were that the women had to care for their children, that their work contracts overseas had expired or that they had been deported. Some ten percent of the migrants has returned home simply because they did not like the foreign country, and a few because they had made the money they had wanted. Around half of the women interviewed reported to have "no problem" with doing sex work overseas, seventeen percent responded negatively to this question. Just under half of the women had managed to help their families with the money they earned overseas, while a quarter of the population felt that they had failed to achieve the goals they has set for themselves (COIN 1994: 40, see also Rosario et al., 1996). This information, the researchers concluded, significantly contradicted dominant ideas about the engagement of Dominican women in the global sex trade. Force and coercion by middlemen to go abroad and ignorance about the type of work once abroad did not play a prominent role in the migration process (COIN 1994: 44).

Insights from the studies conducted over the three-year period in various sites in the country, also led to the formulation of various future directions for COIN. Among them was the need to develop information, education and communication about sexual and reproductive health in the sex industry, particularly basic education about human and civil rights among the sex workers. Ongoing organization among sex workers to defend their rights and raise their consciousness about their situation was defined as necessary for the empowerment of women in the sex trade and to improve the quality of life for the population. Finally the researchers stressed the need to include others in the educational and organizational efforts within the sex industry, such as the boyfriends, lovers, husbands of the sex workers, the "chulos" and pimps, owners and managers of sex businesses, clients and their partners, the military and the police, organized groups of women, legislators and journalists (COIN 1994: 44–45). The COIN team articulated a direction that was underpinned by a recognition of the importance of women in society and the need to guarantee human rights.

The First Sex Workers Congress

In May 1995 COIN organized its first congress on prostitution and sex work. The organizing committee comprised of the director and two health workers at COIN, a UNICEF representative and two "Messengers of Health" (COIN 1996: 216). The aim of the congress was to make the Dominican State and society attentive to the economic and social conditions who determine prostitution or sex work, and to the diversity of issues affecting women that practice the trade. The specific objectives were to analyze the causes of prostitution, to analyze the problems of migration to foreign countries and sex tourism, to discuss working and civil rights of female sex workers and to present alternatives for life and work for women in the sex trade (COIN 1996: 215).

The congress also encouraged the participation and voice of sex workers. Of the five hundred congress participants, around three hundred were female sex workers from different towns and cities in the Dominican Republic. Marisol Blanco—one of the several "Messengers of Health" who addressed the congress—stressed the importance of the congress for the empowerment of sex workers:

> We are viewed negatively by society, in our neighborhoods, by our friends and even by our families. They accuse and persecute us without stopping to think about the reasons that took us into this life. The moment has come to put an end to this and to support each other . . . it's time to stop the violence and injustice, and who could, rather than ourselves, support each other in this struggle (1995).

The congress concluded with various resolutions, around the issues of the causes of prostitution, the legal status of sex work, violence within the sex trade, health and employment alternatives (COIN 1996:195–206). Multiple factors for the cause of prostitution were identified during the congress, such as disruptions within the family, the economic crisis in the country, a failing educational system, changes in social values, and a lack of labor market options for women. Emphasis was given to the fact that many women were independently entering, and staying within, the sex trade and that working conditions within the sector were appalling. The congress demanded that the women's position in society be recognized as similar to that of any other worker. Consequently, "paid vacations, sick leave, maternity leave, a weekly day off, overtime and retirement benefits" for women working in the sex trade were a central part of the congress resolutions (200). The Department of Labor was called upon by congress participants to ensure that owners and mangers of sex businesses comply with regular labor laws. Unions and women's organizations were urged to "include the labor demands of sex workers in their programs" (201). Violence towards sex workers was defined during the congress as multiple violations of their human and civil rights, including physical and verbal abuse from clients and pimps, violations of the right to travel freely throughout the country, being subjected to indiscriminate raids, blackmail and incarceration, and discrimination in laws and social policies designed to protect women. To counter this violence, the congress organizers and participants resolved to "denounce all forms of discrimination against women who exchange sex for money" (201). They demanded from clients, intermediaries and official authorities "an end to the violence against the women and respect for their civil rights" (201). Others were called upon to "work towards the social decriminalization of prostitution, the enforcement of laws against exploitation of sex workers by managers, and an end to the persecution of trafficked women" (204).

In regards to health issues, particularly in the light of AIDS, the congress laid out the need for a specific budget in the existing National AIDS program to guarantee better services for sex workers and to support the educational work already being done by the "Messengers of Health." Discrimination of prostitutes by health-care personnel was also identified as an area that required specific attention. Finally, through recognizing the limited options for women to earn a living in a country pressured by global economic forces and patriarchal laws and ideologies, the government and the private sectors were urged to seek ways to create "infrastructures of work, education and basic support services for women as alternatives to the exchange of sex for money" (203–4).

MODEMU and Sex Worker Autonomy

COIN continues its work and is a valuable organization for sex workers empowerment. As Milagro Martinez describes, "In this institution we have learned to value ourselves as women, to know our rights, to know our bodies, how to protect ourselves and one another, how to build our self-esteem and, the most important thing, how to teach to other women what we have learned" (1995). Nevertheless, an autonomous sex workers organization emerged in 1996 as a result of COIN's projects. Named *Moviemiento de Mujeres Unidas*, MODEMU (The Movement of United Women) its aims are to promote the independent organization of Dominican sex workers, to raise their self-esteem and awareness of their rights as women, citizens and workers, and to develop job alternatives. MODEMU asserts itself as the voice of the Dominican sex workers. It seeks to create mechanisms of solidarity and mutual support, to fight against violence, to prevent sexually transmitted diseases and AIDS, to promote the creation of health services, to provide legal and psychological assistance to victimized members, to train women to find other jobs and to protect their children against stigmatization.

MODEMU and COIN, while successful on many fronts, face several unresolved issues. Among them, as Antonio de Moya points out, are that only the major cities in the Dominican Republic are touched by the initiatives, and a class bias exists in the intervention work. Consequently, middle-class and lower middle-class urban environments are the main targets, with street and rural workers and high risk lower classes being overlooked. In addition, a strong political orientation for the group leadership must still emerge among sex workers in order for the organization to sustain itself, and the high level of dependence on foreign aid, from both governmental and religious groups, could curtail the future development of a wider sex workers movement. All are issues that sex workers and allies in the Dominican Republic will be grappling with in the coming years.

Bibliography

Abaiye–Boateng , I. N .A. "Structural Adjustment Programme (SAP) and Poor Women in Ghana." Paper presented at the African Studies Center/Department of Sociology, University of Liverpool Seminar, November 1992.

Adomoko-Ampofo, A. "Women and AIDS in Ghana: 'I Control my Body (or Do I?).'" Paper presented at IUSSP Seminar on Women and Demographic Change in Sub-Saharan Africa, Dakar, Senegal, 3–6 March, 1993.

Alberts, Tineke. *Je Lust en Je Leven: Een inventariserend Onderzoek naar Relatievorming, Sexueel Gedrag en de Preventie van AIDS op Curaçao.* Curaçao: Nationale AIDScommissie van de Nederlandse Antillen en de Geneeskundige-en Gezondheidsdienst van het Eilandgebied Curaçao, 1992.

Alexander, M. Jaqui, and Chandra Talpade Mohanty eds. *Feminist Geneologies, Colonial Legacies, Democratic Futures.* New York: Routledge, 1997.

Alexander, Priscilla. "Some Considerations Regarding Trafficking in Women and Exploitation of Prostitution in Relation to HIV/AIDS Prevention." Paper presented at the Inter-Sessional Working Group of the Commission on the Status of Women, Vienna, 1992.

————. "Making Sex Safer: a Guide to HIV/AIDS Interventions." Geneva, WHO Global Programme on AIDS, Office of Intervention and Support, unpublished Doc. GUID-TOC:GD4, 1993.

Allison, Anne. *Nightwork: Sexuality, Pleasure, and Corporate Masculinity in a Tokyo Hostess Club.* Chicago: University of Chicago Press, 1994.

Ammelrooy, Anneke van. *Vrouwenhandel: De Internationale Seksslavinnenmarkt.* s'Gravenhage: BZZTôH, 1989.

Anarfi, J. K. "International Labor Migration in West Africa: A Case Study of the Ghanaian Migrants in Lagos, Nigeria." M.A. Thesis, University of Ghana, Legon. 1982

————. "International Migration of Ghanaian Women to Abidjan, Cote d'Ivoire: a Demographic and Socio-Economic Study." Ph.D. Dissertation, University of Ghana, Legon, 1990.

————. "Sexuality, Migration and AIDS in Ghana—A Socio-Behavioral Study." *Health Transition Review,* Supplement to Volume 3, 1993: 45–68.

Anker, R. et al. "Women's Participation in the Labor Force: A Methods Test for India for Improving its Measurement." ILO Women, Work and Development Series, No.16, 1988.

Anderson, Sarah and John Cavanagh. *The Top 200: The Rise of Global Corporate Power.* Washington DC: Institute for Policy Studies, 1996.

Anthias, Floya and Nira Yuval-Davis. *Racialized Boundaries: Race, Nation, Gender, Colour, Class and the Anti-Racist Struggle.* London: Routledge, 1992.

Asia Watch Women's Rights Project. *A Modern Form of Slavery: Trafficking of Burmese Women and Girls into Brothels in Thailand.* Human Rights Watch, 1993.

Assimeng, M. *Social Structure of Ghana*. Accra-Tema: Ghana Publishing Corporation, 1981.

Azize, Yamila, Kamala Kempadoo and Tatiana Cordero. "International Report Project on Trafficking in Women: Latin American and Caribbean Region." Draft Report. Foundation Against Trafficking in Women, December 1996.

Bailey, Beth and David Farber. *The First Strange Place: Race and Sex in World War II Hawaii*. Baltimore: John Hopkins Press, 1992.

Barry, Kathleen. *Female Sexual Slavery*. New York: New York University Press, 1984.

———. *The Prostitution of Sexuality: The Global Exploitation of Women*. New York: New York University Press, 1995.

Bell, Laurie, ed. *Good Girls, Bad Girls: Feminists and Sex Trade Workers Face to Face*. Toronto: Seal Press, 1987.

Bell, Shannon. *Reading Writing and Rewriting the Prostitute Body*. Bloomington: Indiana University Press, 1994.

Bernstein, Laurie. *Sonia's Daughters: Prostitutes and Their Regulation in Imperial Russia*. Berkeley: University of California Press, 1995.

Bindman, Jo, and Jo Doezema. *Redefining Prostitution as Sex Work on the International Agenda*. London: Anti-Slavery International, 1997.

Black, Maggie. *In the Twilight Zone: Child Workers in the Hotel, Tourism and Catering Industry*. Geneva: International Labor Office and NSWP, 1995.

———. "Home Truths," *New Internationalist,* 252, (February 1994).

Blanco, Marisol. "Causas que originan la prostitucion o trabajo sexual." Paper presented at the First Dominican Congress on Prostitution and Sex Work. Santo Domingo, Dominican Republic, May 1995.

Boer, Marga de. *Traffic in Women: Policy in Focus*. Utrecht: Willem Pompe Institute for Criminal Law, 1994.

Bolles, Lynn. "Sand, Sea and the Forbidden." *Transforming Anthropology,* 3 (1992): 30–34.

Bolles, A. Lynne. "Common Ground for Creativity," *Cultural Survival* 16 (Winter 1992): 34–38.

Bonachich, Edna, Lucie Cheng, Norma Chinchilla, Nora Hamilton and Paul Ong eds. *Global Production: The Apparel Industry in the Pacific Rim*. Philadelphia: Temple University Press, 1994.

Bond, George C., John Kreniske, Ida Susser and Joan Vincent. *AIDS in Africa and the Caribbean.* Boulder: Westview Press, 1997

Bourdieu, Pierre. *Outline of a Theory of Practice*. Cambridge University Press, 1977.

Brecher, Jeremy and Tim Costello. *Global Village or Global Pillage: Economic Reconstruction from the Bottom Up*. Boston: South End Press, 1994.

Brockett, L., and A. Murray. "Thai Sex Workers in Sydney." In *Sex Work and Sex Workers in Australia*, (eds) R. Perkins et al, Sydney: UNSW Press, 1994: 191-202

Brussa, Licia. *Survey on Prostitution, Migration and Traffic in Women: History and Current Situation.* Council of Europe. EG/Prost. 1991.

Brussa, Licia. et al. *Tampep: Analyses, the First Year 1993/1994*. Amsterdam, Mr A. de Graaf Stichting. 1995.

Brussa, Licia. et al. *Tampep: Manual.* Amsterdam, Mr. A. de Graaf Stichting. 1994.

Brussa, Licia. "Migrant Prostitutes in the Netherlands." In *Vindication of the Rights of Whores,* ed. Gail Pheterson. Seattle, Washington: Seal Press, 1989. 227–240.

Brussa, Licia et al. *Tampep: Final Report.* Amsterdam, Mr. A. de Graaf Stichting. 1996.

Brydon, L. "Factors Affecting the Migration of Women in Ghana." SSRC Report in British Library, 1977.

Brydon, L. "Ghanaian Women in the Migration Process." In *Gender and Migration in the Third World,* ed. S. Chant, Bellhaven Press. 1992.

Brydon, L. "Women at Work: Some Changes in Family Structure in Amedzofe-Avatime." *Africa* 49 (2) 1979: 97–III.

Brydon, L. "The Dimensions of Subordination: A Case Study from Avatime, Ghana." In *Women, Work and Ideology in the Third World,* ed. H. Ashfar, London: Tavistock, 1985b.

Brydon, L. "Who Moves? Women and Migration in West Africa in the 1980s." In *Migrants, Workers and the Social Order,* ed. J. S. Eades, London: Tavistock, 1987.

Brydon, L. "The Avatime Family and Migration:, 1900–1977." In *Circulation in Third World Countries,* eds. M. Prothero and M. Chapman, London: Routledge and Kegan Paul, 1985a.

Bunch, Charlotte. "Transforming Human Rights from a Feminist Perspective." In *Women's Rights as Human Rights-International Feminist Perspectives,* eds. Julie Peters and Andrea Wolper, London: Routledge, 1996.

Caldwell, J. C. "Determinants of Rural-Urban Migration in Ghana." *Population Studies* 22 (3) 1968: 361–377.

Caldwell, J. C. *African Rural-Urban Migration: The Movement to Ghana's Towns.* Canberra: Australian National University Press, 1969.

Carby, Hazel V. "White Woman Listen! Black Feminism and the Boundaries of Sisterhood." In *The Empire Strikes Back: Race and Racism in 70s Britain.* Centre for Contemporary Cultural Studies. London: Hutchinson, 1982. 183–211.

Center for the Protection of Children's Rights. *The Trafficking of Children for Prostitution in Thailand.* Bangkok: Unpublished manuscript, 1991.

Chancer, Lynn Sharon. "Prostitution, Feminist Theory and Ambivalence: Notes from the Sociological Underground." *Social Text* 37 (Winter 1993): 143–181.

Chanel Ives Marie. "Haitian and Dominican Women in the Sex Trade." *CAFRA News* (June 1994): 13–14. translated by Cathy Shepherd.

Chaney Elsa M. and Mary Carcia Castro. *Muchachas No More: Household Workers in Latin America and the Caribbean.* Philadelphia: Temple University Press, 1989.

Chapkis, Wendy. *Live Sex Acts: Women Performing Erotic Labor.* New York: Routledge, 1997.

Chomsky, Noam. *World Orders Old and New.* New York: Columbia University Press, 1994.

Clark, G. and T. Manuh. *Structural Adjustment and Women Farmers.* Edited by C. Gladin. Florida: University of Florida Press, 1991.

Clemencia, Joceline. "Women Who Love Women: A Whole Perspective from *Kachapera* to *Open Throats.*" Paper presented at the 20th Annual Conference of the Caribbean Studies Association. Curaçao, May, 1995.

Cohen, Jeff. "Cuba Libre," *Playboy,* 38 (March 1991): 69–74

Cohen, Eric."Thai Girls and Farang Men—the Edge of Ambiguity." *Annals of Tourism Research.* 9 (1982): 403–42.

COIN. *La Industria del Sexo por Dentro.* Santo Domingo: COIN, 1994.

COIN. *Juntarnos: Memorias 1er. Congreso Dominicano de Trabajadoras Sexuales* (Proceedings from the First Dominican Congress for Female Sex Workers) Santo Domingo: COIN, 1996.

Collins, Patricia Hill. *Black Feminist Thought: Knowledge, Consciousness and the Politics of Empowerment.* New York: Routledge, 1990.

Convention For the Suppression of the Traffic in Persons and of the Exploitation of the Prostitution of Others. United Nations, 1949.

Convention on the Elimination of All Forms of Sexual Exploitation of Women, by The Coalition Against Trafficking in Women, 1993.

Coomarasway, R. "Report of the Special Rapporteur on Violence Against Women," Geneva, UN document, 1995.

Cooper, Marc. "For Sale: Used Marxism." *Harper's Magazine* (March 1995).

Corbin, Alain. *Women for Hire: Prostitution and Sexuality in France After 1850.* Cambridge, Mass.: Harvard University Press, 1990.

Cortes, Eduardo et al. "HIV-1, HIV-2 and HTLV-I Infection in High Risk groups on Brazil." *The New England Journal of Medicine* 15 (1989).

COSPE. "Cooperazione per lo Sviluppo dei Paesi Emergenti." *Atti del seminario di Bologna sulla mediazione linguistica e culturale.* COSPE, Firenze. 1993.

Danaher, Kevin ed. *Fifty Years is Enough: The Case Against the World Bank and the International Monetary Fund.* Boston, South End Press, 1994.

Darling, Lynn. "Havana at Midnight." *Esquire* (May 1995): 96–104.

David, Tasha *Worlds Apart, Women and the Global Economy.* Brussels: International Confederation of Free Trade Unions, 1996.

David, F. "Overseas Workers in the Australian Sex Industry: Issues and Options for Reform." Canberra. Unpublished paper. 1995.

De Boer, Marga. *Traffic in Women: Policy in Focus.* Utrecht: Willem Pompe Institute for Criminal Law, 1994.

Declaration of Mexico on the Equality of Women, United Nations 1975,

Deere, Carmen Diana, Peggy Antrobus, Lynn Bolles, Edwin Melendez, Peter Phillips, Marcia Rivera and Helen Safa. *In the Shadows of the Sun: Caribbean Development Alternatives and U.S. Policy.* Boulder: Westview, 1990.

Delacoste, Frederique and Priscilla Alexander, eds. *Sex Work: Writings by Women in the Sex Industry.* Pittsburg: Cleis Press, 1987.

Díaz, Elena, Esperanza Fernández, and Tania Caram. "Turismo y prostitución en Cuba." Paper presented at the 21st Annual Conference of the Caribbean Studies Association. Puerto Rico, May 1996.

Dinan, C. "Pragmatists or Feminists? The Professional 'Single' Women of Accra, Ghana." *Cahiers d'Etudes Africaines* 65 (1977): 155–176.

Dinan, C. "Sugar Daddies and Gold Diggers: The White Collar Single Woman in Accra." In *Female and Male in West Africa*, ed. C. Oppong, London: Allen and Unwin, 1983 .

Dirasse, Lasketch. *The Commoditization of Female Sexuality: Prostitution and Socio-Economic Relations in Addis Ababa, Ethiopia.* New York: AMS Press,1991.

Doezema, Jo. "Choice in Prostitution." In *Changing Faces of Prostitution.* Helsinki: Unioni—The League of Finnish Feminists, 1995.

Doezema, Jo. "Sex Worker Delegation to the Beijing Conference." Amsterdam: Network of Sex Work Projects internal communication, March, 1995.

EUROPAP. *European Intervention Projects on AIDS Prevention for Prostitutes: Final Report.* Gent: EUROPAP, 1994.

Fanon, Frantz. *Black Skin, White Masks.* New York: Grove Press, 1967

Farmer, Paul. "Women, Poverty, and AIDS," In *Women, Poverty and Aids: Sex Drugs and Structural Violence,* eds. Paul Farmer, Margaret Conner and Jane Simmons. Monroe, Common Courage Press, 1996. 3–38.

Farmer, Paul, Margaret Conner, and Jane Simmons eds. *Women, Poverty and Aids: Sex Drugs and Structural Violence.* Monroe, Common Courage Press, 1996.

Fereh, Lenke. "Forced Prostitution and Traffic in Persons." In *Combating Traffic in Persons: Proceedings of the Conference on Traffic In Persons,* eds. Marieke Klap, Yvonne Klerk and Jaqueline Smith. Utrecht: IMS, Netherlands Institute of Human Rights, 1995.

Fernández, Nadine T. "The Color of Love: Young Interracial Couples in Cuba." *Latin American Perspectives,* 23 (Winter 1996): 99–117.

Fitzpatrick, Jean, "Using International Human Rights Norms to Combat Violence Against Women." In *Human Rights of Women: National and International Perspectives,* ed. Rebecca J. Cook. Philadelphia: University of Pennsylvania Press. 1994.

Foucault, Michel. *The History of Sexuality: An Introduction.* New York: Pantheon Books, 1978/London: Penguin, 1981.

Friedman, Robert I. "India's Shame." *The Nation* 8 April 1996: 11–20.

GAATW/STV. "A Proposal to Replace the Convention for the Suppression of the Traffic in Persons and of the Exploitation of the Prostitution of Others." Utrecht, 1994.

Gardiner, Judith Kegan. *Provoking Agents: Gender and Agency in Theory and Practice.* Urbana/Chicago: University of Illinois Press, 1995.

Gibson, Mary. *Prostitution and the State in Italy 1860–1915.* New Brunswick: Rutgers University Press, 1986.

Giddens, Anthony. *The Constitution of Society: Outline of the Theory of Structuration.* Cambridge: Polity Press, 1984.

Goldman, Marion S. *Gold Diggers and Silver Miners: Prostitution and Social Life on the Comstock Lode.* Ann Arbor: University of Michigan Press, 1981.

Goldman, E. *The Traffic in Women, and Other Essays on Feminism.* New York: Times Change Press, 1970 [1917].

Gomezjara, Francisco, and Estanislao Barrera. *Sociología de la prostitución.* Mexico, D.F.: Distribuciones Fontamara, S.A., 1992.

Guy, Donna J. *Sex and Danger in Buenos Aires: Prostitution, Family, and Nation in Argentina.* Lincoln: University of Nebraska Press, 1990.

Hanks, Lucien. "Merit and Power in the Thai Social Order." *American Anthropologist* 64 (1962): 1247–1261.

Harrison, Faye V. "Women in Jamaica's Urban Informal Economy: Insights from a Kingston Slum." In *Third World Women and the Politics of Feminism*, ed. Chandra Talpade Mohanty, Ann Russo and Lourdes Torres. Bloomington and Indianapolis: Indiana University Press, 1991: 173–196.

Hartle, Maria. "Traffic in Women as a Form of Violence Against Women." In *Combating Traffic in Persons: Proceedings of the Conference on Traffic In Persons*. eds. Marieke Klap, Yvonne Klerk and Jaqueline Smith. Utrecht: IMS, Netherlands Institute of Human Rights, 1995.

Haverman, R. and J. C. Hes. "Vrouwenhandel en Exploitatie van Prostitutie." In *Het Vrouwenverdrag: Een Beeld van een Verdrag*. A.W. Heringa et. al. eds. Antwerpen and Amersfoort: MAKLU, 1994.

Heng, Geraldine. "'A Great Way to Fly:' Nationalism, the State and Varieties of Third-World Feminism." In *Feminist Geneologies, Colonial Legacies, Democratic Futures*, eds. M. Jaqui Alexander and Chandra Talpade Mohanty. New York: Routledge, 1997. 30–45.

Henrique, Fernando. *Prostitution in Europe and the Americas*. New York: Citadel Press, 1963.

Heringa A.W. et. al. eds. *Het Vrouwenverdrag: Een Beeld van een Verdrag*. Antwerpen and Amersfoort: MAKLU, 1994.

Herman, Edward S. *Triumph of the Market: Essays on Economics, Politics and the Media*. Boston: South End Press, 1995.

Heyzer, Noleen. *Working Women of Southeast Asia: Development, Subordination and Emancipation*. Milton Keynes: Open University Press, 1986.

Heyzer, N. et al. eds. *The Trade in Domestic Workers: Causes, Mechanisms and Consequences of International Migration*, London: Zed Books, 1994.

Hicks, George. *The Comfort Women: Japan's Brutal Regime of Enforced Prostitution in the Second World War*. New York: W.W. Norton, 1994.

Hill, P. *The Migrant Cocoa Farmers of Southern Ghana: A Study in Rural Capitalism* Cambridge: Cambridge University Press, 1963.

Hornblower, M. "Special Report: The Skin Trade," *Time* 8(25) 1993:18-29

Human Development Report 1995. New York: Oxford University Press for the UNDP Program, 1995.

IGCA. *Legal Working Party: Final Report*, Canberra, Commonwealth Dept. of Health, Housing, Local Govt. and Community Services, 1992.

International Agreement for the Suppression of the White Slave Traffic, Paris, 1904 .

International Convention for the Suppression of the Traffic in Women of Full Age, 1933.

International Convention for the Suppression of the White Slave Traffic, 1910.

International Convention to Combat the Traffic in Women and Children, 1921.

Ireland, Kevin. *Wish you Weren't Here*. London: Save the Children Fund, 1993.

IRIP. "Over the Hills and Far Away: Indonesian Migrant Labour." *Inside Indonesia* 42, (March 1995): 27-31

ISIS. "Poverty and Prostitution." *Women's World* 24 ISIS: Geneva, 1990.

JCNCA. *Organised Criminal Paedophile Activity*, Canberra: Senate Printing Unit, 1995.

Jenkins, Philip. *Intimate Enemies: Moral Panics in Contemporary Great Britain*. New York: Aldine de Gruyter, 1992.

Jenness, Valerie. *Making It Work: The Prostitutes' Rights Movement in Perspective.* Hawthorne, NY: Aldine de Gruyter, 1993.

JSC. *A Report on Human Rights and the Lack of Progress Towards Democracy in Burma (Myanmar).* Canberra: Australian Government Publishing Service, 1995.

Kalm, Florence. "The Two 'Faces' of Antillean Prostitution." Paper presented at the American Anthropological Association meeting, November 1975.

Kane, Stephanie C. "Prostitution and the Military: Planning AIDS Intervention in Belize." *Social Science and Medicine* 36 (1993): 965–979.

Kempadoo, Kamala. "Sandoms and Other Exotic Women: Prostitution and Race in the Caribbean" *Race and Reason* (October 1996): 3–54.

———. "Prostitution, Marginality and Empowerment: Caribbean Women in the Sex Trade," *Beyond Law,* 5, 14 (March 1996): 69–84.

———. *Exotic Colonies: Caribbean Women in the Dutch Sex Trade.* Diss. University of Colorado, 1994. 9518632.

Kitzinger, Jenny. "Who Are You Kidding? Children, Power and the Struggle Against Sexual Abuse." In *Constructing and Re-constructing Childhood: Contemporary Issues in the Study of Childhood* eds. A. James and A. Prout. London: Falmer Press, 1990.

Klap, Marieke, Yvonne Klerk and Jaqueline Smith, eds. *Combating Traffic in Persons: Proceedings of the Conference on Traffic In Persons* Utrecht: IMS, Netherlands Institute of Human Rights, 1995.

Kofi, A. R. T. "The Study of Akosombo Dam as a Cause of Prostitution among Krobo Girls at Kodjonya." Department of Sociology, University of Ghana, Legon, 1986.

Konotey-Ahulu, F. I. D. *What is AIDS?* London: Tetteh-A'Domeno Company, 1989.

Koompraphant, Sanphasit. *A Just World for Our Future.* CPCR: Bangkok. n.d.

La Fontaine, Jean. *Child Sexual Abuse.* Cambridge: Polity Press, 1990.

Lagro, Monique and Donna Plotkin, "The Suitcase Traders in the Free Zone of Curaçao." Port-of-Spain: Caribbean Development and Cooperation Committee, Economic Commission for Latin America and the Caribbean, 1990.

Law, L. "Dancing in Cebu: Mapping Bodies, Subjectivities and Spaces in an Era of HIV/AIDS." Diss. Canberra ANU, 1996.

Lea, John. *Tourism and Development in the Third World.* New York: Routledge, 1988.

Lee-Wright, Peter. *Child Slaves.* London: Earthscan Publications, 1990.

Leigh, Carol (aka Scarlot Harlot). "Inventing Sex Work." In *Whores and Other Feminists,* ed. Jill Nagle. New York: Routledge, 1997. 223–231.

Levine, Phillippa. "Veneral Disease, Prostitution and the Politcis of Empire: The Case of British India." *The Journal of the History of Sexuality* 4.4 (1994): 579–602.

Lim, Lin Lean and Nana Oishi. *International Labor Migration and Asian Women: Distinctive Characteristics and Policy Concerns.* Geneva: International Labor Office, 1996.

Little, K. *African Women in Towns* Cambridge: Cambridge University Press, 1973

Longo, Paulo Henrique and Richard G. Parker. *Male Prostitution and the Risk of HIV Transmission.* Final report. Global Program on AIDS. Geneva: World Health Organization, 1992.

Longo, Paulo Henrique. "The Meeting of the Michês." *New Internationalist.* February 1994: 20–21.

Lutjens, Sheryl L. "Reading Between the Lines: Women, the State, and Rectification in Cuba." *Latin American Perspectives*, 22 (Spring 1995): 100(25).

MacDonald, Martha. "What is Feminist Economics?" *Beyond Law*, 5 (March 1996): 11–36.

MacKinnon, C. *Feminism Unmodified: Discourses on Life and Law*, Cambridge: Harvard University Press, 1987.

Marchand, Marianne. "Latin American Women Speak on Development: Are We Listening Yet?" In *Feminism, Postmoderism, Development*, eds. Marianne H. Marchand and Jane L. Parpart. London: Routledge, 1995. 56–72.

Marlowe, Julian. "It's Different for Boys." In *Whores and Other Feminists*, ed. Jill Nagle. New York: Routledge, 1997:141–144

Martinez, Milagro. "Alternativas de vida y de trabajo para las trabajadoras sexuales." Paper presented at the First Dominican Congress on Prostitution and Sex Work. Santo Domingo, Dominican. Republic, May 1995.

Matheson, Angela. "Trafficking in Asian Sex Workers." *Green Left Weekly*, 26 (October 1994): 1.

McClintock, Anne. "Screwing the System: Sexwork, Race and the Law." *Boundary 2* 19 (Summer 1992): 70–95

McClintock, Anne "Sex Workers and Sex Work: Introduction." *Social Text* 37 (Winter 1993): 1– 10.

McGreery, David. "'This Life of Misery and Shame': Female Prostitution in Guatemela City 1880–1920." *Journal of Latin American Studies* 18 (November 1986): 333–353

Metzenrath, S. "The Federal Government's Responsibilites Towards Prostitution," Canberra: WISE discussion paper, 1995.

Miller, Alice M. "United Nations and Related International Action in the Area of Migration and Traffic in Women." In the Report of the International Workshop on International Migration and Traffic in Women. Chiangmai: The Foundation for Women, 1994

Mohanty, Chandra Talpade. "Under Western Eyes: Feminist Scholarship and Colonial Discourses." In *Third World Women and the Politics of Feminism*, eds. Chandra Talpade Mohanty, Ann Russo and Lourdes Torres. Bloomington: Indiana University Press, 1991. 51–80.

————. "Women Workers and Capitalist Scripts: Ideologies of Domination, Common Interest and the Politics of Solidarity." In *Feminist Geneologies, Colonial Legacies, Democratic Futures*, eds. M. Jaqui Alexander and Chandra Talpade Mohanty. New York: Routledge, 1997. 3–29.

Moya, E. A. de, S. Tabet, S. Garris and S. Roasario. "Catamitas y exoletos modernos en Republica Dominicana." *Juntarnos*. Santo Domingo: COIN, 1996: 167–172.

Muecke, Marjorie. "Mother Sold Food, Daughter Sells Her Body: The Cultural Continuity of Prostitution." *Social Science and Medicine* 35 (1992): 891–901.

Murray, Alison. "Minding Your Peers and Queers: Female Sex Workers in the AIDS Discourse in Australia and Southeast Asia." *Gender, Place and Culture* 3.1 (1996): 43–59.

————. "Bondage and Imagined Bodies." Draft manuscript (n.d.).

————. *No Money, No Honey. A Study of Street Traders and Prostitutes in Jakarta.* Singapore: OUP, 1991.

————. "On Bondage, Peers and Queers: Sexual Subcultures, Sex Workers and Aids Discourses in the Asia-Pacific." Draft manuscript (n.d.).

Nabila, J. S. *Migration of the FraFra in Northern Ghana: A Case Study of Cyclical Labor Migration in West Africa.* Diss. Michigan State University, 1974.

Nadel, S. F. "Witchcraft in Four African Societies: An Essay in Comparison." *American Anthropologist* 54 (1952): 18–29.

Nagle, Jill, ed. *Whores and Other Feminists.* New York: Routledge, 1997.

Narayan, Uma. "Contesting Cultures: 'Westernization,' Respect for Cultures and Third-World Feminists." In *The Second Wave: A Reader in Feminist Theory*, ed. Linda Nicholson. New York and London: Routledge, 1996. 396–414.

Network of Sex Work Projects. *European Symposium on Health and the Sex Industry: Final Report.* Edinburgh, 1994.

New Internationalist 292 (July 1997).

NGO Coalition Against Exploitation of Women. "Petition Against Sexual Exploitation." Amherst MA: CATW paper for Beijing, February, 1995.

O'Connell Davidson, Julia. "Sex Tourism in Cuba." *Race and Class*, 38 (July/September 1996): 39–48.

O'Grady, Ron *The Rape of the Innocent, End Child Prostitution in Asian Tourism.* Bangkok: ECPAT, 1994.

————. *Address to the Summit Conference on Child Prostitution of the Vatican Pontifical Council for the Family.* Bangkok: ECPAT, 1992.

Odzer, Cleo. *Patpong Prostitution: Its Relationship to, and Effect on, the Position of Women in Thai Society.* Diss. New School for Social Research, 1990.

————. *Patpong Sisters: An American Woman's View of the Bangkok Sex World.* New York: Arcade Publishing, 1994.

Oldenburg, Veena Talwar. "Lifestyle as Resistance: The Case of the Courtesans of Lucknow, India. *Feminist Studies* 16 (Summer 1990): 259–287.

Ong, Aihwa. "The Gender and Labor Politics of Postmodernity." *Annual Review of Anthropology* 20 (1991): 279–309.

Ortner, Sherry B. *Making Gender: The Politics and Erotics of Culture.* Boston: Beacon Press: 1996.

Orubuloye, I. O., P. Caldwell and J. C. Caldwell. "Commerical Sex Workers in Nigeria and the Shadow of AIDS." In *Sexual Networking and AIDS in Sub-Saharan Africa: Behavioural Research and the Social Context*, eds. I.O. Orubuloye, J. C. Caldwell, P. Caldwell and G. Santow. Canberra: Australian National University, 1994. 101–116.

Painter, T. M. *Migration and AIDS in West Africa.* New York: CARE, 1992.

Palmer, I. *Gender and Population in the Adjustment of African Economies: Planning for Change.* Geneva: ILO, 1991.

Passell, Peter. "Forbidden Sun and Sin, Communist Style." *New York Times Magazine*, Nov. 7, 1993: 66–67.

Pattullo, Polly. *Last Resort: The Cost of Tourism in the Caribbean.* London: Cassell, 1996.

PCV "PCV Statement on Trafficking." St Kilda, unpublished paper, 1995.

Penn State Report, UNESCO and the Coalition against Trafficking in Women. n.d.

Petras James and Tienchai Wongchaisuwan. "Thailand: Free Markets, AIDs, and Child Prostitution." Z *Magazine* September 1993: 35–38.

Pheterson, Gail. *The Prostitution Prism*. Amsterdam: Amsterdam University Press, 1996.

————, ed. *A Vindication of the Rights of Whores*. Seattle, WA: The Seal Press, 1989.

Phizacklea, Annie and Carol Wolkowitz. *Homeworking Women: Gender, Racism and Class at Work.* London: Sage Publications, 1995.

Placencia, Luchy. "El manejo de la problematica de la prostitucion o trabajo sexual en los medios de comunicacion." Paper presented at the First Dominican Congress on Prostitution and Sex Work. Santo Domingo, Dominican Republic, May 1995.

Plant, Martin A., ed. *AIDS, Drugs and Prostitution*. 3rd ed. London: Routledge, 1993.

Porter, Roy. "The Exotic as Erotic: Captain Cook in Tahiti." In *Exoticism in the Enlightenment*. eds. Rousseau G.S. and Roy Porter. Manchester: Manchester University Press, 1990.

Press, Clayton M. Jr. "Reputation and Respectability Reconsidered: Hustling in a Tourist Setting." *Caribbean Issues* 4 (1978): 109–119.

PROS et al. "Alleged Trafficking of Asian Sex Workers to Australia." Sydney: PROS et al., discussion paper for Beijing, 1995.

Pruit, Deborah and Suzanne LaFont. "For Love and Money: Romance Tourism in Jamaica." *Annals of Tourism Research*. 22.2 (1995): 422–440

Reanda, Laura. "Prostitution as a Human Rights Question, Problems and Prospects of United Nations Action." *Human Rights Quarterly* 13 (1991): 209-211.

Rehof, Lars Adam. *Guide to the Travaux Preparatoire of the United Nations Convention on the Elimination of all Forms of Discrimination Against Women*. Dordrecht: Martinus Nijhoff/Kluwer, 1993.

Roberts, Nickie. *Whores in History: Prostitution in Western Society*. London: Harper Collins, 1992.

Rosario Santo, Luis Moreno, Dinnys Luciano, Francisco Ferreira, Mayra Tavares and E. Antonio de Moya. "Trabajadoras sexuales viajeras y no viajeras: Experiencias y expectivas." In *Juntarnos*. Santo Domingo: COIN, 1996: 226–228.

Rosca, Ninotchka. "The Philippines' Shameful Export." *The Nation* 17 April 1995: 522– 527.

Rouch, J. "Notes of Migration into the Gold Coast: First Report of the Mission Carried out in the Gold Coast from March to December 1954." 1956.

Rousseau G.S. and Roy Porter, eds. *Exoticism in the Enlightenment*. Manchester: Manchester University Press, 1990.

Rowbotham, Sheila and Swasti Mitter, eds. *Dignity and Daily Bread: New Forms of Economic Organizing Among Poor Women in the Third World and the First*. London: Routledge, 1994.

Rubin, G. "The Traffic in Women: Notes on the 'Political Economy' of Sex." In *Toward an Anthropology of Women*, ed. R. Reiter. New York: Monthly Review Press, 1975. 157-210

Ryan, Sarah. *Prostitute Women: Status and the Law*. Part 2 Dissertation in Social Anthropology. Cambridge: Cambridge University. n.d.

Safa, Helen I. *The Myth of the Male Breadwinner: Women and Industrialization in the Caribbean*. Boulder: Westview Press, 1995.

Sancho, N., and M. Layador, eds. "Traffic in Women: Violation of Women's Dignity and Fundamental Human Rights." Manila: Asian Women Human Rights Council, 1993.

Sandoval, Chela. "U.S. Third World Feminism: The Theory and Method of Oppositional Consciousness in the Postmodern World." *Genders* 10 (Spring 1991): 1–24.

Sanjeck, R. "New Perspectives on African Women." *Reviews in Anthropology* 3 (2), 1976: 115–134.

Scott, James. *Weapons of the Weak: Everyday Forms of Peasant Resistance.* New Haven and London: Yale University Press, 1985.

Senior, Olive, *Working Miracles: Women's Lives in the English-Speaking Caribbean.* London and Bloomington: James Currey and Indiana University Press, 1992.

Shrage, Laurie. *Moral Dilemmas of Feminism: Prostitution, Adultery, and Abortion.* New York and London: Routlegde, 1994.

Sleightholme, Carolyn and Indrani Sinha. *Guilty Without Trial: Women in the Sex Trade in Calcutta.* New Brunswick: Rugters University Press, 1997.

Stansell, Christine. *The City of Women: Sex and Class in New York 1789 to 1860.* New York: Knopf, 1986.

Stoop, Chris de. *Ze Zijn Zo Lief, Meneer: Over de Vrouwenhandelaars, Meisjesbaletten en de Bende van de Miljardair.* Leuven: Kritak, 1992

Strout, Jan. "Women, the Politics of Sexuality, and Cuba's Economic Crisis." *Socialist Review* 25 (1996): 5–15/ *Cuba Update*, 16 (April–June 1995): 15–18.

Sturdevant, Saundra Pollock, and Brenda Stoltzfus. *Let the Good Times Roll: Prostitution and the U.S. Military in Asia.* New York: The New Press, 1992.

Sudarkasa, N. "Women and Migration in Contemporary West Africa." *SIGNS* 3 (Autumn 1977): 178–189.

Sullivan, B. "Global Prostitution: Sex Tourism and Trafficking in Women." Paper presented at the Annual Meeting of the Law and Society Association, University of Strathclyde, Glasgow, July 11-13, 1996.

Tabet, Paola. "'I'm the Meat, I'm the Knife': Sexual Service, Migration and Repression in Some African Societies." In *Vindication of the Rights of Whores*, ed. Gail Pheterson. Seattle, Washington: Seal Press. 1989. 204–226.

The Human Rights Watch Global Report on Women's Human Rights. New York: Human Rights Watch, 1995.

The International Agreement for the Suppression of the White Slave Traffic, Paris. 1904.

The International Convention for the Suppression of the Traffic in Women of Full Age. 1933.

The International Convention for the Suppression of the White Slave Traffic. 1910.

The International Convention to Combat the Traffic in Women and Children. 1921.

"The Penn State Report," UNESCO/CATW.

"The Traffic in Persons." Report. The Advisory Committee on Human Rights and Foreign Policy. The Hague 1992.

Troung, Than Dam. *Sex, Money and Morality: The Political Economy of Prostitution and Tourism in South East Asia.* London: Zed Books, 1990.

Tyner, James A. "Constructions of Filipina Migrant Entertainers." *Gender, Place and Culture.* 3.1 (1996): 77–93.

UNESCO. "Contemporary Forms of Slavery: Draft Programme of Action on the Traffic in Persons and the Exploitation of the Prostitution of Others," Geneva, UNESCO document, 13 June, 1995.

UNICEF. *Children and Women in Myanmar: A Situation Analysis.* 1995.

United Nations. "Beijing Declaration and Platform for Action Adopted by the Fourth World Conference on Women: Action for Equality, Development and Peace." Beijing: September 15, 1995.

Walkowitz, Judith. *Prostitution and Victorian Society: Women, Class, and the State.* Cambridge: Cambridge University Press, 1982.

Ware, Marilyn. *If Women Counted: A New Feminist Economics.* San Francisco: Harper and Row, 1988.

Weeks, Jeffrey. *Sex, Politics and Society: The Regulation of Sexuality Since 1800.* New York: Longman, 1981.

Wekker, Gloria. *"I am Gold Money (I Pass Through All Hands, But I Do Not Lose My Value):" The Construction of Selves, Gender and Sexualities in a Female Working-Class, Afro-Surinamese Setting.* Diss. University of California, 1992.

Wekker, Gloria, *Ik Ben Een Gouden Munt: Subjectiviteit en Seksualiteit van Creoolse Volksklasse Vrouwen in Paramaribo* Amsterdam: VITA, 1994.

White, Luise. *The Comforts of Home: Prostitution in Colonial Nigeria.* Chicago: University of Chicago Press, 1990.

Wijers, Marjan and Lin Lap-Chew. *Trafficking in Women, Forced Labor and Slavery-like Practices in Marriage, Domestic Labor and Prostitution.* Utrecht: STV, 1997.

World Sex Guide Documents. cuba/faq.2 July 1995. http://www.paranoia.com/faq/prostitution/Cuba.html

Zalduondo, Barbara de and Jean Maxius Bernard. "Meanings and Consequences of Sexual-Economic Exchange: Gender, Poverty and Sexual Risk Behavior in Urban Haiti." In *Conceiving Sexuality: Approaches to Sex Research in a Postmodern World,* eds. Richard G. Parker and John H. Gagnon. New York: Routledge, 1995. 157–180.

Zalduondo, Barbara de. "Prostitution Viewed Cross-Culturally: Toward Recontextualizing Sex Work in AIDS Intervention Research." *The Journal of Sex Research* 28 (May 1991): 223–248.

Newspapers and Periodicals

Bangkok Post, ECPAT Bulletin, Far Eastern Economic Review, Green Left Weekly, Melbourne Sunday Age, The Nation, New York Times, STV News Bulletin, Time, West Australian, The New Internationalist.

Contributors

John Anarfi holds a Ph.D. from the University of Ghana, Legon. He is a demographer and currently a Research Fellow at the Institute of Statistical, Social and Economic Research at the University of Ghana, Legon. He is among the leading researchers in Ghana on the social dimensions of HIV/AIDS in Ghana, and is one of the few to have researched migration of Ghanaians in the West African sub-region.

Jo Bindman is an economist who has worked on a variety of projects associated with the sex industry, particularly in Thailand. She currently works for Anti-Slavery International in London, on the promotion of human and labor rights in the sex industry. She is the author of the 1997 Anti-Slavery International/Network of Sex Work Projects report "Redefining Prostitution as Sex Work on the International Agenda."

Licia Brussa is a sociologist and has worked for many years on migration and prostitution. She is presently general coordinator of TAMPEP, the Transnational Project for AIDS/STD Prevention among Migrant Prostitutes in Europe. She is attached to the Mr. A. de Graaf Foundation, the national Dutch center for research, documentation, public information, policy development and advice of prostitution and related issues.

Amalia Lucía Cabezas is a Ph.D. candidate in the Department of Ethnic Studies at the University of California, Berkeley. Her dissertation examines sex tourism in the Caribbean region.

Jo Doezema first became involved in the sex workers' rights movement through her work with the Red Thread in Amsterdam. She is a former sex worker and Project Officer with the Network of Sex Work Projects. She collaborated in the 1997 Anti-Slavery International/Network of Sex Work Projects report "Redefining Prostitution as Sex Work on the International Agenda."

Coco Fusco is a New York based writer and interdisciplinary artist and author of *English is Broken Here: Notes on Cultural Fusion in the Americas* (New Press). She is an Assistant Professor at the Tyler School of Art of Temple University.

Gordon Isaacs is Associate Professor in the Department of Social Work at the University of Cape Town, a clinician, and a consultant to SWEAT and the National Association of People with AIDS in South Africa.

Kamala Kempadoo is an Assistant Professor of Women's Studies and Sociology at the University of Colorado at Boulder. She has been active in political struggles of Third World, Black and migrant women for many years. She started research on sex work in the Dutch Caribbean in the late eighties, and is currently directing a Caribbean-wide project on tourism and prostitution.

Paulo Henrique Longo is a researcher, activist, and founder/president of NOSS. He also co-coordinates the Network for Sex Work Projects from Brazil.

Heather Montgomery completed her M.Phil. and Ph.D. in social anthropology at Cambridge University. She is affiliated to the Norwegian Center for Child Research at the University of Trondheim, Norway, as a research fellow.

Alison Murray (Ph.D.) is a Research Fellow in Pacific and Asian Studies at the Australian National University, and the author of *No Money No Honey: A Study of Street Traders and Prostitutes in Jakarta* (Oxford University Press). She is also a sex worker, tattoo artist, co-convener of the Queer and Esoteric Workers Union in Sydney, a Scarlet Alliance representative, and an executive member of the Australian Federation of AIDS Organizations.

Shane Petzer is a social worker and the coordinator of the Sex Worker Education and Advocacy Taskforce (SWEAT) in South Africa. SWEAT serves as the contact representative for the Network for Sex Work Projects.

Oumar Tandia is a social worker and has been with ENDA since 1991. He is coordinator of information, education and communication with SYNFEV, and co-coordinator of the ENDA Ecopole West African program.

Satoko Watenabe receievd her M.S. from Cornell University and is presently a Ph.D. candidate in economics at the University of Texas at Austin. She works as an agricultural economist at the International Development Center of Japan.

Marjan Wijers has worked since 1987 for the Dutch Foundation Against Trafficking in Women (STV) and is involved in practical victim support, policy-making, lobbying and campaigning. She is the co-author of the 1997 GAATW/STV international report *Trafficking in Women, Forced Labor and Slavery-like Practices in Marriage, Domestic Labor and Prostitution,* which was commissioned by the UN Special Rapporteur on Violence Against Women.

Contributing Organizations

Anti-Slavery International (ASI)
Unit 4, the Stableyard
Broomgrove Road
London, SW9 9TL, UK
Tel: 44 171 924 9555
Fax: 44 171 738 4110
E-mail: antislavery@gn.apc.org

Asociación de Trabajadoras Autónomas
"22 de Junio" (Association of
Autonomous Women Workers)
Tarqui entre Boyacá y Guabo
Machala, El Oro, Ecuador
Tel: 593 7 962 332

COIN and MODEMU
Aníbal de Espinoza 352
Villas Agricolas
Santo Domingo, Dominican Republic
Fax: 809 245 4336

ENDA/SYNFEV
B.P. 3370
Dakar, Senegal
Tel: 221 22 4529
Fax: 221 22 2695

Foundation Against Trafficking in Women
(STV)
P.O. Box 1455
3500 BL Utrecht, The Netherlands
Tel: 31 30 236 8462
Fax: 31 30 236 4632
E-mail: S.T.V@inter.NL.net

Group Sisterhood
c/o Makiko Tsuboi
3-33-30
Higashikori, Hirakata City
Osaka Pref. 573-0075 Japan
Fax: 81 720 52 7832
E-mail: RXR13611@niftyserve.or.jp

IKHLAS Drop-In Center
P.O. Box 11859
50760 Kuala Lumpur, Malaysia
Tel: 60 3 441 4699
Fax: 60 3 441 5699

Mahila Samanwaya Committee
132/1 Mahatma Ghandi Road
Calcutta 700 007, India
Tel: 91 33 232 21 54

Network of Sex Work Projects (NWSP)
c/o AHRTAG
29–35 Farringdon Road
London EC1 3JB, UK
Tel: 44 181 991 6732
E-mail: sexworkernet@gn.apc.org
Website:
http://walnet.org/csis/groups/nwsp.html

NOSS
Rua Visconde de Piraja 187/403
2210-001
Rio de Janeiro, RJ Brazil
Tel/Fax: 55 21 522 5944

Sex Workers Eduaction and Advocacy
Taskforce (SWEAT)
P. O. Box 373. Salt River,
Cape Town 7925, South Africa
Tel: 9 21 448 7875
Fax: 9 21 448 7867
E-mail: sweat@iafrica.com

SWEETLY
Japan
Tel/Fax: 81 3 5272 3908
E-mail: 6kawabat@ma.kcom.or.jp

TAMPEP
c/o Mr. A. de Graaf Foundation,
Westermarkt 4,
1016 DK Amsterdam, The Netherlands.
Tel: 31 20 624 7149
Fax: 31 20 624 6529
E-mail: mr.a.de.graaf.stichting@pi.net

The Maxi Linder Association
Herenstraat 26
Paramaribo, Suriname.
Tel: 597 42 56 36

The Exotic Dancers Alliance (EDA)
1441 A Walnut Street, Suite 187
Berkeley, CA 94709, USA
Tel: 1 415 995 4745

La Únion Unica
c/o Puente Titla 100-42
Col. Ricarrdo Flores Magón
Deleg. Iztapalapa, Mexico DF
Tel: 52 571 7264

Index

United States, 1, 4, 5, 6, 11, 13, 18, 19, 22, 23,
    36, 52, 57, 72, 82, 94, 154
Uruguay, 20, 199
urbanization, 7, 18
USPROS, 19
Utrecht conference, 63

vagina, 89, 179
veneral disease, 47n 2
Venezuela, 21, 22, 249
victims: Asian workers as, 58, 92–3; of
    organized crime, 74–7; of traffick-
    ing, 46–7, 62, 74–7; passive, 148; pros-
    titutes as, 38, 46, 205, 232, 247; stereo-
    type, 32; Third World, 30; women
    as, 14, 74–7
Vienna Declaration and Program of
    Action of the 1993 World Confer-
    ence on Human Rights, 40
Vietnam, 20
violence, 45, 52, 63, 68, 69, 147; against sex
    workers, 74, 77, 82, 83, 158, 173, 176,
    186, 190, 194, 195, 213, 216, 233, 250, 262,
    264, 265, 266; against women, 34,
    37–9, 53, 62, 74, 133, 190; and traffick-
    ing, 74–5; at work, 65–7; domestic,
    61; sexual, 53, 72, 95, 96, 147

Watenabe, Satoko, 100
West Africa, 14, 25n 4, 99, 104, 108, 110, 113n
    1, 248
West Bengal Sexual Health Project, 170
white slave trade, 35, 36, 44, 60
White, Louise, 7–8
whores, 3–19, 30, 35, 47, 86
Wijers, Marjan, 31–2
women: African, 11; African-American,
    11, 27n 13, 185; Asian, 31, 89, 92–3, 185;
    Black, 131; Brazilian, 221; Burmese,
    30, 43, 54, 57; Carribean, 101; Cuban,

79–86, 102–3, 153, 154, 158, 161–3;
    Curaçaoan, 136; East European, 249,
    250; exploitation of. See exploita-
    tion; from the Dominican Repub-
    lic, 128, 131; Ghanaian, 100, 104–13;
    Haitian, 128, 131; in prostitution,
    72–4; Indian, 46; Japanese, 119, 123;
    Latin American, 131; migrant, 17, 61,
    133. See also migration of women,
    labor migration, migrant women;
    Nigerian, 250; non-western, 11, 26n
    9; of color, 83, 84, 151, 153, 154, 165; of
    the Third World, 10–12, 14, 124; Thai,
    57, 114–16, 122; trafficking of. See
    trafficking of women; victimization
    of, 45; violence against. See violence
    against women; Western, 43; White
    Euro-American, 131; working class,
    4, 81, 83, 132
women's: agency, 9, 83; bodies, 36–7, 53,
    85, 131; movement. See movement,
    women's; oppression, 13, 36, 170;
    organizations, 12, 74, 123, 170; rights.
    See rights, women's; sexuality, 44,
    47, 61, 62, 81, 89
Women's Coordination Committee, 202
Wongchaisuwan, Tienchai, 16
Workers in Sex Employment in ACT,
    49n 37
Working Group on Contemporary
    Forms of Slavery (WGS), 39, 41
World: AIDS Day, 224; Bank, 15, 16, 129;
    Charter for Prostitutes Rights
    (ICPR), 19–20, 37, 82, 195; Trade
    Organization, 15; War II, 14; Whores
    Congress, 19; Whores Summit, 82

yakuzas, 118, 120

ZiTeng, 23